English-Medium Instruction in Higher Education in the Middle East and North Africa

Also Available from Bloomsbury

English-Medium Instruction Practices in Higher Education, edited by Jim McKinley and Nicola Galloway
The Value of English in Global Mobility and Higher Education, Manuela Vida-Mannl
Teaching English-Medium Instruction Courses in Higher Education, Ruth Breeze and Carmen Sancho Guinda
Language and Decoloniality in Higher Education, edited by Zannie Bock and Christopher Stroud
Researching Language Learning Motivation, edited by Ali H. Al-Hoorie and Fruzsina Szabó
Rethinking TESOL in Diverse Global Settings, Tim Marr and Fiona English

English-Medium Instruction in Higher Education in the Middle East and North Africa

Policy, Research and Pedagogy

Edited by
Samantha Curle, Holi Ibrahim Holi,
Awad Alhassan and S. Sergio Saleem Scatolini

BLOOMSBURY ACADEMIC
LONDON • NEW YORK • OXFORD • NEW DELHI • SYDNEY

BLOOMSBURY ACADEMIC
Bloomsbury Publishing Plc
50 Bedford Square, London, WC1B 3DP, UK
1385 Broadway, New York, NY 10018, USA
29 Earlsfort Terrace, Dublin 2, Ireland

BLOOMSBURY, BLOOMSBURY ACADEMIC and the Diana logo are
trademarks of Bloomsbury Publishing Plc

First published in Great Britain 2022
This paperback published in 2024

Copyright © Samantha Curle, Holi Ibrahim Holi, Awad Alhassan and
S. Sergio Saleem Scatolini and Contributors, 2022

Samantha Curle, Holi Ibrahim Holi, Awad Alhassan and S. Sergio Saleem Scatolini
and Contributors have asserted their right under the Copyright, Designs and
Patents Act, 1988, to be identified as Author of this work.

For legal purposes the Acknowledgements on p. xiv constitute an extension
of this copyright page.

Cover design: Charlotte James

Cover image © titoOnz / Alamy Stock Photo

All rights reserved. No part of this publication may be reproduced or transmitted
in any form or by any means, electronic or mechanical, including photocopying,
recording, or any information storage or retrieval system, without prior
permission in writing from the publishers.

Bloomsbury Publishing Plc does not have any control over, or responsibility for, any
third-party websites referred to or in this book. All internet addresses given in this
book were correct at the time of going to press. The author and publisher regret
any inconvenience caused if addresses have changed or sites have ceased
to exist, but can accept no responsibility for any such changes.

A catalogue record for this book is available from the British Library.

A catalog record for this book is available from the Library of Congress.

ISBN: HB: 978-1-3502-3854-1
PB: 978-1-3502-3858-9
ePDF: 978-1-3502-3855-8
eBook: 978-1-3502-3856-5

Typeset by Deanta Global Publishing Services, Chennai, India

To find out more about our authors and books visit www.bloomsbury.com and
sign up for our newsletters.

This book is dedicated to our families.

Contents

List of Illustrations		viii
List of Contributors		x
Acknowledgements		xiv
	Introduction *Samantha Curle*	1
1	EMI in the Arab World: A Decolonial Interrogation *Berrington Ntombela*	7
2	University Students and Instructors' Attitudes towards English-Medium Instruction Courses: Voices from Iran *Ali Derakhshan, Mahboubeh Rakhshandehroo and Samantha Curle*	25
3	The Role of EMI in the Internationalization of Omani Higher Education Institutions (HEIs): Gains and Pains *Holi Ibrahim Holi, S. Sergio Saleem Scatolini and Qasim Salim Al Washahi*	45
4	EMI in Kuwait: Is English a Threat? *Inas Y. Mahfouz*	67
5	EMI in Saudi Higher Education: Challenges and Prospects *Abdulwahid Al Zumor and Habib Abdesslem*	87
6	EMI Programmes in Turkey: Evidence of Exponential Growth *Doğan Yuksel, Mehmet Altay and Samantha Curle*	109
7	Issues of Educational Language Policy and EMI in North Africa *Salah Troudi*	129
8	EMI in Morocco: Attitudes, Merits, Challenges, Strategies, and Implementation *Hassan Belhiah*	147
9	EMI in Sudanese Higher Education: Opportunities and Challenges *Awad Alhassan*	167
Index		191

Illustrations

Figures

2.1	Advantages/opportunities of EMI courses	33
2.2	Disadvantages/challenges of EMI courses	35
2.3	Suggestions for improving the status of EMI courses at Iranian universities	36
4.1	Illiteracy figures in Kuwait	68
4.2	Male corpus: Word sketch difference verbs with Arabic/English as objects	74
4.3	Female corpus: Word sketch difference verbs with Arabic/English as objects	74
4.4	Using Excel to code t-units	85
6.1	A comparison of the full, partial and total number of EMI programmes in 1999 and 2019	120
6.2	Changes in the number of academic programmes in different divisions	121
6.3	Milestones of foreign language MOI development in Turkey	122

Tables

2.1	Demographic information of students	29
2.2	Demographic information of instructors	29
4.1	Percentage of codes	77
6.1	Numbers of full and partial EMI programmes in 1999 according to the universities	116
6.2	Numbers of full and partial EMI programmes in 1999 according to academic division	116
6.3	Top ten academic subjects with the highest number of full and partial EMI programmes in 1999	117
6.4	Numbers of full and partial EMI programmes in 2019 according to the universities	118

6.5 Numbers of full and partial EMI programmes in 2019 according to academic divisions 118
6.6 Top ten academic subjects with the highest number of full and partial EMI programmes in 2019 119

Contributors

Habib Abdesslem is Visiting Professor of Linguistics and Translation Studies at King Khalid University, Saudi Arabia. He graduated from the University of Tunis and the University of Sheffield. He has published research work in journals such as *International Review of Applied Linguistics*, *Journal of Literary Semantics*, *Cahiers de Linguistique d'Ottawa*, *Lettres de Kairouan* and *Arab Journal of Applied Linguistics*, which he co-founded in 2015 and of which he has been Editor-in-Chief since 2016. Professor Abdesslem is former director of the Habilitation and Doctoral Committee at the University of Manouba. He (co)supervised students at the universities of Kairouan, Manouba, KSU, UCLouvain, Starthclyde and Lorraine.

Awad Alhassan is Assistant Professor of Applied Linguistics & TESOL at the Department of English Language and Literature, Dhofar University, Sultanate of Oman. He holds an MA and PhD in applied linguistics from the University of Essex in the United Kingdom. His teaching and research interests include English-medium instruction (EMI) in higher education, TESOL, EAP, academic writing and the use of corpora in translation and translator education. He has presented at numerous international conferences and published in peer-reviewed journals. His research has appeared in journals such as *Language Teaching Research*, *SAGE Open* and *TESOL Journal*.

Holi Ibrahim Holi is Assistant Professor of Applied Linguistics & TESOL, and he is currently Head of the Department of English Language and Literature, UTAS-Rustaq, Sultanate of Oman. He received his PhD from the University of Huddersfield, UK. His teaching and research interests are firmly situated within the field of applied linguistics, English medium of instruction, quality assurance and graduate attributes in HE. He is a member of numerous international professional organizations including the British Educational Research Association (BERA), EMI Oxford Research Group, Global Englishes Network-UK and the IATEFL. He has presented widely and published extensively in peer-reviewed journals.

Qasim Salim Al Washahi received his master's degree in TESOL in 2013 from the University of Sydney, Australia. His current research and teaching areas of interest are instructional design, online assessment, learning autonomy, EMI and educational leadership. He works as the English deputy program director at UTAS, Oman, and lectures at the University of Technology and Applied Sciences-Rustaq in the areas of educational technology and English language teaching. He has presented at several national and international conferences and published in peer-reviewed journals.

Abdulwahid Al Zumor is Associate Professor of Applied Linguistics and a certified Academic Quality Practitioner and Reviewer, currently working at the Department of English, Faculty of Languages and Translation, King Khalid University, Saudi Arabia. He has published research on EFL academic writing, language policy and planning, and English-medium instruction. He has presented in many international conferences in Asia, Africa and Europe. He has eighteen years of experience in teaching English and applied linguistics to undergraduate and postgraduate students in Yemen and Saudi Arabia.

Hassan Belhiah holds a PhD (2005) and an MA (1998) in English from the University of Wisconsin in Madison, United States. He is Associate Professor of English and Linguistics at Mohammed V University in Rabat, Morocco, and Adjunct Professor of North African Studies within the Middlebury C. V. Starr Schools Abroad program. His publications have appeared in *Classroom Discourse*, *Journal of Pragmatics*, *The Modern Language Journal*, *Language Policy* and *Applied Linguistics*. He has recently co-edited a book entitled *English Language Teaching in Moroccan Higher Education* (2020).

Samantha M. Curle is an Assistant professor in the Department of Education at the University of Bath, UK. She completed her DPhil at the University of Oxford, that focused on attitudes towards English-Medium Instruction (EMI) in Japan. She teaches subjects related to applied linguistics and Advanced Quantitative Research Methods (AQM). She is the director of the AQM in Social Sciences MRes Programme. She is also the pathway lead for AQM for the South West Doctoral Training Partnership (SWDTP – funded by the Economic and Social Sciences Research Council (ESRC)). Her main research interest lies in factors affecting academic achievement in EMI. Her research has been published in journals such as *Language Teaching*, *System*, *Studies in Higher Education*, *Applied Linguistics Review*, *International Journal of Bilingual Education and Bilingualism*,

Language Teaching Research and Studies in Second Language Learning and Teaching. She is also an editor for the journal *Data in Brief.* She has published two edited books on EMI: *Research Methods in English Medium Instruction* (by Routledge), and *The Use of Technology in English Medium Education* (by Springer).

Ali Derakhshan is Associate Professor of Applied Linguistics at the English Language and Literature Department, Golestan University, Gorgan, Iran. His publications appear in international journals (*Computers and Education, Language Teaching Research, System, Studies in Second Language Learning and Teaching, ELT Journal, Current Psychology, Frontiers in Psychology*, etc.). His research interests are positive psychology, interlanguage pragmatics, intercultural communication, teacher education, learner individual differences, EMI and cross-cultural interpersonal factors in educational psychology.

Inas Y. Mahfouz joined American University of Kuwait, Kuwait, in fall 2015 as Assistant Professor of English. She earned her PhD in Linguistics in 2008. She contributed chapters to books such as *Choice in Language: Applications in Text Analysis* and *Race/Gender/Media: Considering Diversity across Audiences, Content, and Producers.* Her current research projects include (1) meta-discourse markers in academic writing, a cross-cultural study which she started during her fellowship at the Writing Center at Dartmouth College in summer 2017, and (2) the *Arab Learner English Corpus* (ALEC), a corpus of freshman writing hosted by the Learner Corpus Association.

Berrington Ntombela is an Associate Professor in the Department of Languages, University of Limpopo, South Africa. He is the former Senior Lecturer in the Department of English, University of Zululand, South Africa. He completed his postgraduate studies at the University of Zululand, South Africa. He lectures modules related to English language and linguistics and English academic literacy. He has graduated a number of master's and PhD students. His main research interest is in English language teaching, sociolinguistics, discourse analysis, pragmatics and semantics. He has published in journals such as *Alternation, Reading & Writing, Southern African Linguistics and Applied Language Studies* and *Pertanika Journal of Social Science and Humanities.*

Mahboubeh Rakhshandehroo received her PhD in Human Sciences (Critical Studies in Transformative Education) from Osaka University, Japan. She is currently Associate Lecturer at Kwansei Gakuin University, Japan. She is also the ICLHE East Asia leadership team coordinator. Her research interests include English-medium instruction support, native speakerism and multiculturalism.

S. Sergio Saleem Scatolini, Ph.D., is an assistant professor at Rustaq College of Education within the University of Technology and Applied Sciences, Oman. He holds postgraduate qualifications in theology and educational studies, applied linguistics, and oriental languages and literature: Arab/Muslim World from KU Leuven, Vrije Universiteit Brussel and Université Catholique de Louvain-la-Neuve, Belgium, respectively. His research currently focuses on EMI, QA in education, curriculum and spiritual ecology.

Salah Troudi is an academic at the Graduate School of Education of the University of Exeter, UK, where he is Director of Global Engagement. His teaching and research interests include language teacher education, critical issues in language education, language policy, curriculum development and evaluation, and classroom-based research. He has published articles in several language education journals and edited a number of books. He recently co-edited *Feedback in L2 English Writing in the Arab World: Inside the Black Box*. His latest book is *Critical Issues in Teaching English: International Research Perspectives*.

Doğan Yuksel is an Associate Professor of TEFL at Kocaeli University's Faculty of Education. Areas of interest include Classroom Discourse, English-Medium Instruction, and Vygotskyan Dynamic Assessment. His work has been published in such journals as *International Review of Applied Linguistics (IRAL), Applied Linguistics Review, International Journal of Applied Linguistics, System, ReCALL,* and *Language Teaching Research*.

Mehmet Altay is an Assistant Professor of TEFL at Kocaeli University's Faculty of Education. Areas of interest include English-Medium Instruction, Content-based Instruction, and Content and Language Integrated Learning. His work has been published in such journals as *Applied Linguistics Review, System, Participatory Educational Research*, and *Novitas-Royal*.

Acknowledgements

Our thanks are extended to the blind reviewers for their constructive comments and feedback on the book manuscript. We would also like to extend our deepest gratitude to all the authors who contributed to this volume. This book would not exist without your hard work and commitment.

Introduction

Samantha Curle

Introduction

Providing instruction of academic content through English in higher education is rapidly growing in many countries where English is a second or foreign language (Curle et al., 2020). This global phenomenon is commonly known as English-medium instruction (EMI), defined here as 'the use of the English language to teach academic subjects other than English itself in countries or jurisdictions where the first language of the majority of the population is not English' (Macaro, 2018, p. 18). The focus therefore of this medium of education is the acquisition of academic content, with language learning often being more of an implicit aim. This shift away from the traditional manner of teaching and learning the English language has been motivated by underlying intentions such as (1) to develop students' English competencies, (2) to increase an institution's international ranking, (3) to attract international students, and therefore increase international student revenue, and (4) to implement an 'internationalisation at home' policy (see Pun & Curle, 2021; Fenton-Smith et al., 2017). The Middle East and North Africa have also been affected by this expansion of EMI (Hillman et al., 2021). According to the most up-to-date systematic review on EMI studies from across the globe, the use of EMI has been gaining popularity in higher education institutions (HEIs) in this region; however, few empirical studies have been conducted there (see Macaro et al., 2018). This special edited volume offers a comprehensive overview of EMI in this region. It provides up-to-date insights into EMI education in higher education across the Middle East and North Africa, with chapters focusing on both empirical and critical literature review, therefore making an original contribution to knowledge. The book is split by region covering the Middle East followed by North Africa. It begins by providing an overview of EMI in the Arab world (Chapter 1) and then delves into empirical studies in Iran (Chapter 2), Oman (Chapter 3) and Kuwait (Chapter 4). A critical review of the EMI literature in Saudi Arabia is then provided (Chapter 5), followed by evidence of the exponential growth in EMI programmes in Turkey (Chapter 6). It then presents an analytical review of empirical and theoretical literature on EMI in North Africa (Chapter 7), followed by empirical EMI studies in Morocco (Chapter 8) and Sudan (Chapter 9). Topics covered include investigating the role of EMI in the internationalization of HEIs, the merits, challenges, strategies and implementation issues related to EMI, the perceptions and attitudes towards EMI of both university students and lecturers, as well as EMI practices in these countries. By exploring these issues, this volume hopes to inform EMI practice, as well as the theory underlying EMI research. This volume will be useful for EMI students and lecturers, EMI education curriculum designers, EMI researchers, and higher education policymakers and educators, as well as undergraduate and postgraduate students conducting research in the fields of applied linguistics, language teaching and learning, English for Specific Purposes (ESP), English for Academic Purposes (EAP) and Teaching English to Speakers of Other Languages (TESOL).

In Chapter 1, Ntombela, through the lens of a decolonial critical approach, unpacks the challenges of English medium of instruction in the Arab world. He argues that EMI sets to benefit the English world more than it would ever benefit the Arab world. He further argues that the processes of internationalization and globalization, which are often used as a front to protect the hegemony of the English language, are colonial and serve the imperialistic expansion of the English cultural world view. He concludes by presenting a 'healthier' alternative approach to the coexistence of the English language and other languages in the Arab world.

Derakhshan, Rakhshandehroo and Curle then present an empirical study carried out in the Iranian EMI context in Chapter 2. They note how Iranian universities seem to be behind other Middle Eastern countries in terms of adopting EMI as Persian is almost exclusively still being used as the medium of instruction (MOI). This exploratory qualitative study focuses on the attitudes of university students and instructors towards the use of EMI. Twelve students and twelve instructors filled out open-ended questionnaires and participated in semi-structured interviews. Results showed that while participants mentioned both advantages and disadvantages to implementing EMI, the biggest challenge to its implementation is their lack of English proficiency. The findings of this study are expected to inform university administrators and stakeholders better plan their internationalization strategies in the Iranian context.

Chapter 3 by Ali, Scatolini and Al Washahi draws a link between the use of English as a medium of instruction and the internationalization of higher education in the Omani context. The concept of internationalization in higher education institutions primarily revolves around several goals including promoting global citizenship, building capacity for research, generating income from the recruitment of international students and enhancing institutional prestige and the quality of teaching and learning as well as research. The global spread of English has seen an increase in the importance of not only English language education but also education through English. This chapter presents an empirical study that adopted a qualitative methodology of an open-ended survey. Thirty English as a Foreign Language (EFL) university faculty members were surveyed in Omani HEIs. The study answers the following questions: What are the gains and challenges for Omani HEIs in enacting EMI as a means for internationalization? How do EFL faculty members perceive the role of EMI in the internationalization of Omani HEIs? What could be done to help Omani HEIs to implement EMI as a tool towards internationalization? Findings revealed that respondents held positive views of EMI as a measure to support internationalization. They also reported EMI as a means to smoothly go through the university accreditation process, climb the international university rankings, boost their chances of attracting more international students, as well as increase student employability.

In Chapter 4 Mahfouz elaborates an empirical study that explored Kuwaiti students' attitudes towards EMI. Using task-oriented interviews, she explores young people's perceptions about the use of EMI and the consequences this may have on their Arab identity. A written prompt was designed to encourage students to share their attitudes in relation to the use of English in three interrelated domains: their informal everyday communication, education and leisure time activities. Through these written reflective accounts of their linguistic practices, two corpora were created, one comprising all male students' responses and the other all female students' responses. Results revealed that both male and female students felt that English is needed to function in an international world, as well as to understand science and technology. However, although English was recognized as the global lingua franca that students reported they need for professional and academic reasons, both genders valued Arabic as the language of the Qur'an and their heritage. Nevertheless, gender differences were present: female students used English more often in informal communication and in leisure time activities, and they were more likely to worry about the use of language and their social image, and thought English to be the more 'prestigious' language. Male students on the other hand reported hesitancy to use a foreign language in their daily life for fear of its use being misinterpreted, causing the person to be a social outcast. Implications of this study for EMI pedagogy are then elaborated.

Chapter 5 by Al Zumor and Abdesslem presents a critical review of the EMI literature in Saudi Arabia. The authors discuss the contribution that English can make in achieving Saudi Arabia's ambition of developing a knowledge-based economy. They argue that Saudi Arabia, the cradle of the Arabic language and the birthplace of Islam, has a significant role to play in attenuating the excesses of neoliberalism and the indifferences of globalization. English, the main language of neoliberalism and globalization, presents itself as a means to manage neoliberalism and its values of individualism, competition, secularism and material profit. The authors adopt Dafouz and Smit's (2016, 2020) flexible six-dimensional ROADMAPPING framework for English as a medium of education (EME) to explore the current status of EMI in Saudi Arabia's higher education. They focus their attention on the preparatory year programme (PYP) that Saudi universities offer to high school graduates wishing to study a degree in a 'hard science' discipline. Their review reveals that the PYP does not ensure a satisfactory transition from relying on Arabic as a means of instruction (AMI) at high school to relying on English as a medium of instruction (EMI) at university. They conclude by providing several suggestions of how Saudi Arabia might further globalize its education through EMI and AMI to accelerate to a more knowledge-based economy.

Yuksel, Altay and Curle then present evidence of the exponential growth of EMI programmes in Turkey in Chapter 6. They go about this by elaborating the number of programmes in 1999 and compare it with the most current data in 2019. In order to contextualize this development and expansion, they also review the Turkish Council of Higher Education regulations about foreign language medium of instruction from 1984 onwards. The comparison of EMI programmes in 1999 to 2019 revealed that these programmes increased more than *fourfold* in twenty years. Usefully, universities with the highest numbers of full and partial EMI programmes are listed. The authors then go one step further and compare in which academic subjects these programmes expanded. The top five academic subjects in 1999 (i.e. business administration, electrics and electronics engineering, international relations, computer engineering and economics) remained in the top ten list in 2019. The authors then elaborate implications of these findings for EMI pedagogy.

In Chapter 7, Troudi provides an analytical and critical review of empirical and theoretical literature on EMI in North Africa. In North Africa language policy in general and decisions about what language medium to use in education have been affected on the one hand by discourses of independence and nationalism, as well as development and modernization, and by the inevitable heavy burden of colonialism on the other. In most higher education institutions in North Africa, the medium of instruction for scientific and technological subjects is not Arabic, which is the mother tongue and official language of the entire region. In academia, Arabic has struggled to maintain its position in the social sciences: in Tunisia, Algeria and Morocco, French dominates STEM subjects, while in Egypt and Libya, English dominates 'hard science' subjects. The author reviews studies and discussion pieces that represent a range of ideological and educational positions vis-à-vis the role of English in the North African context, its future and the impact of EMI on the quality of learning experiences of Arab students.

Chapter 8 by Belhiah presents an empirical study that explored the merits, challenges, strategies and implementation issues related to EMI policy in Moroccan secondary and tertiary education. The Moroccan sociolinguistic landscape is characterized by linguistic diversity and multilingualism. Besides the language of Amazigh (also known as Berber) and Standard Arabic (the two official languages), Moroccans use the Moroccan vernacular (or *Darija*), a majority mother tongue, and French, a de facto official language. Nevertheless, over the last two decades, English has gained popularity. This study elaborates results from interviews with secondary school and university students, instructors and administrators. Findings showed that students and instructors alike generally hold positive attitudes towards EMI. Nevertheless, students did express feelings of apprehension, anxiety and low self-esteem as most had not been previously taught academic content through English. The author concludes by providing implications of these views for the effective implementation of EMI policies and the global spread of English in Morocco and North Africa.

Finally, Chapter 9 by Alhassan focuses on an empirical study conducted on EMI in Sudan. In order to gain insight into the perspective of EMI stakeholders, a qualitative, open-ended questionnaire was used to collect data from thirteen EMI content teachers. The author notes that EMI in Sudanese higher education (HE) can be dated back to the early twentieth century, with the beginning of the British colonial rule. It was back then that HE began to modernize and become more formal. Since then, the implementation of EMI has been piecemeal, with a lack of consistency in use and a lack of clear implementation policies. Similar to universities across the globe, Sudanese educators and policymakers have a renewed inclination to expand and sustain the use of EMI in Sudanese higher education institutions. Rationale includes to internationalize, to attract international academic staff and students, to improve student mobility and employability, to increase international university rankings and to gain academic accreditation. However, the author notes a lack of consultation of EMI stakeholders, including lecturers, students, educational managers and policymakers, as to how to achieve these aims of EMI. Findings of the questionnaire showed that participants reported several benefits of EMI. These included international collaboration and academic exchange, and providing students, particularly at the postgraduate level, with research, publication, scholarly and professional development opportunities. Challenges of EMI implementation were also noted. These included low student English language proficiency and a lack of content teacher linguistic and pedagogical training as hindrances to EMI teaching and learning. The author then provides pedagogical implications of these findings for EMI policy, pedagogy and research.

References

Curle, S., Jablonkai, R., Mittelmeier, J., Sahan, K., & Veitch, A. (2020). English medium part 1: Literature review. In N. Galloway (Ed.), *English in higher education (report No. 978-0-86355-977–8)*. British Council. Retrieved from https://www.teachingenglish.org.uk/article/english-higher-education-%E2%80%93-english-medium-part-1-literature-review.

Dafouz, E., & Smit, U. (2016). Towards a dynamic conceptual framework for English-medium education in multilingual university settings. *Applied Linguistics*, *37*(3), 397–415.

Dafouz, E., & Smit, U. (2020). *Road-mapping education in the internationalised university*. London: Palgrave Macmillan.

Fenton-Smith, B., Humphreys, P., & Walkinshaw, I. (2017). *English medium instruction in higher education in Asia-Pacific* (Multilingual Education, 21). Cham: Springer.

Hillman, S., Selvi, A. F., & Yazan, B. (2021). A scoping review of World Englishes in the Middle East and North Africa. *World Englishes*, *40*(2), 159–175. doi: 10.1111/weng.12505

Macaro, E. (2018). *English medium instruction*. Oxford: Oxford University Press. doi:10.30687/978-88-6969-227-7/001.

Macaro, E., Curle, S., Pun, J., An, J., & Dearden, J. (2018). A systematic review of English medium instruction in higher education. *Language Teaching*, *51*(1), 36–76. doi:10.1017/S0261444817000350

Pun, J., & Curle, S. (Eds.) (2021). *Research methods in English medium instruction*. Retrieved from https://www.waterstones.com/book/research-methods-in-english-medium-instruction/jack-k-h-pun/samantha-m-curle/9780367457556.

1

EMI in the Arab World
A Decolonial Interrogation
Berrington Ntombela

Introduction

The Arab world, like many parts of the world, is being swept by the power and dominance of the English language. This dominance is meticulously organized through the imperial expansion of the English-speaking world, particularly the United States. Skutnabb-Kangas and Phillipson (2010, p. 3) argue that 'the project of global dominance has been articulated since before the USA achieved its independence', where George Washington saw the United States as the rising empire. Thus, '[t]he project of establishing English as the language of power, globally and locally, is central to this empire' (2010). It would, therefore, not appear anomalous for the empire to establish cultural and linguistic dominance as part of expanding its soft power to the world. In this case, English is set as the most effective vehicle to accomplish such expansion.

While globalization and internationalization have been in most cases reported positively, at the centre of these phenomena is the English language in the guise of lingua franca and medium of instruction; this has posed challenges for local languages. In the context of this chapter, such challenges are experienced by the Arabic language. This challenge is further exacerbated by several educational policy changes in the Gulf Cooperation Council (GCC) countries as it will be discussed later in the chapter. In a nutshell, educational policy changes across GCC countries seem to have in the centre the promotion of English as the medium of instruction. Since English as a medium of instruction is commonly located in contexts where English is not the mother tongue (Curle et al., 2020) among the speakers, it is often contrasted with mother-tongue instruction (Ntombela, 2020; Nyika, 2015). Such contrast, interestingly, tends to exclude

English as part of mother-tongue instruction for its first language speakers, to the extent that the logical necessity and benefit of mother-tongue instruction are not read as equally beneficial to English first language speakers (Ntombela, 2020; UNESCO, 2016).

This chapter, therefore, interrogates the challenges of the English medium of instruction in the Arab world through a decolonial lens. A decolonial perspective has been adopted to counter the effects of a colonial ethos, which is behind the expansion of the English language at the expense of the Arabic language in the context of this chapter. The chapter is organized around the themes of Arabization, internationalization and globalization, English medium of instruction, the case of GCC and concludes with decolonization.

Arabization

The spread and dominance of Arabic in the Arab world, which constitutes most of the Middle East and Northern Africa, were arguably a result of religious zealotry. In other words, the spread of Arabic as a language was packaged in the spread of Islam since Arabic is regarded as the sacred language of the Qur'an, the holy book for Muslims. But with the assimilation of Arabic as a language, the religious and cultural world view of the Oriental was also cultivated as encapsulated in the language. The result was that the cultural identification that had previously dominated the areas conquered by Islam disappeared and those places were effectively 'Arabized'. The success of Arabization is seen in the fact that all the GCC countries are bound by the same Modern Standard Arabic language. This is unlike similar corporations such as the Association of Southeast Asian Nations (ASEAN) where English is used as a working language (Barnawi, 2018).

The spread of English in recent times in the Arab world has not occurred in the same religious zealotry as Arabization, but the impact would not be very different. Unlike the process of Arabization that had religious undertones, Anglicization was facilitated by a colonial dominance of the British Empire. In the scramble for Africa, for instance, Britain arguably had the largest piece of the cake (Pakenham, 2014). Similarly, five GCC countries – that is Oman, Qatar, Bahrain, Kuwait and UAE – were colonized by Britain (Barnawi, 2018). Britain went on to colonize most parts of the world, which earned her the description of an empire on which the sun never sets. Through colonial escapades, English was spread to most parts of the world. It is no surprise, therefore, that the growth of English as a medium of instruction cuts across Anglophone and non-Anglophone countries (Curle et al., 2020).

Long after the colonial expansion, English continues to dominate many parts of the world especially in the areas of education, commerce, technology and entertainment. The dominance of English in education means that subjects and programmes in institutions are perceived to be of world standard if they are offered in English (Salomone, 2015). This means that in the Arab world, even though Arabic is the common language with all the amenities of offering sophisticated intellectual materials in science and technology, it is not regarded as having the same value as English. The repercussions of such perception are dire in the fact that those whose immediate benefits are wrapped up in the Arabic language are sadly put backwards and have to start afresh catching up in the English language. The burden of learning a second language weighs heavily on the shoulders of second language learners than first language speakers could ever appreciate (Nyika, 2015). The unfortunate part is that only a minority will ever attain what is set as the standard in English – the majority carry the perpetual second-class label of being English second or foreign language users (or speakers).

The other sad reality is that there does not seem to be any signs of English relinquishing its dominance or sharing its power with other languages. The new neocolonial process seems to have the effects of reinvigorating the hegemony of English at a scale equal to if not more than the period of colonization. Canagarajah (2005) puts it succinctly that while the non-Western communities were busy with the project of decolonization, the other project of globalization has pulled the carpet from underneath their feet, which necessitates that we shift our focus to the processes of internationalization and globalization discussed in the next section.

Internationalization and Globalization

With the emergence of the global market, the modern world came to be regarded as a global village. In this village, citizens are deemed to be connected closer than before. The transport system has become more accessible and cheaper; and technologies have connected even the remotest parts of the world. Most importantly, communication has meant that the world can be on the same page with a minimal threat of miscommunication. This has been largely facilitated by a common language. It is interesting, on that note, to observe that the common language is not explicitly stated but is often interpreted to be English. Curle et al. (2020), for instance, report that the expansion of English as a medium of instruction in Europe coincided with the Bologna Agreement, which was set to promote freedom of movement among higher education students, even though there is no mention of language in the policy.

English, as the common language among other things, is bolstered by the power of the American economy in the world. This means, at the world level, most high-stakes interactions are carried out in English. This has resulted in English being regarded as lingua franca – the language for global communication. Lingua franca English means that interlocutors adapt into English common code, which is often laced with individual situatedness. Everyday communication of individuals from diverse backgrounds is facilitated through lingua franca English. Nonetheless, there have been attempts to bring lingua franca English into the classroom and mainstream education (Canagarajah, 2007, 2014; Taguchi, 2014).

On the one hand, standard English is ideal in the academic environment. Serious academic activities such as assessment, research reports and publications are carried out in standard English. Academic writing is laced with expectations of a standardized form of English. Even academic literacy carries with it expectations of a standard form of English. On the other hand, lingua franca English tolerates regional, national and individual differences while standard English strives for a common code – the prestigious code. Needless to say, the custodians of this code are the first speakers of English in the centre (Harmer, 2006). On the contrary, there is no singular or fixed location of lingua franca English whose speakers outnumber native speakers of English (Canagarajah, 2007).

Lingua franca English could also be associated with English as a second language. In this case, the speakers are brought together by a common need to communicate in English because they do not share a common language. It is usually the case that such speakers bring with them individual differences in pronunciation as influenced by their first languages. The goal among these speakers is to achieve communication with each other. There is no aspiration to attain some ideal standard English. On the other hand, English as foreign language could be associated with standardized English. Speakers who learn English as a foreign language are usually bound by a common language. In this case, the motivation to learn English does not come from a need to communicate with each other than to emigrate to a country where English is spoken for educational or work purposes (Ntombela, 2020). There is, therefore, a heightened aspiration to learn standard English as spoken in the target country.

Interestingly, English as a second language and English as a foreign language sometimes coexist in the same environment. In the GCC countries, for example, expatriates generally outnumber the natives. English becomes a lingua franca among expatriates themselves and with the host country nationals. However, natives are bound by the same language but need English for educational purposes either locally or abroad – English is a foreign language to them.

While globalization could be arguably regarded as the driver for English as a lingua franca, the process of internationalization in higher education institutions (HEIs) is arguably responsible for the expansion of standard English in the academy. More HEIs are opting for English in offering various programmes of study to attract the international student population (Curle et al., 2020; Ntombela, 2017). This is lucrative because those international students would mostly come from countries that were formerly colonized by English and, therefore, have a basic command of the language. This is different from the cases where individuals have to learn English from scratch. Nevertheless, the prevailing perception of English as a language equal to education in general means that many forfeit the comfort and utility of their languages in education and choose to learn English from scratch. This contributes to the growth of English as a lucrative business and commodity. In the GCC countries, for instance, the revenue generated by English-medium schools runs into trillions of dollars (Barnawi, 2018).

Additionally, internationalization also means that those institutions that do not offer programmes in the medium of English lose out in the scientific citations of their work because the scientific community is being taken over by the dominance of English. The heavy price that is paid by communities is that local languages are left into a state of intellectual disuse – a step that triggers the process of language attrition. As with Arabization where many local languages eventually died and with colonization where many local languages still suffer marginalization, the process of internationalization, through the spread of English as a language of instruction in various programmes in HEIs, is intellectually murdering other languages and the bits of knowledge embedded in those languages.

English as a Medium of Instruction

As argued earlier, the spread of English was facilitated by the British imperial expansion and the colonization agenda. As a result, English was entrenched in the formerly colonized states, in the same way that French and Portuguese were entrenched in the francophone and lusophone countries respectively. The dominance of these colonial languages continued even after the colonized states had gained independence. Such dominance played itself in the education system, the judiciary, commerce, business, communication and all forms of government transactions. This was all facilitated by a neocolonial regime (Prah, 2018). Unfortunately, such a regime had bought into the fallacy of colonial languages as the only means of carrying out sophisticated academic and scientific thought.

The result was that all formal education was planned and offered in a colonial language. The most dominant of the colonial languages was English simply because of the number of colonies established under British rule. There are very few countries in the world that did not experience British imperialism. Education was also a tool used by colonialists to construct a citizen that would contribute to the economic expansion of the empire. The colonial language was, therefore, sold as the only viable language especially given the reality that those who were masters possessed this language. The conqueror of colonies also meant the conqueror of their cultural milieu and linguistic expression (Ntombela, 2012). The colonized were meant to feel that their languages were inferior.

This rhetoric of inferiority has persisted such that the economic and cultural muscle of English, stretching through countries in the centre, such as the United Kingdom, the United States, Canada, Australia and New Zealand, presents English as the indomitable currency through which education could be purchased. The result is that many students from English non-speaking countries increasingly idealize that English-speaking countries are their educational paradise. At the same time, non-English-speaking countries, realizing that they are losing student enrolment to English-speaking countries, bought into the rhetoric of internationalization which simply resulted in changing the medium of instruction into English.

There are complicated subtleties in the promotion of English as a medium of instruction in various countries, which are often presented in the form of benefits by some scholars. For instance, in multilingual contexts, the choice of English as a medium of instruction is justified based on being an 'arbiter' among native languages (Ntombela, 2017; Nqoma et al., 2017). In GCC countries, the varying demographics caused by the diverse nationalities that live and work in the Gulf countries present English as both appealing and a readily available language (Hopkyns, 2020). The logical progression to this reality finds its expression in the educational policy that promotes English as the language of education. This explains why Curle et al. (2020) suggest that the rise of English as a medium of instruction is influenced by various educational policy changes that, among other things, seek to catch up with institutional world rankings, invite more international students and change the workplace into an international arena by adopting English. It is now fitting to zoom into the Gulf Cooperation Council countries as a case in point.

The Case of Gulf Cooperation Council Countries

The Gulf Cooperation Council consists of six countries: Saudi Arabia, Oman, Qatar, Bahrain, UAE and Kuwait. The GCC is bound together by a common Arabic language, which has been in place for curricular and economic development (Hopkyns, 2020). However, the advent of English has been tied with neoliberal and capitalist orientation. English has been viewed as holding linguistic, economic and cultural capital sold as employability and economic mobility (Barnawi, 2018, p. xii). Each of the six GCC countries has been sold into the dominance of English as it shall be apparent further.

While Arabic has been the dominant medium of instruction in Saudi Arabia, events following 9/11 witnessed drastic changes to an educational policy where, among other things, English was introduced in schools as early as grade 4. Some higher education institutions increased programmes offered in English as a medium of instruction (Barnawi, 2018, p. 57). It must be highlighted here that such policy changes seem to have been driven by political influences than sound pedagogical considerations. Saudi Arabia increasingly found herself under pressure from the West, following the 9/11 events, to move from what is conceived by the West as a conservative education system to a liberal system. It would appear that such a liberal education system would only be attained through the adoption of English. In other words, the shift from the Arabic medium of instruction, which is the mother tongue for the majority of Saudis, did not consider the importance of being schooled in your first language, nor did it consider the ramifications of cultural and identity loss that come with language change.

Among other reasons, the shift into the use of English as a medium of instruction in Saudi Arabia is seen as a means of closing the gap between the job market requirements and outputs in higher education. It is also seen as a means of accomplishing Saudi Arabia's vision 2030 of having at least five universities ranked among the world's top 200 and having students perform above average internationally (Saudi Press Agency, 2016). From this perspective, it is clear that English is regarded as the passport to world recognition, even if it means abandoning the utility of local languages. Again, the job market is constantly viewed as dependent on English proficiency. Such a view would most likely be driven by the overwhelming presence of the expatriate community – the backbone of the economic activity in Saudi Arabia – which uses English in the workplace and for social interaction.

In UAE, there has been heavy local investment in education with an international presence. Ironically, the continued unemployment of Emirati youth is believed to be linked to their lack of English language skills. Their inability to speak English fluently makes them economically sidelined (Barnawi, 2018, p. 72). The situation in the UAE is exacerbated by the fact that Emiratis are outnumbered by expatriates in the workplace where only 10 per cent of employees are UAE nationals (Hopkyns, 2020). Similarly, expatriates operate in the English language which immediately sets nationals at a disadvantage.

This heavy educational investment in UAE has been mainly directed to the English language to which some scholars such as Al-Issa and Dahan (2011) have complained that this would jeopardize the Arabic language. There is a growing concern that young Emiratis are gradually growing up in English and are losing Arabic inter alia due to the pressure to attend English-medium schools that do not teach Arabic (Hopkyns, 2014). In other words, there is a growing generation of Emiratis that is pointing to the direction of monolingual English, to which Hopkyns (2014) recommends a move towards a bilingual situation. Nonetheless, however viable such a recommendation might seem, a bilingual situation involving English has usually served to promote the power and dominance of English as both languages are usually set on equal footing. That said, the direction of language maintenance and loss is sometimes unpredictable; for instance, some immigrants immediately lose their home language while others retain and maintain it perpetually (Spolsky, 1998).

Another fact that explains the heavy investment in English is that UAE seeks to diversify its economy by moving towards the global knowledge-based economy (Barnawi, 2018). In this arrangement, English is seen as the commodity through which a knowledge-based economy could be purchased. The result is that the whole educational experience and activity are reduced into a business venture where English is the currency. Unfortunately, the effects of such an approach are miscalculated – investment into English also means disinvestment into Arabic. It remains paradoxical that the nation's vision of building and maintaining (or preserving) the Emirati heritage and identity (Barnawi, 2018) is yoked with the promotion of English.

Qatar also reformed its education by promoting English as a medium of instruction, replacing Arabic, which is the language of the Qur'an and of Islam (Karmani, 2005). Although this move was praised by the West, local scholars and Muslims remained critical, arguing that English symbolized interference from the outside, thus undermining local culture and Arab and Muslim identity (Abdel-Moneim, 2016, p. 101). Indeed, there is no doubt that the replacement of Arabic by English is framed on the notion of replacing conservative Islam with a liberal system embodied by the English language. In this instance, there does not seem to be any pedagogical explanation except for the apparent appeasement of Western powers and the liberal system. The outspoken nature of these developments testifies to the interference of the outside world – the neocolonial regime – into local affairs.

Unfortunately, this heavy investment in English as a medium of instruction has not stopped the widening gap between the job market and the education system. Students were reported to be underachieving in science, math and English at all levels (Qatar Education and Training Sector Strategic Plan, 2011). This should serve as a testament to the fact that the introduction of English as a medium of instruction was not negotiated on sound pedagogic principles but was the brainchild of the Western liberal system that undermines the utility of Arabic as a viable local language. In fact, as Barnawi (2018) reports, the introduction of English as a replacement for Islam has created another social stratum where learners with high English proficiency are sent to prestigious Ivy League institutions and thereafter recruited into top jobs. There is no doubt that this situation creates stiff competition among learners who must ultimately sacrifice their Arabic or Islamic identity to be welcomed in the English-run job market.

In Oman, the government has been pushing private education providers to internationalize their programmes by benchmarking curricula and adopting English as a medium of instruction to their programmes (Barnawi, 2018). This has resulted in many Omani private education providers affiliating with international higher education institutions, for example in the United States, the United Kingdom and Australia. The obvious ethos in such a move is that only curricula designed and presented in the English language from an English-speaking world equal real education. It might as well be argued that prestige seems to be determined by the place of affiliation than by the programme of affiliation. That is, educational institutions seek to affiliate with institutions from the English-speaking world.

Such an arrangement has been criticized as selling a false idea that only an English-delivered education is efficient and that authentic education is with

Western collaboration (Al-Bakri, 2013, p. 19). Unfortunately, from a political perspective, there seems to be very little manoeuvre in arguing against such falsity. The policies that instigate such collaborations are based on subtle influences and lobbying by world powers that pose as standing for modernity, progress and transformation. Thus, resistance to adopting English as central to the modern world is likely to be seen as backwardness.

Unfortunately, such prestige attached to English has resulted in more opportunities and economic participation by young Omanis who are proficient in English while leaving many of them who are not proficient in economic hardships and social suffering. In addition, the promotion of English is influenced by the expatriate community that occupies most of the private sector jobs (Barnawi, 2018). Expatriates operate in English, which means the economy in which they are participants relies on English. There is, therefore, no way of escaping the dominance of English since the Omani society seems to have been organized along with the notions of giving access to English skills that are viewed as a passport to the job market (Barnawi, 2018).

In Kuwait, English has become a requirement for anyone wishing to gain entry into the job market (Dashti, 2015). This forces Kuwaiti citizens to seek proficiency in English if they want to take part in the country's economy. Linking English proficiency with the requirements for the job market is in sync with a neoliberal system (Barnawi, 2018). Furthermore, the fact that such proficiency must be exported from the English-speaking world also speaks of the neocolonial position of the English language (Prah, 2018). In other words, we could argue that the Kuwaiti economic system is being captured by English. And English has become the essential 'technicized skill' that reduces learners into future capital producers (Barnawi, 2018).

Moreover, since expatriates outnumber Kuwaiti citizens, Kuwaities are forced to find schools that can teach English to their children if they are to compete with expatriates in the private sector job market (Barnawi, 2018). But this is complicated by the fact that Kuwait has adopted policies that privatize the national economy, which is expected to entrench the dominance of English through private companies and conglomerate corporations. In the education sector, about 40 per cent of Kuwaiti youth are being educated by the private sector, which is growing faster than the public sector (Barnawi, 2018).

Since the Kuwaiti government took the direction of revising the educational policy by appealing to English as a medium of instruction, the result so far has produced social suffering, contradiction and false promises instead of liberating individuals (Barnawi, 2018). This is expected because the adoption of English as a medium of instruction creates unequal social classes, where those who gain proficiency, perhaps through private English tuition, are immediately placed at a better position than those who have a poor command of English.

The Kuwaiti private higher education institutions, which outnumber public institutions in the ratio of 9:1, are required to benchmark their curricula with international institutions and offer all their programmes in the medium of English. As a result, there is stiff competition between Kuwaiti private higher education institutions that benchmark their curricula with Western institutions and seek academic accreditation from Western providers (Barnawi, 2018).

In Bahrain, citizens find themselves at an economic disadvantage against expatriates because of low English proficiency (Barnawi, 2018). To exacerbate the situation, the Bahraini government adopted English as the medium of instruction as part of restructuring the education system, which amounted to the westernization of the educational system. In this situation, the disparity caused by the overwhelming majority of the expatriate community contributes to the obliteration of citizens' language which is not spoken by the expatriates. While the government should be seen to work for the citizens, it does not seem to be the case as the dominant English language used predominantly among the expatriates is extended to the citizens.

This adoption of English as a medium of instruction in Bahrain has resulted in the replacement of the Arabic language, culture and heritage with the dominance of academic monolingualism (Phan, 2017). Such replacement is facilitated by the adoption of the Western form of education without interrogating the hegemony of the English language. Instead, English is sold as the solution to the realization of the expansion of the economy (Barnawi, 2018). What puts Bahraini citizens in a dire situation is that English is adopted as not only the medium of instruction but also the whole Western pedagogy and practice. There is, therefore, no way of stopping the disappearance of the Arabic language, culture and identity in such a situation.

Bahrain is also keen to catch up in the world rankings of universities, which are seen as only possible through internationalization that involves the adoption of English as a medium of instruction (Barnawi, 2018). Unfortunately, the Bahraini government has not seen that the education system that has adopted English as a medium of instruction does not seem to have produced the envisaged workforce among Bahraini youth. Part of the problem is that the Bahraini youth seems to have been denied epistemic access which could reportedly be solved by involving the Arabic language.

Discussion

There is no doubt that the linguistic dominance of Arabic in the Arab world is being replaced by English. The dominance of English is encroaching on other former colonial languages such as French and Portuguese. There is a growing trend among French-speaking colonies in Africa to opt for English. Even in France (and Germany), the English language in higher education is penetrating through internationalization. This is not without local complaints that the intellectual space is being taken over by the Anglo-Saxon pattern of thought (Doiz et al., 2011; Salomone, 2015). The biggest outcry is that local languages are not allowed to develop, because intellectual linguistic development is invested in English. In the context of this chapter, Arabic is continuously undermined through the hegemony of English.

Although Arabization was a religious penetration that forcefully advanced into different territories, there is no doubt that the capitalist neocolonial project is behind the advancement of English. For instance, there is no coincidence that the United States influences Saudi Arabia's change of education policy to allow more English as a medium of instruction. In addition, the involvement of Britain in the education systems of many GCC countries is not coincidental. English has been successfully re-engineered as an educational commodity. Economic woes have been conveniently explained as resulting from less English. Paradoxically, the shift to more English did not seem to have improved the economic participation of many natives in GCC countries; instead, more problems of English incompetence have affected the educational advancement of citizens. At the same time, the academic enterprise of English language teaching continues to generate revenues, which benefits mostly the providers and not the learners.

It is also obvious that English is at the centre of internationalization and globalization. This coincides with the political dominance of the English-speaking countries, chiefly the United States and United Kingdom, in the world. English is, therefore, sold as the global and international language (Crystal, 2012). The unfortunate part is that those who buy the English language do so to the detriment of their languages, culture and identity. For instance, the growing demand for English in GCC countries among citizens is already relegating Arabic into a second-class language, which might ultimately be reduced into a religious language and eventually lose its currency and die out.

While globalization is arguably linked to English as a lingua franca where communication in English is essentialized for business, travel, entertainment and so on, internationalization emphasizes the utility of English as the medium of instruction in formal educational transactions. English as a medium of instruction has been equated with a prestigious education, academic literacy and modernization (Lin & Martin, 2005). Epistemic access has been denied to those who use a different language other than English in higher education. Rather than based on sound linguistic and sociolinguistic realities, English as a medium of instruction shows linkages with a capitalist, neocolonial and neoliberal agenda. In other words, the main beneficiaries of English as a medium of instruction are not students who use English as a second or foreign language but the native speakers of English who are immediately set at an advantage of epistemic access and by default are the providers of tuition to students who want access to native-like proficiency of English. This equates to trillions of dollars of revenue.

In GCC countries, while on the one hand, Arabic has been conceived by the West as representative of Islam and thus seen as complicit with a terrorist agenda, on the other hand, English seems to have been presented as a symbol of democracy, freedom and modernity (Skutnabb-Kangas & Phillipson, 2010). This, unfortunately, bears all the marks of neocolonial arrangements where local languages are associated with backwardness to the effect that locals are reduced into begging for a foreign language.

The youth, in particular, is made to believe that the Western society, represented by the English culture, is the ideal society. Barnawi (2018), for instance, reports how Saudi youth try to emulate the American culture through dress code and mannerisms with the hope that it would speed up their assimilation of the English language. A similar trend is also visible among young Emiratis who are drifting more into the Western dress code and culture (Hopkyns, 2014). All this happen perhaps to confirm that language is linked to social identity – which means English cannot be adopted solely for instrumental purposes but will come with all its cultural orientations. The question that persists is whether there is anything that can be done to alter this situation. Perhaps, the attempt to address that question lies in decolonization.

Decolonization

Decolonization in its simplest form means reversing the effects of colonization. For example, if lands were usurped during the colonial regime, decolonization seeks to restore the lands to their original owners. If, for instance, the dignity and value of certain groups of people were lost during the colonial regime, decolonization works towards restoring that dignity and value. But that is easier said than done. One of the reasons for that is the brutality of colonialism which implies that similar pain would be experienced during the decolonization project (Skutnabb-Kangas & Phillipson, 2010). Those who benefited from the exploits of colonization would not wish to part with those gains. But also, those who were formerly exploited during colonialism and had subsequently benefited from it through neocolonialism would not want to invest in the project of decolonization (Luke, 2005). Another pertinent assertion by Canagarajah (2005, p. 196) is that 'decolonisation entails resisting English in favour of building an autonomous nation state', which he contrasts with globalization that has reinvigorated the importance of English in all communities through popular culture, markets, new technologies and so forth.

In the context of this chapter, Arabic in the Arab world is set on a downward spiral as English unleashes its dominance in the linguistic terrain (Skutnabb-Kangas & Phillipson, 2008). Although it might seem that such a downward spiral is a natural phenomenon, it is clear that the promotion of English is a deliberate plan to advance the cultural dominance of the English-speaking world (Skutnabb-Kangas & Phillipson, 2010). For instance, the rise of the political, economic and cultural dominance of America has been directly linked to the promotion of English as a global language (Skutnabb-Kangas & Phillipson, 2010). Skutnabb-Kangas and Phillipson (2010, p. 3) aptly state that '[i]n US colonies and in the British Empire, English was privileged and other languages marginalized. Today's global ruling class tend to be proficient in English'.

It should be noted that the shift from education in the native language to education in a foreign language such as English has negative ramifications for the majority. Learners who are schooled in a foreign language struggle to reach their full potential – as a result, they are either often labelled as unintelligent or end up dropping out and cannot join the job market. Therefore, the heavy investment in English in the GCC countries that promises to assist the youth gain employment has not produced the desired outcomes. The reason is that the introduction of English as a medium of instruction at the expense of Arabic represents a misdiagnosis of the problem. Instead of increasing the employability of the youth, the imposition of English as a medium of instruction in education has created harmful psychological, social, political and economic problems (Skutnabb-Kangas & Phillipson, 2010).

There is undoubtedly not much that can be done to lessen the power of English in the world. However, there is a lot that can be done to prevent the linguistic annihilation of local languages. In fact, while the expansion of English is driven by the ethos of monolingualism, sociolinguistic realities point to the multilingual situation of the world in general. The plurality of languages, from the biblical metaphor of Babel, recognizes diversity as an organizing factor. In that respect, Skutnabb-Kangas and Phillipson (2008) argue that subtractive language planning, where local languages are replaced by the powerful English language, is at odds with linguistic human rights. This contributes to linguistic genocide, which can be seen in cases such as the disappearance of Hokkien that used to be the mother tongue of the majority of Chinese in Singapore (Lin & Martin, 2005). It also contributes to the disempowerment of local languages such as the case of Nenets in the Russian Federation, where the medium of instruction is Russian to the extent that students who go through the whole educational system exit with the only option of speaking Russian (Skutnabb-Kangas & Phillipson, 2010). Those who tend to be proficient in Nenets are those who either did not go to school or could not finish school – in this way, Nenets is inversely proportional to education (Skutnabb-Kangas & Phillipson, 2010).

The solution to the decline of indigenous languages is additive multilingualism. In the case of the GCC countries, Arabic should remain the medium of instruction for the majority of the citizens. This will reduce the negative ramifications already associated with English as a medium of instruction where the intellectual capability of citizens is measured by their proficiency in English. There should be a realization that English, contrary to the prevailing rhetoric, is not a panacea to socio-economic woes. The promotion of Arabic, which is a well-established language capable of handling sophisticated intellectual and technological advances, will ensure that the neocolonial agenda of the West does not lead to the decline and ultimate death of the Arabic language, culture and identity.

In addition, there should be an acknowledgement that the present subtractive education is based on colonial top-down planning. This planning does not take into account the aspirations and linguistic realities of the general language users. Additive multilingualism should, therefore, be organized from the ground up. In other words, it first takes into account the linguistic make-up of the general public or citizenry and then only adds to that rather than subtract. In this way, linguistic human rights would get protected and language planning would be decolonized.

Conclusion

This chapter has traced the spread and dominance of English in the Arab world by drawing similarities with the process of Arabization. It argued that while

Arabization contributed to the spread of Islam, just as Russian contributed to Soviet communism, English is set to expand the American empire (Skutnabb-Kangas & Phillipson, 2010).

The spread of the empire is facilitated through the processes of internationalization and globalization. Through these processes, English is regarded as lingua franca and as the medium of instruction in education. Global communication and high-stakes transactions are carried out in the medium of English. At the same time, HEIs are pressurized to offer programmes in the medium of English in the race to attract international students or remain competitive in the academic enterprise.

GCC countries have been used to illustrate the penetration and hegemony of the English language in education. In these countries, English as a medium of instruction is promoted with the rhetoric of modernity and internationalization. Proficiency in English is sold as a solution to the economic participation of the youth. However, it appears that instead of solving socio-economic problems, the English-medium instruction brings with it other problems such as stigmatization of those who are not proficient in English and loss of identity resulting from the relegation of Arabic into a second-class language.

While English on its own as a language is not problematic, the problem is brought by subtractive education which is set to replace indigenous languages with the powerful English language. Subtractive education contributes to violations of linguistic human rights. In GCC countries, this is seen through the replacement of Arabic with English as the medium of instruction. This replacement is the first step towards the murder of the language. Subtractive education works in tandem with the colonial top-down planning where the rights of those on the ground are not recognized.

The chapter has proposed that diversity should be acknowledged as the necessary ingredient in the survival of languages and cultures. It is, therefore, possible for multiple languages to coexist healthily. Additive multilingualism organized from the ground up is proposed as a solution where in the case of the Arab world, Arabic is not disturbed as the medium of instruction but English is added. In this way, the culture, identity and language of the Arab people are preserved and developed.

References

Abdel-Moneim, M. (2016). *A political economy of Arab education: Policies and comparative perspective*. London: Routledge.

Al-Bakri, S. (2013). Problematising English medium of instruction in Oman. *International Journal of Bilingual & Multilingual Teachers of English*, *1*(2), 55–69.

Al-Issa, A., & Dahan, L. S. (2011). Global English and endangered Arabic in the United Arab Emirates. In A. Al-Issa & L. S. Dahan (Eds.), *Global English and Arabic: Issues of language culture and identity* (pp. 1–22). Oxford: Peter Lang.

Barnawi, O. Z. (2018). *Neoliberalism and English language education policies in the Arabian Gulf*. London: Routledge.

Canagarajah, A. S. (2005). Accommodating tensions in Language-in-Education policies: An afterword. In M. Y. Lin & P. W. Martin (Eds.), *Decolonisation, globalisation: Language-in-education policy and practice* (pp. 194–201). Clevedon: Multilingual Matters.

Canagarajah, S. (2007). Lingua franca English, multilingual communities, and language acquisition. *The Modern Language Journal*, *91*, 923–939.

Canagarajah, S. (2014). In search of a new paradigm for teaching English as an international language. *TESOL Journal*, *5*(4), 767–785.

Crystal, D. (2012). A global language. In P. Seargeant & J. Swann (Eds.), *English in the world: History, diversity, change* (pp. 151–177). London: Routledge.

Curle, S., Jablonkai, R., Mittelmeier, J., Sahan, K., & Veitch, A. (2020). English medium part 1: Literature review. In N. Galloway (Ed.), *English in higher education*. British Council. https://www.teachingenglish.org.uk/sites/teacheng/files/L020_English_HE_lit_review_FINAL.pdf.

Dashti, A. (2015). The role and status of the English language in Kuwait. *English Today*, *31*(3), 28–33.

Doiz, A., Lasagabaster, D., & Siera, J. M. (2011). Internationalization, multilingualism and English-medium of instruction. *World Englishes*, *30*(3), 345–359.

Harmer, J. (2006). *The practice of English language teaching*. Harlow: Longman.

Hopkyns, S. (2014). The effects of global English on culture and identity in the UAE: A double-edged sword. *Learning and Teaching in Higher Education: Gulf Perspectives*, *11*(2), 1–20.

Hopkyns, S. (2020). Linguistic hybridity and cultural multiplicity in Emirati identity construction. In M. Karolak & N. Allam (Eds.), *Gulf Cooperation Council culture and identities in the new millennium* (pp. 179–199). Contemporary Gulf Studies. doi:10.1007/978-981-15-1529-3_10.

Karmani, S. (2005). TESOL in a time of terror: Towards an Islamic perspective on applied linguistics. *TESOL Quarterly*, *39*(4), 738–744.

Lin, A. M. Y., & Martin, P. W. (2005). From a critical deconstruction paradigm to a construction paradigm: An introduction to decolonization, globalization and language-in-education policy and practice. In A. M. Y. Lin & P. W. Martin (Eds.), *Decolonisation, globalisation: Language-in-education policy and practice* (pp. 1–19). Clevedon: Multilingual Matters.

Luke, A. (2005). Foreword: On the possibilities of a post-colonial language education. In A. M. Y. Lin & P. W. Martin (Eds.), *Decolonisation, globalisation: Language-in-education policy and practice* (pp. xiv–xix). Clevedon: Multilingual Matters.

Ntombela, B. (2012). Literature and culture: Literature and identity building. In A. Roscoe & R. Al Mahrooqi (Eds.), *Literacy, literature and identity* (pp. 136–151). Newcastle upon Tyne: Cambridge Scholars Publishing.

Ntombela, B. X. S. (2017). 'The double-edged sword': African languages under siege. In V. Msila (Ed.), *Decolonising knowledge for Africa's renewal* (pp. 161–179). Randburg: KR Publishing.

Ntombela, B. (2020). Switch from mother tongue to English: A double-jeopardy. *Studies in English Language Teaching, 8*(2), 22–35. doi:10.22158/selt.v8n2p22.

Nyika, A. (2015). Mother tongue as the medium of instruction at developing country universities in a global context. *South African Journal of Science, 111*(1/2), 1–5.

Nqoma, L., Abonglia, J. A., & Foncha, J. W. (2017). Educators and learner's perceptions on English first additional language speaker's use of English as medium of instruction. *Gender & Behavior, 2017*, 8830–8841.

Pakenham, T. (2014). *The scramble for Africa.* London: Abacus.

Phan, L. H. (2017). *Transnational education crossing 'Asia' and 'the West': Adjusted desire, transformative mediocrity and neo-colonial disguise.* London: Routledge.

Prah, K. K. (2018). *The challenge of decolonizing education.* Cape Town: CASAS.

Qatar Education and Training Sector Strategic Plan. (2011). *Education and Training Sector Strategic Plan 2011-2016.* http://planipolis.iiep.unesco.org/sites/planipolis/files/ressources/qatar_etss_2011-2016.pdf.

Salomone, R. (2015). The rise of global English-medium of instruction and language rights. *Language Problems and Language Planning, 39*(3), 245–268.

Saudi Press Agency. (2016). Kingdom of Saudi Arabia's vision 2030 Riyadh 16. https://www.spa.gov.sa/viewstory.php?lang=en&newsid=1493792.

Skutnabb-Kangas, T. & Phillipson, R. (2008). A human rights perspective on language ecology. In A. Creese, P. Martin, & N. Hornberger (Eds.), *Encyclopedia of language and education* (pp. 3–14). New York: Springer.

Skutnabb-Kangas, T. & Phillipson, R. (2010). The politics of language in globalisation: Maintenance, marginalization, or murder. In N. Coupland (Ed.), *Handbook on language and globalization* (pp. 77–100). Maiden: Blackwell.

Spolsky, B. (1998). *Sociolinguistics.* Oxford: Oxford University Press.

Taguchi, N. (2014). English-medium education in the global society. *International Review of Applied Linguistics in Language Teaching, 52*(2), 89–98.

UNESCO. (2016). *If you don't understand how can you learn?* Global Education Monitoring Report (Policy Paper). UNESCO.

2

University Students and Instructors' Attitudes towards English-Medium Instruction Courses

Voices from Iran

Ali Derakhshan, Mahboubeh Rakhshandehroo and Samantha Curle

Introduction

In today's globalized higher education (HE) sphere, internationalization is closely linked with Englishization (Chang, 2010; Kirkpatrick, 2011). English has been identified as a 'killer language' (Coleman, 2006, p. 1), due to its rapid adoption as an international lingua franca and, more importantly, as the medium of instruction (Carrió-Pastor, 2020; Dearden, 2014; Macaro et al., 2018). While the use of English as a language of instruction can have both political and cultural consequences in countries where the first language is not English, the internationalization of education and the desire to compete globally have contributed to the rise of English-medium instruction (EMI) in higher education around the world (Macaro et al., 2018). Since English is one of the most extensively used languages today, EMI has often been seen as a way of getting access to an international academic community whose lingua franca is English (Vinke, 1995). Teaching courses in English enables educational institutions to attract international students and faculty members while providing students and instructors the opportunity to engage in an international research community, where a substantial amount of scientific research is written in English (Graddol, 2000).

EMI in Asia started through a partner collaboration with English-speaking countries and/or launching brunch campuses. Gradually, Asian governments and universities have developed their own EMI programmes. Many Asian ministries of education, including in Japan, Korea, China and other Asian countries, have supported their HE sectors to implement EMI, through a number of internationalization initiatives (Barnard, 2014).

In Iran, nonetheless, EMI has not been encouraged by the Ministry of Education, and there has been no evidence of EMI implementation in Iran's HE sector in the literature. Nevertheless, university faculty members and students have shown positive attitudes towards promoting the use of English as an internationalization strategy (Khorasani & Zamani Manesh, 2012; Rassouli & Osam, 2019), as well as towards EMI implementation (Ghorbani & Alavi, 2014; Hejazi & Zare-ee, 2017; Zare-ee & Gholami, 2013).

This chapter seeks to contribute to the literature by shedding light on the current status of EMI implementation in Iran's HE and illustrating that EMI has been recently introduced and implemented at a few Iranian universities. It attempts to address the current attitudes and perceptions of university students and instructors towards EMI courses running at Iranian universities. The following three main research questions are addressed:

(1) What are the university students and instructors' perceptions towards the advantages/opportunities of the EMI courses?
(2) What are the university students and instructors' perceptions towards the disadvantages/challenges of the EMI courses?
(3) How can the status of EMI be improved at Iranian universities?

Literature Review

The first non-English universities that offered EMI programmes were in Europe in the 1980s. The Bologna Declaration (1999) created a mobile space throughout Europe and facilitated the expansion of EMI (Phillipson, 2009). In Asia, the countries that used to be colonized by English-speaking countries have adopted EMI faster than other Asian countries without this experience (Byun et al., 2011). The rationale for offering EMI in Asia differs widely but has been focused on avoiding falling behind in the competitive global market and international rankings (Barnard, 2014). Many Asian ministries of education have launched internationalization initiatives to encourage and facilitate EMI adoption (Hommond, 2016).

Alongside the rapid EMI implementation, much research attention has been focused on the challenges and negative outcomes of EMI (Aizawa et al., 2020; Al-Bakri, 2013; Byun et al., 2011; Huang, 2012; Lei & Hu, 2014; Phuong &

Nguyen, 2019; Pun & Thomas, 2020; Soe et al., 2020; Ter-Vardanyan, 2021). For instance, Byun et al. (2011), in an exploratory survey study, attempted to investigate the challenges and disadvantageous sides of EMI classes. To this end, using surveys and focus group interviews, they gathered Korean students' perceptions towards EMI courses. Analysing the verbal and textual data, researchers mentioned inadequate English proficiency of students and instructors as the main challenge of EMI courses experienced by students at Korean universities. Similarly, Phuong and Nguyen (2019) set out to probe the challenges and drawbacks of EMI courses by administering a close-ended questionnaire to 136 Vietnamese students. The analysis of students' responses illuminated that they perceived 'difficulty in comprehending the specialized textbooks written in English' as the most important challenge of EMI courses. Subsequently, Soe et al. (2020) explored the challenges of EMI courses experienced by 120 Myanmar teachers and students at the University of Mandalay using questionnaire surveys and semi-structured interviews. The findings from qualitative and quantitative data analysis indicated that both teachers and students viewed 'low language proficiency levels' and 'confidence levels of EMI practitioners' as the most significant challenges of EMI classes, respectively. Gradually, the opportunities and positive outcomes of EMI have also been addressed in research projects (e.g. Başibek et al., 2014; Brown, 2018; Diezmas & Barrera, 2021; Tamtam et al., 2012; Wallitsch, 2014; Xie & Curle, 2019).

Although many Asian ministries of education are encouraging the universities to rapidly adopt EMI, they are sometimes criticized for being too government-led and forcing the HE sectors to implement EMI without carefully considering the students and faculty members' linguistic limitations and planning for curriculum design. In contrast with the literature, Iranian HE seems to be missing this support from the Iranian government, despite the fact that Iranian students and faculty members give the impression of being ready to take part in EMI programmes (Khorasani & Zamani Manesh, 2012; Rassouli & Osam, 2019). In Iran, Persian (Farsi) has been used as the official language in the HE sector. Starting from 2013, a small number of studies have addressed the feasibility of EMI implementation in Iran. Zare-ee and Gholami (2013) reported that due to the widespread use of English as an international language, EMI implementation would be beneficial in communication with English-based scholars and avoiding content loss that often occurs during the translation process of research studies, particularly in science, technology, engineering and mathematics (STEM) subjects.

A year later, Ghorbani and Alavi's (2014) study documented that the potential advantages of EMI in Iran's HE can be twice more than its disadvantages. Among the advantages, using EMI as 'a means for scientific communication' and its role in 'facilitating the use of internet and computer software' (Ghorbani & Alavi, 2014, p. 8) were highly ranked. As for the disadvantages, the challenges associated with comprehension of class materials in English were frequently mentioned. The study found that before implementing EMI, emphasis should be placed on students' English skills through systematic 'modifications in the school educational system' (Ghorbani & Alavi, 2014, p. 9) and that EMI needs to be supported hand in hand by the university and the government.

Hejazi and Zare-ee's (2017) study results were in line with those of the previous two studies. They specifically focused on the positive outcomes of EMI, including its role in facilitating the participation of Iranians in academic events, avoiding unessential translation and a better academic communication opportunity with the world. These studies showed no significant differences between students (both undergraduate and graduate) and faculty members' positive attitudes towards EMI.

In the reviewed literature, several studies in Asia have examined the challenges and opportunities of EMI courses (e.g. Aizawa et al., 2020; Byun et al., 2011; Lei & Hu, 2014; Wallitsch, 2014; Xie & Curle, 2019), but there is insufficient evidence for the advantages and disadvantages of such courses in Iran. To put it differently, a scant number of studies have been done to explore the benefits and drawbacks of EMI classes at Iranian universities (e.g. Ghorbani & Alavi, 2014; Zare-ee & Gholami, 2013). In addition, much of the previous research in this era has focused on university students' perceptions (e.g. Kym & Kym, 2014; Phuong & Nguyen, 2019); hence, the voices of university instructors are not extensively heard. Consequently, this study seeks to fill these gaps by surveying both the university students and instructors' perceptions regarding the challenges and opportunities of EMI courses at Iranian universities.

Methodology

Participants

As put forward by Nassaji (2020), using multiple data sources, known as triangulation, can help researchers 'to achieve a more accurate and complete understanding of the issue under investigation, thus increasing the validity and

Table 2.1 Demographic information of students

Participants	Gender	Age	Nationality	University
1	Female	23	Iraqi	Ferdowsi University of Mashhad
2	Female	25	Iraqi	Ferdowsi University of Mashhad
3	Female	27	Iraqi	Ferdowsi University of Mashhad
4	Female	20	Lebanese	Tehran University of Medical Sciences
5	Female	25	Iraqi	Tehran University of Medical Sciences
6	Male	26	Iraqi	Tehran University of Medical Sciences
7	Male	20	Tanzanian	Tehran University of Medical Sciences
8	Male	22	Lebanese	Tehran University of Medical Sciences
9	Male	24	Iranian	Tehran University of Medical Sciences
10	Female	33	Afghan	Allameh Tabataba'i University
11	Female	23	Afghan	Allameh Tabataba'i University
12	Male	33	Iranian	Isfahan University of Medical Sciences

Table 2.2 Demographic information of instructors

Participants	Gender	Age	Nationality	University
1	Male	55	Iranian	Isfahan University of Medical Sciences
2	Female	32	Iranian	Isfahan University of Medical Sciences
3	Female	52	Iranian	Isfahan University of Medical Sciences
4	Male	33	Iranian	Isfahan University of Medical Sciences
5	Male	29	Iranian	Ferdowsi University of Mashhad
6	Female	33	Iranian	Ferdowsi University of Mashhad
7	Female	34	Iranian	Allameh Tabataba'i University
8	Male	36	Iranian	Allameh Tabataba'i University
9	Female	29	Iranian	Tehran University of Medical Sciences
10	Female	48	Iranian	Tehran University of Medical Sciences
11	Female	42	Iranian	Tehran University of Medical Sciences
12	Male	30	Iranian	Tehran University of Medical Sciences

credibility of the findings' (p. 428). Accordingly, two groups of participants, including twelve university students (Table 2.1) and twelve university lecturers (Table 2.2) took part in this study. They were selected based on the purposive sampling method. The primary objective of purposive sampling, which is the most recommended sampling technique in qualitative inquiry, is to handpick a sample that can reasonably be deemed to be representative of the target population (Ary et al., 2018). To increase the representativeness of the findings, the participants were chosen from both genders, different age levels, different nationality (i.e. Afghan, Iraqi, Iranian, Lebanese, Tanzanian) and different universities (i.e. Ferdowsi University of Mashhad, Tehran University of Medical Sciences (TUMS), Allameh Tabataba'i University, Isfahan University of Medical Sciences).

The participants were selected based on their willingness to participate in the study. Prior to initiating the inquiry, respondents were asked to fill out the consent forms. They were assured that their valuable information would be employed for research purposes and would be kept confidential. They were also informed that their biographical information would not be divulged, and pseudonyms would be used in the research.

Data Collection Instruments and Procedure

Open-ended Questionnaire

To gather students and instructors' perceptions towards the opportunities and challenges of the EMI courses, an open-ended questionnaire containing two different sections was employed (see Appendix). In the first section, participants were invited to write about their demographic information, namely gender, age, nationality and university. In the second section, participants were asked to answer three open-ended questions about EMI courses they have experienced in their universities. The rationale of employing open-ended questionnaire in this inquiry was that 'they are easier to administer (notably when conducted online), provide more time for respondents to complete questionnaires, and do not need to be transcribed' (Friedman, 2012, p. 190).

To enhance the trustworthiness of the questionnaire, three non-participant university students and instructors filled out the first draft of the questionnaire. The required revisions were made on the basis of piloting outcomes. To finalize the questions, two university instructors in the field of applied linguistics who have conducted some studies on EMI courses were invited to check the appropriateness of the questions in terms of language and content. Based on their comments, the open-ended questions were finalized. The finalized version of the questionnaire was sent through social networks such as WhatsApp and Telegram to the respondents.

Semi-structured Interviews

For the sake of triangulation which enhances the credibility of qualitative findings (Lincoln & Guba, 1985; Nassaji, 2020), semi-structured interviews were also held with half of the participants. Prior to initiating the interview sessions, the researchers prepared an interview guide encompassing three predetermined questions and some follow-up ones. Before interviewing the participants of the study, some interview sessions were held with some non-participants in order to pilot the interview guide that helps researchers to detect the possible problems of the interview prompts (Friedman, 2012).

The researchers interviewed each participant individually. Since all participants had a good command of English, the interview sessions were conducted in English. Due to the Covid-19 pandemic, to obey the health protocols stated by the World Health Organization (WHO) to decrease the chance of spreading the coronavirus, the interview sessions were held through the online platform of Adobe Connect. The interview sessions were recorded, and the interviewees' perceptions towards EMI courses were transcribed verbatim for further content analysis.

Data Analysis

Content analysis was employed as the method of data analysis in this inquiry. Content analysis as a widely used qualitative data analysis approach involves 'coding data in a systematic way in order to discover patterns and develop well-grounded interpretations' (Friedman, 2012, p. 191). As put forward by Cole (1988), content analysis is a common approach for analysing various modes of data, including textual, visual and verbal. As such, it was employed in this study to analyse both verbal and textual data gathered from participants' responses.

Overall, there are two main approaches to content analysis, namely deductive approach and inductive approach. In the deductive approach, analysis is operationalized on the basis of some theoretical frameworks, while in inductive content analysis, there is no prior theoretical framework, and the codes and sub-codes are derived entirely from the obtained data (Elo & Kyngäs, 2008). In the present study, the researchers implemented the inductive approach to analyse participants' perceptions towards EMI courses. Both inductive and deductive approaches of content analysis proceed in three phases: preparation, organization (i.e. coding process) and reporting (Burnard, 1996).

To increase the credibility of the study, all phases of content analysis have been implemented by two applied linguists. At the preparation phase, the analysts initiated the process by selecting sentences as the unit of analysis. Prior to initiating the organization phase, the analysts decided to examine only the manifest data. Then, to become acquainted with the depth and breadth of the gathered data, the analysts read and reread participants' responses. In the organization phase, they went through three stages: open coding, creating categories and abstraction in order to code the obtained data. The coding process in this study was done through MAXQDA software (version 2020) due to the fact that 'using a Computer-Assisted Qualitative Data Analysis Software (CAQDAS) can improve the credibility of the coding process' (Baralt, 2012, p. 228). At the first stage of the coding process (i.e. open coding), the analysts went through the data line by line and freely generated some initial codes. In the stage of creating categories, they drew connections among the generated codes and grouped them under higher-order headings. Finally, in the abstraction stage, the analysts named each category through 'content-characteristic words'. During this stage, subcategories (sub-themes) with similar statements were grouped together as categories (themes), and categories were classified as main categories. As the result of analysing process, eleven themes and four sub-themes were extracted from participants' perceptions towards the opportunities and challenges of the EMI courses. Employing Krippendorff's alpha (α), an inter-coder agreement coefficient of 0.91 was reached, which represented a high consensus between the coders.

Due to the fact that member checking can increase the trustworthiness of qualitative findings (Lincoln & Guba, 1985; Rolfe, 2006), at the end of this three-phase approach, the derived themes and sub-themes were returned to ten participants to verify their accuracy on the basis of their personal experiences in EMI courses.

Findings

The findings of the present study represent the opportunities and challenges of the EMI courses experienced by students and instructors at Iranian universities. Based on the research questions of the study, three general patterns emerged: the advantages/opportunities of EMI courses, the disadvantages/challenges of EMI courses and the suggestions for improving the status of EMI courses at Iranian universities. These patterns are demonstrated by several themes and sub-themes. Each theme is closely related to a specific pattern associated with a particular research question. In the following sections, the derived themes and sub-themes were portrayed through some hierarchical models.

Advantages/Opportunities of EMI Courses

As the first question, participants were asked to express their perceptions regarding the advantages/opportunities of EMI courses. The analysis of both verbal and textual responses provided by students and instructors resulted in

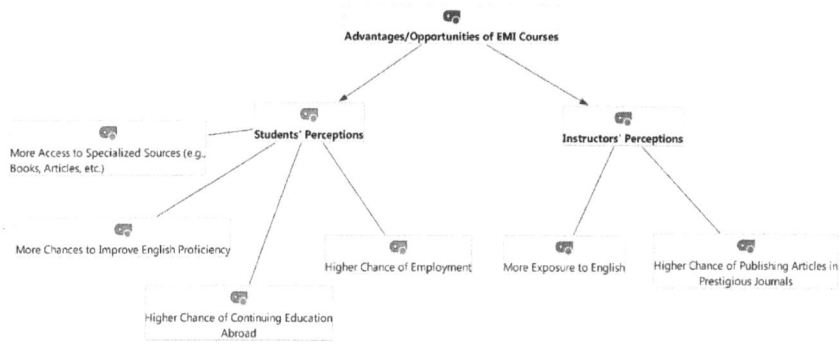

Figure 2.1 Advantages/opportunities of EMI courses.

six themes (Figure 2.1): more access to specialized sources, more chances to improve language proficiency, higher chance of continuing education abroad, higher chance of employment, more exposure to English and higher chance of publishing articles in prestigious journals.

More access to specialized sources as the first advantage of EMI courses refers to resource availability. Most of the students stated that EMI enables them to access various specialized sources that are not available in their mother tongue. They illustrated that 'EMI helps us to access more valuable resources because most of the specialized textbooks and reliable articles are published in English' (P6).

Regarding the second advantage of EMI courses, students highlighted the role of EMI in improving their English proficiency. They explicated that due to more exposure to English in EMI courses, their English language proficiency would be considerably enhanced. For instance, some of the participants stated,

> P9: In addition to learning the subject matter, we can improve our English proficiency in EMI courses.
>
> P12: EMI provides more exposure to English which leads us to become more proficient users of English language.

As another advantage of EMI courses, students noted that EMI increases their chance of continuing education abroad. Some statements demonstrating this advantage of EMI courses are as follows:

> P8: EMI gives us more opportunities to continue our studies abroad.
>
> P9: Due to the fact that having a good command of English is a necessity for educating abroad, I think EMI offers higher chances for university students to pursue their studies overseas.

Students also mentioned *higher chance of employment* as the last advantage of EMI courses. They believe that being a more proficient user of English can dramatically increase their chances of employment.

> P4: Our chances of employment can be enhanced as the result of EMI courses because those who have good command of English will be offered more employment opportunities.

In line with the second advantage of EMI courses mentioned by students, many instructors stated that EMI offers university students *more exposure to English*, which causes improvements in their level of English proficiency. To illustrate,

> P2: One of the advantages of running a class in English is that the students are exposed to English, and the higher the input and exposure, the more output will occur accordingly.

> P10: The main advantage of EMI courses would be that the use of English as the medium of instruction ideally increases the amount of exposure to English. More exposure to English is likely to exert great influence on students' English language proficiency.

The second theme extracted from instructors' responses regarding the advantages of EMI courses is *higher chance of publishing articles in prestigious journals*. They declared that 'EMI enables students to write in English, helping them to publish their academic articles in peer-reviewed journals' (P6).

Disadvantages/Challenges of EMI Courses

As the second question, respondents were asked about the disadvantages/challenges of EMI courses. Analysing the gathered data culminated in five themes and four sub-themes (Figure 2.2). Among them, three themes were derived from students' responses. *Difficulty in expressing the ideas/opinions* is one of the important challenges raised by students. Many students noticed that they face difficulties in expressing their ideas during classroom discussions. For instance, participant 12 expressed,

> P12: In EMI courses, due to insufficient English proficiency, it is difficult to share our ideas and opinions with others.

Students also mentioned that they encounter some challenges in comprehending the materials for the same reason. This challenge of EMI can directly be demonstrated through the following statements.

P6: I am not personally interested in EMI courses since I cannot comprehend the academic contents very well.

P7: It is difficult for us to fully grasp the information provided in our specialized textbooks.

As the third disadvantage of EMI courses, students stated that EMI decreases the amount of their participation in classroom activities. To illustrate,

P8: Since we are not skilled enough in English language, it is not possible for us to participate in classroom tasks and activities.

As Figure 2.2 depicts, instructors' perceptions towards the disadvantages of EMI courses were categorized into two main themes, namely *instructor-related factors* and *student-related factors*. *Instructor-related factors* encompass a single sub-theme, which is *inadequate English proficiency of instructors*. Instructors expounded that some EMI instructors are not proficient enough to transmit content through English language.

P3: I assume that the main problem of EMI courses is teachers' lack of English proficiency.

P10: One of the most prevalent challenges of EMI courses is the inadequate level of English language proficiency of lecturers and professors while they're trying to run a full class in foreign language.

Student-related factors generated from instructors' responses comprised three sub-themes –*inadequate English proficiency of students, lack of motivation and interest* and *lack of confidence*. As for English proficiency of students, some instructors stated,

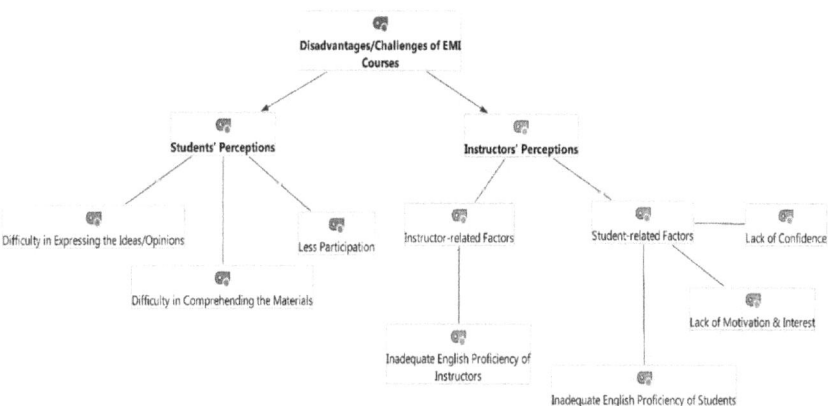

Figure 2.2 Disadvantages/challenges of EMI courses.

P3: Sometimes learners do not understand what I say and I have to explain in their mother tongue.

P8: Due to inadequate English proficiency, some students may find it difficult to understand the ideas and information presented in English.

For the next sub-theme, *lack of motivation and interest*, some participants mentioned that 'immersion in a foreign language may demotivate some students who are not proficient language users' (P2). Finally, for the last sub-theme in this regard, instructors reported that 'due to low English levels, students are not confident to learn content through English language' (P10).

Suggestions for Improving the Status of EMI Courses at Iranian Universities

As the last question, participants were asked to suggest some ways through which the status of EMI courses can be improved. Their responses were grouped into two main categories: *students' suggestions* and *instructors' suggestions*. As Figure 2.3 reveals, university students proposed two solutions including *train instructors for EMI courses* and *employ some English native instructors for EMI courses*. The following responses of students explicate these two practical solutions respectively:

P9: Since EMI courses are somehow different from other specialized courses, university administrators should provide some teacher training courses for university lecturers to equip them with the knowledge of teaching content through English language.

P7: To improve the efficiency of EMI courses, university administrators should ask some English native speakers to run such courses.

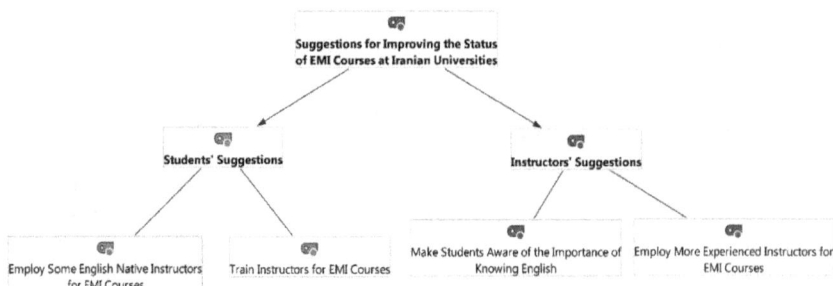

Figure 2.3 Suggestions for improving the status of EMI courses at Iranian universities.

Two important solutions were also identified from instructors' responses: *employ more experienced instructors for EMI courses* and *make students aware of the importance of knowing English*. They stated,

> P9: Experienced teachers who are interested in teaching EMI courses ought to be taken into account as the most effective type of aid here.

> P2: I do believe that one of the best ways to improve the status of EMI courses at Iranian universities is to make students aware of the importance of acquiring English language.

Discussion and Conclusions

This research study was intended to examine how students and instructors of Iranian universities perceive EMI courses. To put it differently, how EMI courses are advantageous and disadvantageous for university students. It also aimed at suggesting some practical ways to improve the current status of EMI courses at Iranian universities.

Concerning the first research question, content analysis represented that the advantages/opportunities of EMI courses can be grouped under six themes: more chances to improve language proficiency, more access to specialized sources, higher chance of continuing education abroad, higher chance of employment, more exposure to English and higher chance of publishing articles in prestigious journals.

Most of these themes are directly/indirectly tied with improvements in English language proficiency of students. As the result of *more exposure to English*, students' English proficiency will be improved, which leads them to a brighter future (i.e. *higher chance of continuing education abroad, higher chance of employment*). This result may be explained by the fact that since English is an international language, being skilled in it can be considered a prerequisite for almost every occupation in the future. Hence, it is quite natural if students and instructors enumerate *higher chance of employment* as one of the main advantages of EMI courses. This finding is consistent with the ideas of Tamtam et al. (2012), who suggested that 'bilingualism is the root of career and studying opportunities' (p. 1423). They explicated that those who have a good command of English would be offered more employment and promotion prospects. This finding is also supported by the ideas of Phuong and Nguyen (2019), who stated that since there is a growing number of foreign companies in several countries around the world, being a proficient language user can be deemed as a key to career opportunities.

Some participants also mentioned that attending EMI courses helps them access different specialized books and articles written in English. Similar findings were also reported by some previous studies (e.g. Başibek et al., 2014; Diezmas & Barrera, 2021; Phuong & Nguyen, 2019; Soe et al., 2020; Zare-ee & Gholami, 2013). Additionally, some participants, in both open-ended questionnaires and semi-structured interviews, assume that the EMI course gives university students the ability to write in English, helping them to publish their academic manuscripts in high-quality journals. This might be due to the fact that the language of many peer-reviewed journals is English. Hence, to publish the manuscript in these prestigious journals, one should be skilled in English writing.

Regarding the second research question, findings demonstrated the disadvantages/challenges of EMI courses with five themes and four sub-themes: *difficulty in expressing the ideas/opinions, difficulty in comprehending the materials, less participation, instructor-related factors (inadequate English proficiency of instructors) and student-related factors (inadequate English proficiency of students, lack of motivation and interest and lack of confidence)*.

The first two challenges mentioned by students can be justified by the fact that university students' English proficiency is not good enough to be able to comprehend the materials written in English or to express their ideas in English. This finding is in agreement with Phuong and Nguyen's (2019) findings, which showed that in EMI courses, most students encounter some difficulties in sharing their ideas with others and comprehending the specialized textbooks written in English. The last challenge reported by students, *less participation*, may also have something to do with their level of English proficiency. As put forward by Soe et al. (2020), during EMI courses, since students are not skilled at the English language, they rarely participate in classroom activities.

Among the aforementioned challenges, *inadequate English proficiency of instructors, inadequate English proficiency of students, lack of motivation and interest and lack of confidence* were mentioned by instructors. Many instructors believe that the main problem of EMI courses is teachers' lack of English proficiency. This finding accords with Zare-ee and Hejazi's (2017) findings, which showed that some instructors are not proficient enough to transmit information through the English language. Additionally, several instructors perceived *inadequate English proficiency of students* as another important challenge of EMI courses. They assume that many university students do not have a good command of English. Similar challenges were also found by some previous studies (Al-Bakri, 2013; Huang, 2012; Phuong & Nguyen, 2019; Soe et al., 2020).

Finally, some instructors referred to students' lack of motivation, interest and confidence as other disadvantageous points of EMI courses. Similar challenges can also be found in a study by Ter-Vardanyan (2021).

Ultimately, the last research question was addressed by investigating participants' views on how challenges of EMI courses can be minimized in Iranian universities. Four important solutions were gathered from participants' responses in total: *train instructors for EMI courses, employ some English native instructors for EMI courses, employ more experienced instructors for EMI courses* and *make students aware of the importance of knowing English*. Based on the suggested solutions, it can be inferred that participants held university administrators and instructors responsible for the challenges of EMI courses; hence, they provided them with some solutions to minimize the existing challenges. It is in agreement with Ter-Vardanyan's (2021) findings, which represented that students put the blame for EMI challenges on university administrators and stakeholders.

Overall, the findings from qualitative data analysis suggest that along with several opportunities provided by EMI courses, participants encountered some severe challenges which were mainly caused by their inadequate English proficiency. Besides the advantageous and disadvantageous aspects of EMI courses, participants were also asked to suggest some practical ways through which the status of EMI courses can be improved. Their suggested solutions reveal that most participants put the blame of EMI challenges on university administrators. These findings offer some valuable information on the opportunities and challenges experienced by the instructors and students of the EMI courses at four Iranian universities being investigated. The university administrators may wish to revisit the way EMI courses are being conducted to enhance its benefits and reduce its drawbacks. The findings of the current study are also informative for EMI instructors. Obviously, instructors should be aware of the potential opportunities and challenges of EMI courses to ensure more efficient instruction.

Like any other study, the findings of the current study are subject to some limitations. First, the number of participants was relatively small; hence, future studies are recommended to be carried out on a larger scale. Second, the instruments used in this inquiry were restricted to open-ended questionnaires and semi-structured interviews. Future studies are advised to use other data collection techniques such as diary writing and observation to obtain deeper insights into the essence of EMI. Third, this study employed a purely qualitative method. Future studies are recommended to use the mixed-methods approach to examine the depth and breadth of the subject under investigation. Finally, this study was conducted in Iran. As the findings might not be transferable to other contexts, further studies on the current subject are required to be conducted in other EFL countries.

References

Aizawa, I., Rose, H., Thompson, G., & Curle, S. (2020). Beyond the threshold: Exploring English language proficiency, linguistic challenges, and academic language skills of Japanese students in an English medium instruction programme. *Language Teaching Research*, 1362168820965510. doi:10.1177/1362168820965510.

Al-Bakri, S. (2013). Problematizing English medium instruction in Oman. *International Journal of Bilingual and Multilingual Teachers of English*, 1(2), 55–69.

Ary, D., Jacobs, L. C., Irvine, C. K. S., & Walker, D. (2018). *Introduction to research in education*. Boston: Cengage Learning.

Baralt, M. (2012). Coding qualitative data. In A. Mackey & S. M. Gass (Eds.), *Research methods in second language acquisition* (pp. 222–244). Oxford: Blackwell.

Barnard, R. (2014). English medium instruction in Asian universities: Some concerns and a suggested approach to dual-medium instruction. *Indonesian Journal of Applied Linguistics*, 4(1), 10–22.

Başıbek, N., Dolmacı, M., Cengiz, B. C., Bür, B., Dilek, Y., & Kara, B. (2014). Lecturers' perceptions of English medium instruction at engineering departments of higher education: A study on partial English medium instruction at some state universities in Turkey. *Procedia-Social and Behavioral Sciences*, 116(1), 1819–1825.

Brown, H. G. (2018). *Getting started with English-medium instruction in Japan: Key factors in program planning and implementation* (Unpublished doctoral dissertation). University of Birmingham.

Burnard, P. (1996). Teaching the analysis of textual data: An experiential approach. *Nurse Education Today*, 16(4), 278–281.

Byun, K., Chu, H., Kim, M., Park, I., Kim, S., & Jung, J. (2011). English-medium teaching in Korean higher education: Policy debates and reality. *Higher Education*, 62(4), 431–449.

Carrió-Pastor, M. L. (2020). English as a medium of instruction: What about pragmatic competence. In M. L. Carrió-Pastor (Ed.), *Internationalizing learning in higher education: The challenges of English as a meduim of instruction* (pp. 137–153). Cham:Palgrave Macmillan.

Chang, Y. Y. (2010). English-medium instruction for subject courses in tertiary education: Reactions from Taiwanese undergraduate students. *Taiwan International ESP Journal*, 2(1), 53–82.

Cole, F. L. (1988). Content analysis: Process and application. *Clinical Nurse Specialist* 2(1), 53–57.

Coleman, J. A. (2006). English-medium teaching in European higher education. *Language Teaching, 39*(1), 1–14.

Dearden, J. (2014). *English as a medium of instruction – A growing global phenomenon.* Oxford: British Council.

Diezmas, E. N. M., & Barrera, A. F. (2021). Main challenges of EMI at the UCLM: Teachers' perceptions on language proficiency, training and incentives. *Alicante Journal of English Studies/Revista Alicantina de Estudios Ingleses, 34*(1), 39–61.

Elo, S., & Kyngäs, H. (2008). The qualitative content analysis process. *Journal of Advanced Nursing, 62*(1), 107–115.

Friedman, D. A. (2012). How to collect and analyze qualitative data. In A. Mackey & S. M. Gass (Eds.), *Research methods in second language acquisition* (pp. 180–200). Oxford: Blackwell.

Ghorbani, M. R., & Alavi, S. Z. (2014). Feasibility of adopting English-medium instruction at Iranian universities. *Current Issues in Education, 17*(1), 1–18.

Graddol, D. (2000). *The future of English.* British Council.

Hammond, C. D. (2016). Internationalization, nationalism, and global competitiveness: A comparison of approaches to higher education in China and Japan. *Asia Pacific Education Review, 17*(4), 555–566.

Huang, Y. P. (2012). Design and implementation of English-medium courses in higher education in Taiwan: A qualitative case study. *English Teaching & Learning, 36*(1), 1–51.

Khorasani, A., & Zamani Manesh, H. (2012). Effective strategies in internationalization of universities and institutes of higher education in Iran. *Education Strategies in Medical Sciences, 5*(3), 183–189.

Kirkpatrick, A. (2011). English as an Asian lingua franca and the multilingual model of ELT. *Language Teaching, 44*(2), 212.

Kym, I., & Kym, M. H. (2014). Students' perceptions of EMI in higher education in Korea. *Journal of Asia TEFL, 11*(2), 33–61.

Lei, J., & Hu, G. (2014). Is English-medium instruction effective in improving Chinese undergraduate students' English competence? *International Review of Applied Linguistics in Language Teaching, 52*(2), 99–126.

Lincoln, Y. S., & Guba, E. G. (1985). Establishing trustworthiness. *Naturalistic Inquiry, 289*(331), 289–327.

Macaro, E., Curle, S., Pun, J., An, J., & Dearden, J. (2018). A systematic review of English medium instruction in higher education. *Language Teaching, 51*(1), 36–76.

Nassaji, H. (2020). Good qualitative research. *Language Teaching Research, 24*(4), 427–431.

Phillipson, R. (2009). *Linguistic imperialism continued.* New York: Routledge.

Phuong, Y. H., & Nguyen, T. T. (2019). Students' perceptions towards the benefits and drawbacks of EMI classes. *English Language Teaching, 12*(5), 88–100.

Pun, J. K., & Thomas, N. (2020). English medium instruction: Teachers' challenges and coping strategies. *ELT Journal, 74*(3), 247–257.

Rassouli, A., & Osam, N. (2019). English language education throughout Islamic republic reign in Iran: Government policies and people's attitudes. *SAGE Open, 9*(2). doi:10.1177/2158244019858435.

Rolfe, G. (2006). Validity, trustworthiness and rigour: Quality and the idea of qualitative research. *Journal of Advanced Nursing, 53*(3), 304–310.

Soe, T., Ko, T., & Myint, S. (2020). Attitudes towards English as a medium of instruction (EMI): A case study of University of Mandalay. *Research Journal, 11*(1), 108–115.

Tamtam, A. G., Gallagher, F., Olabi, A. G., & Naher, S. (2012). A comparative study of the implementation of EMI in Europe, Asia and Africa. *Procedia-Social and Behavioral Sciences, 47*(1), 1417–1425.

Ter-Vardanyan, Z. (2021). The challenges of EMI courses in Armenian higher education institutions (HEIs). In M. L. Carrió-Pastor & B. B. Fortuño (Eds.), *Teaching language and content in multicultural and multilingual classrooms* (pp. 157–189). Cham: Palgrave Macmillan.

Vinke, A. A. (1995). *English as the medium of instruction in Dutch engineering education* (Unpublished doctoral dissertation). Delft University.

Wallitsch, K. N. (2014). *Internationalization, English medium programs, and the international graduate student experience in Japan: A case study* (Unpublished doctoral dissertation). University of Kentucky.

Xie, W., & Curle, S. (2019). Success in English medium instruction in China: Significant indicators and implications. *International Journal of Bilingual Education and Bilingualism*, 1–13. doi:10.1080/13670050.2019.1703898.

Zare-ee, A., & Gholami, K. (2013, March 11–12). Academic justifications for preferring English as a medium of instruction by Iranian university teachers. *Paper Presented at the Proceedings of the Global Summit on Education*, Kuala Lumpur.

Zare-ee, A., & Hejazi, Y. (2017). University teachers' views on English as the medium of instruction in an Iranian higher education institution. *Arab World English Journal (AWEJ), 8*(4), 1–19.

Appendix

1. Biographical Information

Name:
University:
Gender:
Age:
Nationality:

2. Interview Protocol

1. What do you think are the advantages/opportunities of running EMI courses?
2. What do you think are the disadvantages/challenges of running EMI courses?
3. Do you have any further comments on the growing trend of English as a medium of instruction in Iran?

3

The Role of EMI in the Internationalization of Omani Higher Education Institutions (HEIs)

Gains and Pains

Holi Ibrahim Holi, S. Sergio Saleem Scatolini and Qasim Salim Al Washahi

Background

Internationalization in education may be defined as the 'process of integrating an international, intercultural, or global dimension into the purpose, functions or delivery of post-secondary education' (Knight, 2004, p. 11); alternatively, it is defined as a plan that 'promotes a university-wide approach to the development and integration of international, intercultural and global perspectives in institutional policies, programmes, and initiatives', including 'a commitment, confirmed through action, to infuse international and comparative perspectives throughout the teaching, research and service missions' of the HEI (Whitsed & Green, 2013).

Internationalization in education, which has been happening for centuries in one way or another,[1] has undeniably become a distinct concept and practice in the last decades (Jones and de Wit, 2012; Dimova & Kling, 2020; Earls, 2016). It has even become a criterion for ranking HEIs worldwide. For example, the Times Higher Education World University Rankings scores HEIs on their international outlook in terms of international staff, students and research. Internationalization has an administrative dimension, such as trends in curriculum design (e.g. how many credit hours should degrees comprise) or recognition of foreign degrees. Following Teichler (2010), we can say that internationalizing is manifested at different levels: (1) staff and student mobility, (2) internationally valid (i.e. recognized) accreditation, (3) the transfer of knowledge across borders (as in publications, patents and, now, online teaching and learning), (4) the curriculum (e.g. language of instruction and prestigious textbooks) and the nature of education (e.g. the importance of comparative enquiry), (5) international agendas (e.g. fostering global understanding or enhancing the competitive edge of one's HEI by learning from the best/one's competitors) and (6) increasing uniformity among education policies and systems, even in disparate countries. The incidence of internationalizing discourses is so strong that internationalization has become 'an argument for almost any higher education reform' these days (p. 265) (see also Altbach, 2013). Internationalization as mobility has had clear benefits.

> The increase in student mobility is associated with: the introduction of a more international curriculum in many subject areas in universities across the world; greater diversity of student bodies in many HEIs; new cross-national friendships; and a more cosmopolitan outlook amongst those who choose to study overseas (and, perhaps, amongst those with whom they come into contact). It is also the case that for some students, increased opportunities for mobility have allowed them to secure better financial support and/or pay lower fees for their study abroad than if they had remained within their own country. (Brooks & Waters, 2011, p. 137).

Nonetheless, despite the global commitment to internationalization, neither policymakers nor HEIs share the same understanding of it. Consequently, Jones and de Wit (2012) were warranted in suggesting that 'It is time to consider whether this variety of interpretation is a barrier or a benefit and to question whether we are learning sufficiently from other global contexts' (p. 35). According to Maringe et al. (2013), there are three internationalization models: *(1) the commercial-driven model*, mostly in the affluent West; *(2) the cultural-integration model*, especially in the Far East and the Arab Middle East; and *(3) the curriculum-driven model*, usually in the less prosperous South. Whatever the model, governments and HEIs have attempted to internationalize HE by internationalizing the curriculum, student and staff recruitment, professional development (including research and publication) and funding (Maringe, 2009; David et al., 2016).

These different models are the result of *geopolitical variables*, examples of which are the Bologna Process that homogenized the European educational landscape and the OECD's Programme for International Student Assessment (PISA) that gauges and compares the abilities of fifteen-year-olds from countries as diverse as Qatar, Tunisia, Uruguay and Belgium in problem-solving, reading, math, and science knowledge and skills. These developments have resulted in the existence of a 'new constellation of actors' in education policy and evaluation next to but also beyond the nation states (Martens et al., 2014, p. 5) not only in the West but also in the East (Chan, 2011; McPherron, 2017). In fact, 'This new kind of "co-management" relationship between state and non-state sectors has altered the public-private partnership in the delivery of social services in general, and that of educational services in particular' (Chan, 2011, p. 12).

At the same time, the aforementioned models respond also to *socio-economic factors* (Hébert & Abdi, 2013). Mobility for the sake of international experience and intercultural understanding (the 'multicultural self') has given rise to internationalization as a way to enhance one's competitive edge (the 'strategic cosmopolitan') (Mitchell, 2003; Brooks & Waters, 2011). Furthermore, internationalization often enacts one-directional movements: 'good education' comes from the North and thousands of fee-paying students come from the South (De Vita & Case, 2003). In this dynamic, the defining categories are those of the rich countries, particularly the English-speaking ones (De Wit et al., 2017). For example, Hyatt reported that 'non-EU student numbers increased from 126,720 in 2000/2001 to 280,760 in 2009/2010, representing a rise of 121.6%. This is partly policy-driven and partly an expression of an international movement towards the marketisation of higher education' (2013, p. 844). In 2018/2019, the figures were twice as much: 485,645 international students, approximately 20.4 per cent of the then total of 2,383,970 tertiary students (Study-in-uk.org, 2020).

Internationalization – understood as comparable internationally harmonious and homologous education systems, curriculums and practices – implies criteria and presuppositions, based upon which comparisons can be made. High performance and equality of opportunity seem to underscore the OECD's PISA measurements and tables. Of course, the countries that outperform the others become international models. However, as the Educational Prosperity Framework (Willms, 2018) suggests, performance is more closely related to actual equity than formal equality.

This phenomenon fits within neoliberal agendas whereby universities and colleges in the rich North market their mostly English-medium programmes internationally as products without any link to the societies from which their customer-students hail. In the knowledge economy, HEIs are service providers and, as such, they must compete by attracting increasing numbers of fee-paying international students (Eaton, 2013; Gayton, 2020). In other words, education replicates the market economy and favours decentralization, privatization (or, at least, private funding), profitability and cost-effectiveness. Higher education has become 'a significant export industry' (De Vita & Case, 2003, p. 385, see also Kerklaan et al., 2008): colleges and universities are 'certificate factories with financial self-sufficiency as a condition for existence' (De Vita & Case, 2003,

p. 387), and curricula are market commodities, goods and services (Chan, 2012). As far as competition boosts quality, this would not necessarily constitute a serious problem. However, given that HEIs do not sell products that can be exported globally and accompanied with user's manuals in the buyers' languages, education programmes and courses are essentially language-dependent services. They do not only demand sufficient knowledge of the language medium, but they also generate research and publications in privileged languages, especially English (Doiz et al., 2011; Palmer et al., 2011; Haberland et al., 2013; Cots et al., 2014; O'Neill & Chapman, 2015; Carrió-Pastor, 2020; Kuteeva et al., 2020). For example, some have noted that the internationalization of EMI education, regardless of 'the willingness and ability of teachers to use English as part of their professional and pedagogical practice' (Duong & Chua, 2016, p. 670), 'not only endanger[s] the role of Asian languages in academia but also impedes the development of social sciences and humanities in the region' (Duong & Chua, 2016, p. 669; Sun et al., 2017).

International English-medium qualifications take on a significance that goes far beyond education. As Ha and Barnawi (2015) have expressed it, the 'intersection of English and the internationalization of HE is played out in education policy, practice, and pedagogy at all levels and with varying degrees and intensities across global contexts and settings, including the Middle East' (p. 545; see also Huo, 2020). This phenomenon has often resulted in the creation of elites of sorts that end up undermining the local production of indigenous knowledge in their communities' languages.

While internationalization has often meant either bringing foreigners into one's HEI or sending one's staff or students to foreign HEIs (through scholarships, recruitment, the Erasmus programme in Europe, etc.), another approach has also emerged: internationalization at home. There has been *a shift from mobility to the curriculum* (Beelen, 2019). Consequently, internationalization has gradually become the responsibility not only of the staff at the International Offices at the HEIs but also of the curriculum designers, academics and policymakers (Whitsed and Green, 2013; Beelen, 2015; Soler & Gallego-Balsà, 2019). From the 1990s and, especially, in the last decade, HE curriculums around the world have become increasingly internationalized in response to the globalization of quality assurance standards taken from the rich North, Australia and New Zealand, learning outcomes, intercultural skills, transversal employability skills and HE rankings.

However, there are myths about internationalization in HE. Knight pointed out five of them (2011):

- Myth 1: Foreign students are internationalization agents. In reality, domestic students do not often interact with them, and foreign students remain at the margins of the HEI.
- Myth 2: International reputation is a proxy for quality. Although world rankings contribute to this idea, internationalization is not always the causal element in an HEI's high-quality curriculum or appeal.
- Myth 3: International institutional agreements make an HEI more attractive. This is not the case. The reputation of an HEI is much weightier than its international outlook.
- Myth 4: International accreditation makes an HEI more international. This is not the case as such accreditations are often marketing strategies and do not impact the nature of international outreach and flavour of an institution's culture and outlook.
- Myth 5: Global branding is secured through internationalization strategies. The problem with this idea is that it redefines internationalization as a marketing strategy rather than as the means for the realization of educational, intercultural, and civilizational targets. So, even if it was true, it would betray the argument that renders ethical and educational validity to internationalization.

At this point, questions need to be raised (Bowles & Murphy, 2020). First, has the HE internationalization forgotten its 'why and wherefore'? In other words, has internationalization become one more tradition that marketizes education rather than a force and channel of innovation, and a promise of more inclusive and diverse global futures, as suggested by Brandenburg and de Wit (2011)? Second, has too much emphasis been placed on activities rather than results (Whitsed & Green, 2013)? Third, has the globalization of online environments and online education as a result of the Covid-19 pandemic initiated a new phase in the internationalization of HEIs, or has it, instead, merely re-thickened the divide between the developing South and the developed North and (South) East including China, South Korea, Singapore, Australia and New Zealand?

The Internationalization of IELTS, Not Just English

IELTS is allegedly 'recognized by over 9,000 institutions worldwide' including 'over 2,000 universities in the US, and many universities in the UK and Ireland, Canada, Australia, New Zealand, and South Africa, as well as numerous professional organizations around the world' (Collier, 2021). One of the greatest advantages of IELTS is that it provides general and clear language proficiency standards for both the institutions and the test-takers. One of the critical repercussions of its popularity is 'the gatekeeping function of IELTS for higher education, employment, and immigration' (Noori and Mirhosseini, 2021, p. 3). A test focused on an inner-circle variant of English (albeit in many accents) has been attributed a decisive role all around the world. In Oman, IELTS is used as a screening gatekeeper and plays a crucial role in helping Omani students meet job requirements (Holi et al., 2020). Therefore, a decision was made by the Omani Ministry of Education to set Band 6 on the academic IELTS test as an official standard for hiring English language teachers (Al-Issa et al., 2016). In Oman and elsewhere, IELTS is a criterion-referenced test that adequately predicts the test-takers language proficiency levels. It is used to inform the decisions of higher education institutions and is also used by employers to assess prospective employees' ability to function in a workplace. It also plays a significant role in the language-proficiency-selection process for English-medium programmes for international higher education institutions (Green, 2019; Pearson, 2019).

The Omani Experience with Internationalization

The global spread of English has had a great impact on language policies all over the world and the Arab world, and especially Gulf countries are no exception. The policies seem to be driven by the belief that English prepares students best for the multicultural world of employment (Al Bakri, 2017). Therefore, as a response to globalization and regional integration, HEIs around the world have adopted various strategies to internationalize their programmes and accelerate the process and bring intercultural understanding (Doung & Chua, 2016; Fabricius et al., 2017).

In Oman, English has played a central role in the country's education system (Al-Mahrooqi & Denman, 2016). It has been the only official foreign language in Oman since then. Different domains and sectors such as education, tourism, media and business have institutionalized English (Al-Issa & Al-Bulushi, 2012). Oman has viewed English as an important part of its development and an essential key to integrate with the wider community and modern world (Al-Issa & Al-Bulushi, 2012; Al-Mahrooqi, 2012). Al-Issa (2007, pp. 199–200) stated that 'Oman needs English – the only official foreign language in the country as a fundamental tool for "modernization", "nationalization", and the acquisition of science and technology'. Additionally, English has become such an intrinsic part of Omani life that most Omanis do not have any misgivings about the phenomenon. This is partly because English has never been a colonial imposition on them. On the contrary, it has been a conscious choice on the part of the policymakers, mostly in response to the country's needs, and the benefits of it are palpable. Nevertheless, any quick perusal of job advertisements at the main universities and colleges will confirm Brooks and Waters's (2011) assertion that 'a degree awarded by a "Western", Anglophone country often has considerably higher status within the labour markets of many "Eastern" countries than an equivalent domestic qualification' (p. 145). On the other hand, in 'those countries such as the UK from where prestigious degrees often emanate, calculations are different; indeed, an overseas qualification may be seen by employers as of less value than one secured from a British university' (2011). This is not a pro-Western attitude, as it also discriminates against other European degrees, as much as it is a pro-Anglophone bias. Such a mindset could easily work against local qualifications and 'may encourage assumptions amongst graduate recruiters about the "superior" quality of a UK qualification' (2011). Given that this strong preference is not simply for a lingua franca or language of instruction but for specific countries and their qualifications factories and brand of knowledge and curriculums, some may wish to describe this as a state of 'voluntary academic colonization', and the incidence of IELTS in sectors for which it was neither designed nor meant might prove them right.

EMI as a Necessity after the Omani Renaissance

The widespread use of English as a medium of instruction by many HEIs in Asia and elsewhere is an outstanding example of internationalization (Duong & Chua, 2016; Ha, 2013; Duong & Chua, 2016). The impact of the global spread of English has affected language policy and language education policy in many countries all over the world (Al Bakri, 2017). English in Oman is widely used in education, the health care system and business. The prominence of English is because the most educated private sector is still largely dominated by non-Omani and non-Arabic-speaking labour force. English in Oman is also important for tourism, which has flourished since the beginning of the current millennium (Al-Issa, 2020).

English has been viewed as an important aspect of Oman's continued development. Al-Jadidi (2009) argued that English has become a central part of Omanization, the government's ambitious plan to gradually replace the expatriate labour force with Omani nationals. Thus, a good command of English is an important requirement for undergraduate education and employment

(Al-Jadidi, 2009). Oman has realized that English is not only the dominant language of science, research and technology in the twenty-first century, but it is an essential means for the country to integrate and engage with the international academic community (Al-Mahrooqi, 2012). Upon laying down the foundations of HE in Oman, the late Sultan Qaboos's government needed lecturers who could teach thousands of Omani students across the Sultanate. However, HEIs were meant to not only produce the local engineering, business and IT specialized workforce that the oil, gas, banking and information and communications technology (ICT) sectors needed but also introduce them to careers in which English would be the lingua franca (Holi, 2018), at least, for as long as much of the workforce was not made up of Omanis or Arabic speakers. There is a need for enhancing EMI teachers' capabilities and skills to assist in enacting greater internationalization. Although Oman is an Arabic-speaking country, most of its higher education is in the English medium. As a result, General Foundation Programmes (GFPs) have become an integral part of the tertiary education landscape to the point that only a few people could imagine students directly transitioning to college from post-basic, or secondary, education. The government adopted EMI as the norm in most cases in the Sultanate's tertiary education sector. As soon as enough Omanis were qualified, it could have turned back to Arabic-medium education, but it did not. That would certainly have had its gains, but the internationalization process would not have gone far enough. The Sultan seems to have wanted Oman to fully join the community of nations, not only that of the Arab nation or the Arab League. English was much better positioned to achieve this goal. Some countries like South Korea have adopted an EMI policy for the aim of bringing down the number of enrolments of domestic students for programmes in English-speaking countries and boosting the number of international students coming to Korea to join EMI programmes (Green, 2015).

The Study

Methodology and Design

The study adopted a qualitative approach because qualitative research paradigms can be an apt tool for understanding the participants' views of the reality under study from their perspectives. Hence, this study interprets the participants' prescriptions about and possible answers to the research questions. As with other case study research, this, too, examines a given phenomenon within its real-life context (Creswell, 2012), thus enabling the exploration of a particular group of settings, peoples and societies to generate rich and detailed information (Gray, 2009). The qualitative method was chosen here because it helps identify the target group that can more effectively contribute to answering the research questions (Marshall & Rossman, 1999), within which purposive sampling plays an important role. Purposive sampling was utilized which enabled this study to target EFL faculty members from a particular area, thirty participants in total, who responded to an open-ended survey about their views of and perceptions about the internationalization of HEIs through EMI. This open-ended answer survey was aimed to generate detailed and in-depth information while being less concerned about objective facts (Creswell, 2012). The data were analysed using the thematic method, that is comparing and contrasting themes within the text to establish similarities and differences among the responses (Saunders et al., 2012). This kind of analysis was suitable for this research because validating the perceptions and perspectives of faculty members about the link between EMI and the internationalization of HEIs is answered better by comparing and contrasting the information received from respondents. All ethical considerations and measures were taken into account. The participants were informed about the purpose and objectives of the study and consented to the methodology. The participants were also told that their participation was voluntary and that they could withdraw from the study at any stage in line with ethical research practices. Anonymity was ensured, and confidentiality was maintained during the process of data collection and analysis.

Findings and Discussion

This study utilized thematic analysis as it suits the study aims and objectives which investigated faculty members' views on the role of EMI in the internationalization of HEIs in Oman and what could be done to enact EMI for 'greater' internationalization. The researchers familiarized themselves with the collected data and then initial codes were created and reviewed.

Faculty Members' Perspectives on the Role of EMI in the Internationalization of HEIs

This section aims to analyse and discuss how faculty members view EMI as a tool for internationalizing HEIs in Oman. The data showed that most of the participants have positive views on EMI as a means of internationalization. For example, one participant reported:

> Using EMI in higher education is a good decision that will enable future generations to take part in international commerce and science. It was practical at the time (1) to modernize and internationalize Oman and (2) find up-to-date syllabi, materials, and faculty. It is useful but challenging. It's essential to have English as the medium of instruction. Without English, the educational standards in Omani institutions won't come at par with the international ones. It is the global language that is used as a medium of communication and instruction all over the world. It's the right and wise decision. (P1)

The points made by the interviewee underline that EMI is important as it helps Omani HEIs to partner up with other HEIs around the world. Besides, the previous extract also highlights the impact of EMI on the teaching and learning process.

> EMI will help Omani institutions to bridge the gaps there may exist between the standards of Omani and western institutions, especially in the field of science and technology. If the institution wishes to achieve higher educational standards and accreditation, it should focus on higher standards one of which is using English. Education should meet the state local needs and compete internationally as well. (P3)

This response consolidates the previous interviewee's comments and demonstrates the importance of EMI in helping to meet both local needs and internationally recognized standards in HE. Furthermore, EMI as a transmission tool or bridging measure may encourage HEIs to interact and collaborate in more effective ways with foreign counterparts.

It is apparent that most of the participants have positive views on EMI and its importance in internationalizing HEIs. This agrees with what other researchers have seen elsewhere (e.g. Al Bakri, 2017; Duong & Chua, 2016; Beelen, 2019; Maringe et al., 2013; Teichler, 2010; Knight, 2004).

A similar point was made by another participant:

> Of course, since English [is] the language of most of the international organizations that give accreditation to institutions worldwide. It is easier to judge the credibility and validity of the practices of the HEIs based on international standards when EMI is deployed. I think using English as a medium of instruction is an important criterion in the accreditation process. Because most of the evaluation and accreditation agencies belong to the West. (P13)

At least one of the respondents disagreed. They remarked:

> Quality could be high even if the subjects were taught in other languages, e.g.: Japanese. Yet, English is the preferred language of instruction at the international universities which both the Omani government and individuals prefer, such as those in the UK, USA, Australia, New Zealand, and Ireland, where English is the main language. (P8)

This perspective, albeit valid, is held by a small number of participants. For them, EMI and the internationalization of HEIs are two separate issues. Quality education can be maintained and sustained using mother tongues or other languages, as is the case in most countries around the globe.

Gains for Omani HEIs from Enacting EMI

The survey revealed that the absolute majority of our respondents focus on the gains of the current EMI policy. For example:

> EMI enables Omani youth to have access to the latest scientific, technological, and commercial innovations in the world secure training a capable workforce. Easy progression to further studies abroad, 2) exposure to new ideas, 3) a variable talented foreign workforce. EMI creates more jobs for graduates, offers better standards and accreditation, modern research-oriented approaches, being recognized internationally and being academically accredited, and it enables Omani students and graduates to be international and can fit anywhere for postgraduate studies or employment. (P10)

International academic accreditation, research production, dissemination of knowledge, pursuing postgraduate studies overseas and getting jobs overseas are some of the opportunities that EMI creates. Besides these academic benefits, the respondents saw other advantages associated with EMI such as communicative competencies.

> EMI may cater to and accommodate diverse student population. What follows EMI is fostering communicative competence amongst students (as the key stakeholders) in the target language, as well as facilitating wider opportunities for them to engage in authentic discourse and access authentic resources, all of which contribute to better recognition as well as a sense of professionalism of the HEI to compete in the local and global markets. Overall, I would also think EMI has contributed to better financial incomes for the HEIs. (P12)

Additionally, EMI offers students opportunities to be exposed to the English language, and this can help them to improve their language proficiency and competencies. Since most of the academic resources for different fields and disciplines are in English, especially on the Internet, EMI also helps students to access this reservoir of knowledge.

Despite the real benefits of EMI in Oman, it can also be argued that local and international employers expect more from graduates than mere English language proficiency. EMI may be an asset but not always the weightiest one.

Challenges for Omani HEIs with Enacting EMI

The participants indicated that despite the benefits of EMI and its role in internationalizing HEIs, it can also present several linguistic and pedagogic challenges to the content teachers and the students, both of whom must deal with not only the disciplinary content but also English. For example:

> Low English proficiency among students often contributes to reduced class participation and inhibits optimum progression through course areas/requirements, which reflects negatively on teachers' attitudes towards the efficiency of EMI. Often, students are less confident about their language competency level, which often results in low engagement levels in and out-class activities. Many seem to perceive English as an obstacle to acquiring content/subject areas, which they can acquire more optimally in Arabic. For those students who haven't been educated at international schools, just comprehending the lectures alone is a daunting task. They have to limp their way through the levels till they finish foundation programs and beyond. This weakness often keeps them back from advancing in their studies. (P7)

As a result of the doubling of challenges, less proficient students may be – indeed, often are – disadvantaged and see their classroom participation reduced due to their having to communicate in English. Additionally, EMI can make lecture comprehension more difficult, especially if the lecturer's command of English is also deficient. As a result, students may have to delay their graduation or may even drop out of college. Some of this conundrum was articulated by one of our respondents as follows.

> Students' comprehension depended on their English proficiency. They need to understand English before they can understand their subjects. They will be having a problem with comprehension, writing skills, and anxiety and failing to achieve really and productively. It will be a new practice and a new experience for them taking into account that the majority of students come from government schools with a not adequate level of English that enables them to study the program, so they need to spend at least their first year to study English. The

most frequently associated challenge with EMI to content teachers is the English Language. (P17)

EMI does represent comprehension challenges for the students. Most of them had their schooling in Arabic and must, suddenly, conduct themselves in English as soon as they start college. To make the transition as smooth as possible, students spend approximately a year in the General Foundation Programme to improve their language proficiency, and math, IT and study skills. However, becoming fluent in English is not the end of the road. They need to acquire English for academic and special purposes, too, next to the language used in each of their degree courses. Understandably, some succumb under the weight not of their degree courses but of their English courses. The silver lining is that despite their failures, students leave college better equipped to function in English-speaking contexts, such as those at work, in intercultural situations and during holidays abroad.

EMI as a Tool for (Greater) Internationalization in Omani HEIs

Apart from the current EMI strategy, there are other measures that HEIs in Oman could take to reach greater degrees of internationalization. They could:

(1) Use a standardized test such as IELTS to place students across levels.
(2) Reform the schooling system by adopting EMI in the last two pre-college grades (i.e. 11 and 12).
(3) Opt for CLIL in delivering some school subjects in grade 10 to prepare students for EMI in grades 11 and 12 (as suggested in no. 2).
(4) Design and enact content-based syllabi.
(5) Adopt EMI in all Omani HEIs.
(6) Train content teachers to function well in English.
(7) Build ties and enter into collaboration schemes with international universities, and
(8) Attract non-Arabic-speaking international students.

Some of these suggestions were also put forward by the respondents:

> Omani HEIs may require more internationally-oriented programs to enable better EMI integration. This may include the facilitation of cross-continent programs, collaborative projects with global bodies, etc. (P2)
>
> Instead of 'in-house' testing, use standardized tests at the beginning of the foundation program so the student is placed in a level that truly reflects their level of expertise in English. This requires all students to undergo a level exit

exam at the end of the foundation program and also HEIs should provide rigorous training in study skills for both students and content teachers. (P21)

Start EMI from primary school and train teachers at the school level for EMI, actively follow up with students at home through online learning forums. They should focus more on the English language at the school level. Using content-based syllabuses where the content of the other subjects at schools are delivered in English however, is costly but it is a suggestion. (P5)

Indeed, enhancing internationalization in Oman requires reforming and making changes to the current school assessment policies, procedures and instruments in school and, particularly, in grades 11 and 12 (just before youngsters are admitted to college). Additionally, it appears that the GFP entry and exit standards need to be revised and benchmarked with the internationally recognized standards to foster and sustain greater internationalization. Finally, content teachers ought to be trained on how to deliver their content in English, as already suggested by others (Al Bakri, 2017).

Discussion

This is an open-ended survey-based study set out to investigate the perceptions and views of EFL faculty members about the role of EMI in internationalizing Omani HEIs. This section refines the discussion of the data and synthesizes the key findings and their significance concerning the study research questions: What are the gains and challenges for Omani HEIs in enacting EMI? How do faculty members perceive the role of EMI in the internationalization of Omani HEIs? What could still be done to help Omani HEIs to implement EMI as a tool towards (greater) internationalization? The study participants in their response used repeatedly words such as 'accreditation', 'language proficiency', 'international collaboration', 'international ranking' 'challenges' and 'employment'. EMI programmes attract international students and help to produce graduates who can contribute to the workforce and promote the international profile of the HEIs (Ishikura, 2015). However, the implementation of the EMI policy has a negative impact on the students, particularly students with low English language proficiency and on the content subject teachers. These findings seem to be consistent with other findings in the literature (e.g. Holi, 2020, 2021; Beelen, 2019; Willms, 2018; Al Bakri, 2017; Lueg & Lueg, 2015; Dearden, 2015; Belhiah & Elhami, 2014; Wilkinson, 2013; Airey, 2012; Kirkpatrick, 2011).

The themes identified in the study findings lead to the question of the current EMI practices and policies whether they serve the greater internationalization of Omani HEIs or not. The participants' responses indicated that internationalization has several values for HEIs such as it helps in accreditation and offers employment opportunities for graduates. These findings seem to be in line with other findings in the literature (e.g. Fabricius et al., 2017; Green, 2015; Knight, 2004).

Conclusions, Implications and Recommendations

This study utilized an open-ended answer survey and organized the layers of the responses into thematic clusters as a way to gauge EFL faculty members' perceptions of EMI in relation to internationalization in HEIs in Oman. The study sought to elucidate three aspects: (1) the gains and challenges that EMI represents for Omani HEIs, (2) faculty members' perceptions of the role played by EMI in the internationalization of Omani HEIs and (3) plausible strategies for enhancing EMI's impact on a college's degree of internationalization. The findings showed that respondents hold positive views of and are optimistic about EMI as a measure supporting internationalization (as well as employability). The analysis of the responses revealed that despite the challenges that EMI brings with it for both teachers and students, the participants deemed adopting English as a medium of instruction in Oman a golden opportunity for HEIs to become more international and score some points during accreditation or programme review audits, attracting more international students and faculty and climbing in the international HE rankings.

Consequently, this study cannot but corroborate the incidence, reputation and level of acceptance that EMI has evidential gains in Oman. Despite the view of thirty participants that internationalization would be attained by using another foreign language in instruction, the country's models and main foreign education destinations are English-speaking countries (United Kingdom, United States, Australia and New Zealand). Also, since English is often the lingua franca in the health, banking and oil and gas sectors, it does have not only international allure but also local usefulness. Yet, more studies are needed to gauge the efficiency and returns from the immense investments in EMI in Oman. One indeed ought to ask whether EMI has contributed to the production of Omani indigenous knowledge in their mother tongue or hindered it. In other words, has Oman found its voice in English and Arabic (i.e. authentic, non-colonial internationalization), or is it simply an echo of people in another people's language? Answering these questions might help to steer the future course in EMI in Oman by recalibrating the existing EMI infrastructure, policies and pre-university preparation programmes. Special attention should be paid to finding ways to better help Omani students to overcome the difficulties associated with the implementation of EMI.

It is undeniable that our data strongly suggest that the adoption of EMI is being perceived as beneficial for HEIs in Oman and elsewhere. Despite acknowledging the challenges posed by EMI, the participants appreciated EMI and viewed it as something that should stay in place. The benefits mentioned included EMI's potential for improving one's position in the international rankings, attracting international students and valuable teachers, boosting one's credentials for accreditation, creating graduate employment opportunities and helping both students and disciplinary teachers to improve their English language proficiency. However, EMI also presents challenges for ESL/EFL students as it makes it more difficult for them to comprehend lectures and textbooks and forces them to spend a lot of time focusing on language rather than content. These challenges have caused many students to fail the General Foundation Programmes or to drop out of their degree programmes.

Finally, since internationalizing HEIs often comes down to regional and global integration (Fabricius et al., 2017), HEIs in Oman need not only focus on EMI as a quasi-extrinsic 'magical' strategy but also intrinsically become the sort of partners with which reputable international HEIs might want to exchange students and faculty members and join research collaboration schemes (Fabricius et al., 2017). Intrinsic internationalization requires more than the adoption of EMI. For example, it includes designing innovative, competitive and impactful academic programmes; dynamic and flexible teaching and research environments; career paths with growth perspectives for valuable foreign scholars and experts who want to join HEIs in Oman; and, above all, the right kind of students who want more from themselves than merely get a degree. At the same time, HEIs must bear in mind that true talent may be lost due to the quasi-universal EMI practice. There should be academic, professional and vocational educational and training pathways for those students whose English language proficiency is low but could do much better if they studied in Arabic. EMI should not be the cause of high dropout figures and exam failures (Lueg & Lueg, 2015) at a time when Oman seeks to implement its Vision 2040 for the establishment of a competitive local knowledge economy.

Although the study achieved its aims, it has some limitations which are worth acknowledging. The sample of the study was rather small, and the study relied on an open-ended survey as its main data collection tool. Therefore, the findings cannot be taken as representative of all EFL faculty members across the Sultanate. Other studies are needed, especially ones that are based on interviewing faculty members as well as other stakeholders.

Note

1 Think of the international travels within the medieval world that resulted from people's search for knowledge, for example, in the Muslim world (between Al-Andalus, Qayrawan, Egypt, Damascus, Medina, Baghdad and beyond) or in China (e.g. in the Taishi, Yingtianfu, Yuelu and Shigu Academies, or Shuyuan). Similar movement of people occurred in Europe and the Levant between Christian universities and monasteries, and other Christian and non-Christian centres of learning. During the modern colonial times, there was also a flux of students from the colonies to the metropolis, for example, from the Americas, Africa and the Indian subcontinent, on the one hand, to the Iberian Peninsula, France or England, on the other.

References

Airey, J. (2012). I don't teach language: The linguistic attitudes of physic lecturers in Sweden. *AILA Review, 25*(1), 64–79.

Al-Bakri, S. (2017). *Effects of English medium instruction on students' learning experiences and quality of education in content courses in a public college in Oman* (Unpublished PhD thesis). University of Exeter, UK.

Al-Issa, A. (2007). English language teaching at the College of Law – Muscat, Sultanate of Oman: Analyzing needs and understanding problems. *Asian Journal of English Language Teaching, 17*, 65–86.

Al-Issa, A. (2020). The language planning situation in the Sultanate of Oman. *Current Issues in Language Planning*, 1–68. doi:10.1080/14664208.2020.1764729.

Al-Issa, A., & Al-Bulushi, A. (2012). English language teaching reform in Sultanate of Oman: The case of theory and practice disparity. *Educational Research for Policy and Practice, 11*(2), 141–176. doi:10.1007/s10671-011-9110-0.

Al-Issa, A., & Al-Zadjali, R. (2016). Arab English language candidates climbing the IELTS mountain: A qualitatively driven hermeneutic phenomenology study. *The Qualitative Report, 21*(5), 848–863.

Al-Jadidi, H. (2009). *Teaching English as a foreign language in Oman: An exploration of English language pedagogy in tertiary education* (Unpublished PhD thesis). Victoria University, Australia.

Al-Mahrooqi, R. (2012). English communication skills: How are they taught at schools and universities in Oman? *English Language Teaching, 5*(4), 124–130. doi:10.5539/elt.v5n4p124.

Al-Mahrooqi, R., & Denman, C. (2016). *Bridging the gap between education and employment: English language instruction in EFL contexts.* Peter Lang.

Altbach, P. G. (2013). *The international imperative in higher education.* Sense Publishers.

Belhiah, H., & Elhami, M. (2014). English as a medium of instruction in the Gulf: When students and teachers speak. *Language Policy, 14*(1), 3–23.

Beelen, J. (2015). Left to their own devices: The role and skills of academics in partnerships for the future. *Higher Education Partnerships for the Future, 47*–61.

Beelen, J. (2019). Internationalisation at home: Obstacles and enablers from the perspective of academics. In E. Hillebrand-Augustin, G. Salmhofer & L. Scheer (Eds.), *Responsible University. Verantwortung in Studium und Lehre* (Sammelband Tag der Lehre 2017 der Karl-Franzens-Unversität Graz; Grazer Beiträge zur Hochschullehre, Band 9) (pp. 29–54). Grazer Universitätsverlag.

Bowles, H., & Murphy, A. C. (Eds.) (2020). *English-medium instruction and the internationalization of universities.* Palgrave Macmillan.

Brandenburg, U., & Hans de Wit, H. (2011). The end of internationalization. *International Higher Education, 62,* 15–17.

Brooks, R., & Waters, J. (2011). *Student mobilities, migration and the internationalization of higher education.* Palgrave Macmillan.

Carrió-Pastor, M. L. (Ed.) (2020). *Internationalising learning in higher education: The challenges of English as a medium of instruction.* Palgrave Macmillan

Chan, D. K. (2011). Internationalization of higher education as a major strategy for developing regional education hubs: A comparison of Hong Kong and Singapore. In J. D. Palmer, Y. Ha Cho, & Gregory S. C. (Eds.), *The internationalization of East Asian higher education: Globalization's impact* (pp. 11–39). Palgrave Macmillan.

Chan, S.-J. (2012). Shifting patterns of student mobility in Asia. *Higher Education Policy, 25*(2), 207–224. doi:10.1057/hep.2012.3.

Collier, S. (2021). IELTS: The basics. Retrieved from https://www.topuniversities.com/student-info/placement-tests/ielts-basics. (Written in 2010, updated on 5 March 2021).

Cots, J. M., Llurda, E., & Garrett, P. (2014). Language policies and practices in the internationalisation of higher education on the European margins: An introduction. *Journal of Multilingual and Multicultural Development, 35*(4), 311–317. doi:10.1080/01434632.2013.874430.

Creswell, J. (2012). *Educational research: Planning, conducting, and evaluating and qualitative research.* London: Pearson.

David, S. A. Taleb, H., Scatolini, S. S., Al-Qallaf, A., Al-Shammari, H. S., & George, M. A. (2016). An exploration into student learning mobility in higher education among the Arabian Gulf Cooperation Council countries. *International Journal of Educational Development, 55,* 41–48.

Dearden, J. (2015). *English as a medium of instruction – A growing global phenomenon.* UK: British Council. Retrieved November 2015, from www.teachingenglish.org.uk.

De Vita, G., & Case, P. (2003). Rethinking the internationalization agenda in UK higher education. *Journal of Further and Higher Education, 27*(4), 383–398. doi:10.1080/0309877032000128082.

De Wit, H., Gacel-Ávila, J., Jones, E., & Jooste, N.(2017). Introduction. In H. de Wit, J. Gacel-Ávila, E. Jones, & N. Jooste (Eds.), *The globalization of internationalization: Emerging voices and perspectives* (pp. 1–3). Routledge.

De Wit, H., Gacel-Ávila Jones, E., & Jooste, N. (2017). *The globalization of internationalization: Emerging voices and perspectives.* Routledge.

Dimova, S., & Kling, J. (Eds.) (2020). *Integrating content and language in multilingual universities.* Springer.

Doiz, A., Lasagabaster, D., & Sierra, J. M. (2011). Internationalisation, multilingualism and English-medium instruction. *World Englishes, 30*(3), 345–359.

Duong, V. A., & Chua, Catherine S. K. (2016). English as a symbol of internationalization in higher education: A case study of Vietnam. *Higher Education Research & Development, 35*(4), 669–683. doi:10.1080/07294360.2015.1137876.

Earls, C. W. (2016). *Evolving agendas in European English-medium higher education: Interculturality, multilingualism and language policy.* Palgrave Macmillan.

Eaton, S. E. (2013). The administration of English as a Second Language (ESL) program in higher education: Striking the balance between generating revenue and serving students. In Yvonne Hébert & Ali A. Abdi (Eds.), *Critical perspectives on international education* (pp. 165–180). Sense Publishers.

Fabricius, A., Mortensen, J., & Haberland, H. (2017). The lure of internationalization: Paradoxical discourses of transnational student mobility, linguistic diversity and cross-cultural exchange. *Higher Education, 73*(4), 577–595. doi:10.1007/s10734-015-9978-3.

Gayton, A. M. (2020). Exploring the widening participation-internationalisation nexus: Evidence from current theory and practice. *Journal of Further and Higher Education, 44*(9), 1275–1288. doi:10.1080/0309877X.2019.1678014.

Gray, D. E. (2009). *Doing research in the real world* (2nd ed.). London: SAGE.

Green, C. (2015). Internationalization, deregulation and the expansion of higher education in Korea: A historical overview. *International Journal of Higher Education, 4*(3), 1–13. Retrieved from http://www.doi.10.5430/ijhe.v4n3p1.

Green, A. (2019). Restoring the perspective on the IELTS test. *ELT Journal, 73*(2), 207–2015.

Ha, P. L. (2013). Issues surrounding English, the internationalisation of higher education and national cultural identity in Asia: A focus on Japan. *Critical Studies in Education, 54*(2), 160–175. doi:10.1080/17508487.2013.781047.

Ha, P. L., & Barnawi, O. Z. (2015). Where English, neoliberalism, desire and internationalization are alive and kicking: Higher education in Saudi Arabia today. *Language and Education, 29* (6), 545–565. doi:10.1080/09500782.2015.1059436.

Haberland, H., Lønsmann, D., & Preisler, B. (Eds.) (2013). *Language alternation, language choice and language encounter in international tertiary education.* Springer.

Hébert, Y., & Abdi, A. A. (2013). *Critical perspectives on international education.* Sense Publishers.

Holi, I. H. (2018). *Omani engineering students' experiences of learning through the medium of English* (Unpublished PhD thesis). University of Huddersfield, UK.

Holi, I. H. (2020). Lecture comprehension difficulties experienced by Omani students in an English medium engineering programme, *Cogent Arts & Humanities, 7*(1), 1–17. doi:10.1080/23311983.2020.1741986.

Holi, I. H. (2021). Impact of EMI on Omani engineering students' academic performance. *Arab World English Journal, 12*(1), 309–324. doi:10.24093/awej/vol12no1.21.

Holi, I. H, AlWashahi, Q., & Alhassan, A. (2020). Unpacking the challenges and accommodation strategies of Omani English-major students on IELTS academic reading tests. *Journal of Language and Linguistic Studies, 16*(3), 1621–1636. doi:10.17263/jlls.803922.

Huo, X. (2020). *Higher education internationalization and English language instruction: Intersectionality of race and language in Canadian Universities.* Springer.

Hyatt, D. (2013). Stakeholders' perceptions of IELTS as an entry requirement for higher education in the UK. *Journal of Further and Higher Education, 37*(6), 844–863. doi:10.1080/0309877X.2012.684043.

Ishikura, Y. (2015). Realizing internationalization at home through English-medium courses at a Japanese university: Strategies to maximize student learning. *Higher Learning Research Communications, 5*(1). doi:10.18870/hlrc.v5i1.237.

Jones, E., & de Wit, H. (2012). Globalization of internationalization: Thematic and regional reflections on a traditional concept. Special edition on rethinking internationalization. *AUDEM: International Journal of Higher Education and Democracy,* 35–54.

Kerklaan, V., Moreira, G., & Boersma, K. (2008). The role of language in the internationalisation of higher education: An example from Portugal. *European Journal of Education, 43*(2), 241–255.

Kirkpatrick, A. (2011). Internationalization or englishization? medium of instruction in today's universities. Hong Kong. *Centre for Governance and Citizenship. Working Paper Series 2011/003.* Institute of Education.

Knight, J.(2004). Internationalization remodeled: Definition, approaches, and rationales. *Journal of Studies in International Education, 8*(1), 5–31.

Knight, J.(2011). Five myths about internationalization. *International Higher Education*, 62, 10–15.

Kuteeva, M., Kaufhold, K., & Hynninen, N. (Eds.) (2020). *Language perceptions and practices in multilingual universities*. Palgrave Macmillan.

Lueg, K., & Lueg, R. (2015). Why do students choose English as a medium of instruction? A Bourdieusian perspective on the study strategies of non-native English speakers. *Academy of Management Learning & Education*, 14(1), 5–30.

Maringe, F. (2009). Strategies and challenges of internationalization in HE: An exploratory study of UK universities. *International Journal of Educational Management*, 23(7), 553–563.

Maringe, F., Foskett, N., & Woodfield, S. (2013). Emerging internationalisation models in an uneven global terrain: Findings from a global survey. *Compare: A Journal of Comparative and International Education*, 43(1), 9–36. doi:10.1080/03057925.2013.746548.

Marshall, C., & Rossman, G. (1999). *Designing qualitative research*. Sage Publications.

Martens, K., Knodel, P., & Windzio, M. (Eds.) (2014). *Internationalization of education policy: A new constellation of statehood in education?* Palgrave Macmillan.

McPherron, P. (2017). *Internationalizing teaching, localizing learning: An examination of English language teaching reforms and English use in China*. Palgrave Macmillan.

Mitchell, K. (2003). Educating the national citizen in neoliberal times: From the multicultural self to the strategic cosmopolitan. *Transactions of the Institute of British Geographers*, 28, 387–403.

Noori, M., & Mirhosseini, S. (2021). Testing language, but what? Examining the carrier content of IELTS preparation materials from a critical perspective. *Language Assessment Quarterly*, 1–16. doi:10.1080/15434303.2021.1883618.

O'Neill, M., & Chapman, A. (2015). Globalisation, internationalisation and English language: Studies of education in Singapore, Malaysia and Australia. *Education Research and Perspectives*, 42, 1–24.

Palmer, John D., Roberts, Ami, Cho, Young-Ha, & Ching, Gregory S. (Eds.) (2011). *The internationalization of East Asian higher education: Globalization's impact*. Palgrave Macmillan.

Pearson, W. S. (2019). Critical perspectives on the IELTS test. *ELT Journal*, 73(2), 197–206.

Saunders, M., Lewis, P., & Thornhill, A. (2012). *Research methods for business students* (6th ed). London: Pearson Education Limited.

Soler, J., & Gallego-Balsà, L. (2019). *The sociolinguistics of higher education: Language policy and internationalisation in Catalonia*. Palgrave Macmillan.

Study-in-uk.org (2020). International student statistics in UK 2020. Retrieved from https://www.studying-in-uk.org/international-student-statistics-in-uk.

Sun, J. J.-M., Hu, P., & Ng, S. H. (2017). Impact of English on education reforms in China: With reference to the learn-English movement, the internationalisation of universities and the English language requirement in college entrance examinations.

Journal of Multilingual and Multicultural Development, 38(3), 192–205. doi:10.1080/01434632.2015.1134551.

Teichler, U. (2010). Internationalising higher education: Debates and changes in Europe. In Dimitris Mattheou (Ed.), *Changing educational landscapes: Educational policies, schooling systems and higher education – A comparative perspective* (pp. 263–283). Springer.

Whitsed, C., & Green, W. (2013). Internationalisation begins with the curriculum. *University World News*. 26 January 2013. Retrieved 2 April 2021, from https://www.universityworldnews.com/post.php?story=20130123121225469.

Whitsed, C., & Wright, P. (2013). English language learning in the Japanese higher education sector: Towards internationalisation. *Intercultural Education, 24*(3), 222–236. doi:10.1080/14675986.2013.793033.

Willms, J. D. (2018). Learning divides: Using data to inform educational policy (Information Paper No. 54, September) UNESCO-UIS.

Wilkinson, R. (2013). English-medium instruction at a Dutch university: Challenges and pitfalls. In A. Doiz, D. Lasagabaster, & J. M. Sierra (Eds.), *English-medium instruction at universities: Global challenges* (pp. 3–24). Multilingual Matters.

4

EMI in Kuwait

Is English a Threat?

Inas Y. Mahfouz

Background

My six-year-old came to me with a disappointed look on his face and asked, 'Why do we study English?' I paused for a few minutes to overcome my shock and replied, 'because it's important'. This disappointment of a young child who struggled with English spelling made me wonder about the feelings of older students. What about my undergraduate students who are mostly eighteen plus and are forced to take all their subjects in English? English is a foreign language to most of them. Do they face the same struggles? Is their experience any better than my child's? Although they have studied it most probably since their early childhood, it is likely not their home language. It may not be their preferred language when they hang out with friends, watch TV or play PlayStation. So, I started thinking that maybe the perceptions of these youngsters might enrich our educational policies.

In Kuwait, we often discuss the challenges students face while studying in English but seldom pay any attention to their attitudes towards the language. Therefore, I shall focus more on young people's perceptions of EMI and its consequences for their identity. I shall set off with the questions: 'Do people love English? Is the farmer right in assuming that English can make you "a king"?'. Next, I shall examine the role of English in everyday communication, education and entertainment/leisure activities. Using task-oriented interviews, students will reflect on their language practices and reveal their attitudes towards EMI. Subsequently, the responses will be compiled and analysed quantitatively and qualitatively.

EMI Situation in Kuwait and the Arabian Gulf

The Arabian Gulf is a region known for its small area and great wealth based on oil revenues. In the Gulf Cooperation Council (GCC) countries, the growing incidence of English as a lingua franca can be attributed to two main reasons: the spread of literacy and a sharp increase in foreign workers and educators. These reasons are both related to the discovery of oil. More wealth entailed spending more on education and attracting foreigners from different parts of the world to work and do business. As a result, the oil-rich Arab countries have lured people from Western and Asian countries searching for better-paid jobs towards countries like Kuwait, either alone or with their families.

First, the newly found wealth has changed the lives of the citizens of these countries. Citizens have benefited from increased expenditure on education. According to a report on investing in Kuwait, '[e]ducation expenditure in Kuwait crossed USD 6.8 Bn in 2013 and [was] expected to reach USD 10.5 Bn by 2019' (Kuwait Direct Investment Promotion Authority, n.d., p. 25). Immediately after discovering oil, a significant increase in literacy took place in the last few decades in the GCC countries. For example, according to UN figures, in 1985, the illiteracy rate among Kuwaitis aged fifteen to twenty-four was 23,040 among females and 14,340 among males. However, illiteracy dropped to 960 for females and 2,880 for males in 2015 (Kuwait, 2016) (Figure 4.1).

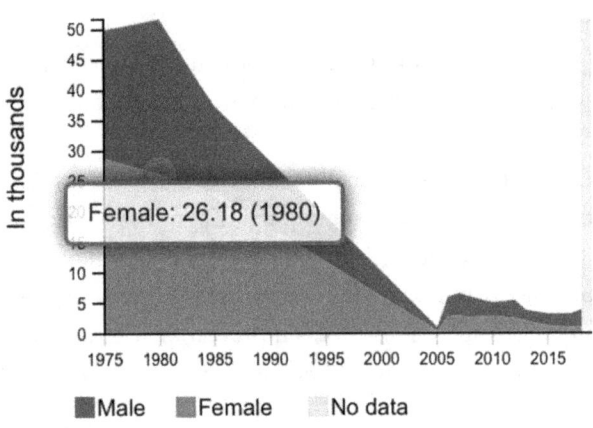

Figure 4.1 Illiteracy figures in Kuwait.

In 2020, Kuwait budgeted 12.3 per cent of its government expenditure for the education sector, ranking third among the GCC countries after Saudi Arabia and the UAE ('GCC: Government spending on education as a share of total expenditure by country 2020', 2021). The discovery of oil in the 1960s would subsequently fuel investments in education to bridge the gap between GCC countries and Western civilization. Consequently, more and more Gulf countries, including Kuwait, started to adopt the American model of higher education where English-medium instruction is the norm (Weber, 2011). In higher education, internationalization is often seen as synonymous with higher quality in education, as the 'white knight of higher education' (Kertz-Welzel, 2018).

By 2011, the number of Australian, British and American campuses in the Middle East had almost doubled, going from 140 to 260 campuses, compared to a few decades back (Weber, 2011). These institutions serve the growing population of these countries, both citizens and expats, who have no access to public education institutions as they are reserved for the nationals. According to the World Population Review, expats represent 70 per cent of the population in Kuwait (Kuwait Population, 2021; Demographics, Maps, Graphs, 2021). Since many expats do not speak Arabic fluently, the internationalized English-medium model serves them well and provides their offspring with the education they need.

On the social level, the presence of people who speak different languages in one place often imposes upon them the need to use a lingua franca in their day-to-day tasks. In Kuwait and most of the Arabian Gulf, English fulfils this function. Whether you are shopping or dining out with friends, you will probably communicate with the shop assistant or the waiter in English. This phenomenon often happens in the domestic sphere, where foreign domestic workers and nannies use a mixture of English and pidgin Arabic. As a result, children below the age of five are exposed to more than two languages at home daily. Such prevalence of English has caused contradictory responses from the citizens. Some accept its use and hail it as a channel of modernization, while others remain suspicious and worry about their national identity. Similarly, the attitudes of youngsters vary significantly, shaping their language practices and choices as they communicate.

Some of the attitudes towards the spread of English in Kuwait are reminiscent of linguistic imperialism. Robert Phillipson (1992) raised the issue of the international dominance of English as a kind of linguistic imperialism, much to the detriment of other languages. According to Phillipson, such dominance is 'asserted and maintained by the establishment and continuous reconstruction of structural and cultural inequalities between English and other languages' (1992, p. 47). In fact, in some cases, EMI has widened the inequality gap between English and other languages in society, that is, at a society's cultural heart. So, in some cases, English may be seen as a killer language, for, as some would argue, 'no language is a neutral medium; the adoption of any language has a range of cultural and conceptual consequences' (Gregory et al., 2009). Consequently, there are people in Kuwait, especially older generations, who worry about the status of Arabic not only as the language of the Qur'an but also as *the* living language to interpret and describe *their* own lived experiences as Kuwaitis.

Given this social context, it is imperative to focus on young people's use of English and Arabic and their attitudes towards both languages. This controversy is not new. In February 2007, a conference was organized to discuss the future of the Arabic language, especially Standard Arabic, by UNESCO in collaboration with five other leading organizations (the Arab League (AL), the Arab Council of Childhood and Development, the Arab Gulf Programme for United Nations Development Organization, the Kuwaiti Fund for Arab Economic Development and the Islamic Organization for Education, Science and Culture (ISESCO)).

For quite some time, Arab countries have dreaded the decline of their mother tongue and felt threatened by the precedence of English (Bassiouney, 2020). In response to those feelings, some have started taking extra steps to protect the Arabic language. For example, in 2012, Qatar mandated Arabic-medium instruction at Qatar University (Belhiah & Elhami, 2015).

In Kuwait, public schools teach sciences and math in Arabic, while some private schools do it in Arabic and others in English. In higher education, however, all private institutions adopt EMI. In addition, all fourteen private institutions adopt the international model of higher education, and, in many cases, they are also affiliated to Western universities. Kuwait's two public higher education institutions, Kuwait University (KU) and the Public Authority for Applied Education and Training (PAAET), use English in teaching sciences and math. As a result, Kuwaiti students enrolled in public schools will study science and math in Arabic first and then switch to English in their undergraduate programme at the faculty of education at KU. After graduation, they will be expected to teach these subjects in Arabic in public schools (Alazemi, 2017). This discrepancy between the medium of instruction in public schools and higher education institutions represents a challenge, which many Kuwaiti students struggle with and may hinder their progress as undergraduates and their professional development after graduation.

Review of Literature

The prevalence of EMI in higher education has intrigued scholars in the twenty-first century because '[t]he rise of English as the dominant language of scientific communication is unprecedented since Latin dominated the academy in medieval Europe' (Altbach et al., 2009, p. iv). In a 300-page report for the UNESCO 2009 World Conference on Higher Education, Altbach et al. (2009) discussed the internationalization of higher education, access to it, equity in it and its impact on students' experience and assessment. Dearden (2014) argues that using EMI enables universities to attract students from different nationalities. However, she also wonders if EMI is associated with upper social classes since most institutions that rely on English are private ones.

In the Arabian Gulf, EMI has attracted much attention from researchers, including Troudi and Jendli (2011), Belhiah and Elhami (2015), Solloway (2016), Alazemi (2017), Ali (2018, 2020) and Graham et al. (2021). Burden-Leahy (2009) reports on higher education in the UAE and laments the exclusion of the Gulf countries from the comparative education literature only because of their high-income status. Belhiah and Elhami (2015) examined EMI in six different universities in the UAE using questionnaires and structured interviews. They concluded that the linguistic challenges students face hinder their performance in other courses. They recommended reliance on bilingual education to ensure the preservation of national identity. Along the same lines, Solloway (2016) drew on the same tools to highlight the perspectives of Emirati undergraduate females on EMI and recommended pursuing studies that focus on the students and their attitudes. Alazemi (2017) and Daniel et al. (2018) shed light on Kuwaiti students' challenges while learning English and emphasized parental encouragement in motivating students.

Alhassan et al. (2021) have recently used structured interviews to investigate the challenges which both teachers and students face in an EMI master's degree programme in business administration (MBA) in Sudan. Other studies like Habbash and Troudi (2015), Al-Wadi (2016), Ahmadi (2017) and Mustafawi and Shaaban (2019) have focused on language policy and the question of whether English should be used as the language of instruction in the Gulf at all.

In short, the factual ubiquity and dominance of English in educational policy and practice in the Arabian Gulf are not wholly uncontested among scholars.

Methodology

Data Collection: Procedures

This chapter represents a study on Kuwaitis' perspectives on the linguistic situation in their country and the Arabian Gulf that dates back to 2019. In May 2019, a preliminary survey was distributed among undergraduate students about their perceptions of the English language in their lives. Although most of them acknowledged its importance, the statistical information collected was not enough to reflect the students' attitudes and perspectives. To fill this gap, I spent more than a year informally observing students enrolled in the private university in Kuwait where I teach. According to the university policy, English is the medium of communication on campus, and all students, faculty and staff should use English at all times.

Initially, I planned to interview some students individually and discuss their attitudes towards our university's language policy. However, I realized that students might hesitate to complain or express discontent because I am one of the English instructors. Eventually, I decided to rely on task-based interviews. The respondents were given a few questions and encouraged to express their views on English, not just as a medium of instruction but as a possible threat to their social or cultural life as young Arabs. The prompt here was developed and shared among undergraduate students.

The Prompt. Please write a 500–1000-word paper where you describe your language practice.

In the first half, it would be best if you tried to answer these questions:

1. What is your preferred language of literacy?
2. Would you study math and science in English or Arabic instead?
3. Do you read books in Arabic?
4. Do you watch talk shows or movies in Arabic or English? Do you listen to Arabic songs?
5. Which language, or variety of it, do you use on social media platforms?
6. In your opinion, what are the common perceptions of English and Arabic in Kuwait? For example, is there a language that makes you feel/seem more powerful or be perceived as more prestigious than others?

Refer to your own opinion and give examples from your own experience.

In the second half, discuss which language practices would best help you as an Arab to protect your identity and achieve personal growth. Let the questions here guide your reflection:

1. Which language(s) should schools in Kuwait use in science classes?
2. Which language should be used in talk shows?
3. Should schools teach foreign languages?
4. How many hours should students spend studying Arabic and any foreign language every day?
5. What about higher education? Which language(s) should be used there?
6. Should international models of higher education be adopted? Why?

While answering these questions, always try to give reasons for your answers.

Participants

In February 2021, the prompt was shared with sixty junior students. These undergraduates are English majors, so most of their courses, except for a few GenEd ones, focus on English literature. They were asked to submit a short paper electronically in response to the previous questions within two weeks. They were also encouraged to include their personal experience where relevant. The total number of submissions received was fifty-nine (twenty-three males and thirty-six females).

Corpora, Concordance and Segmentation

First, the collected submissions were divided into two corpora based on the gender of the respondents. This division was needed to find out whether gender influences the perceptions of young people, especially since most previous studies disregarded gender-based differences — the male corpus consists of 7,551 words and the female corpus of 9,145 words. The second step involved removing any personal information about the respondents, such as age and nationality, to anonymize the corpora. The submissions for analysis would thus protect the respondents' privacy.

As reflected in this chapter, the study combines both quantitative and qualitative analyses tools to interpret the most frequent themes and the perceptions they denote more comprehensibly. For the quantitative analysis, I used *Sketch Engine* ('Create and search a text corpus', 2016), while for the qualitative analysis, I segmented the corpora and entered each segment into a *Microsoft Excel* file. Most previous studies that approached users' perceptions relied on surveys with multiple choice or Likert scale questions. In some cases, when qualitative analysis was used, the researchers focused on recurrent themes and their frequency (Ahmadi, 2017). In this study, combining quantitative and

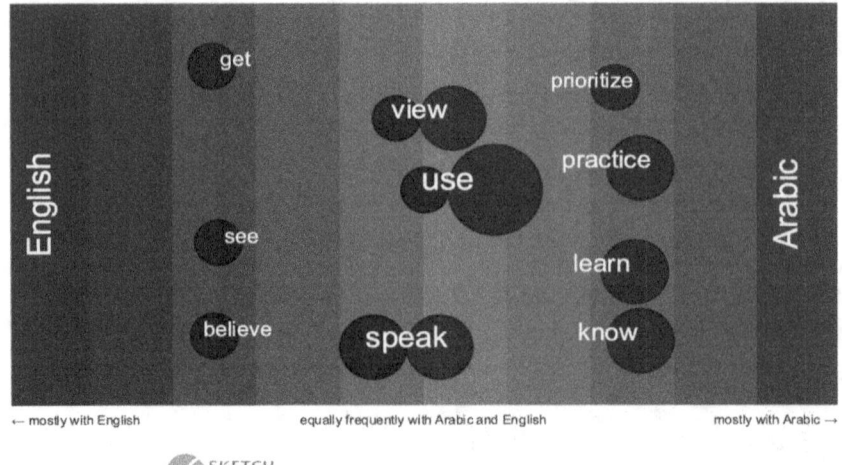

Figure 4.2 Male corpus: Word sketch difference verbs with Arabic/English as objects.

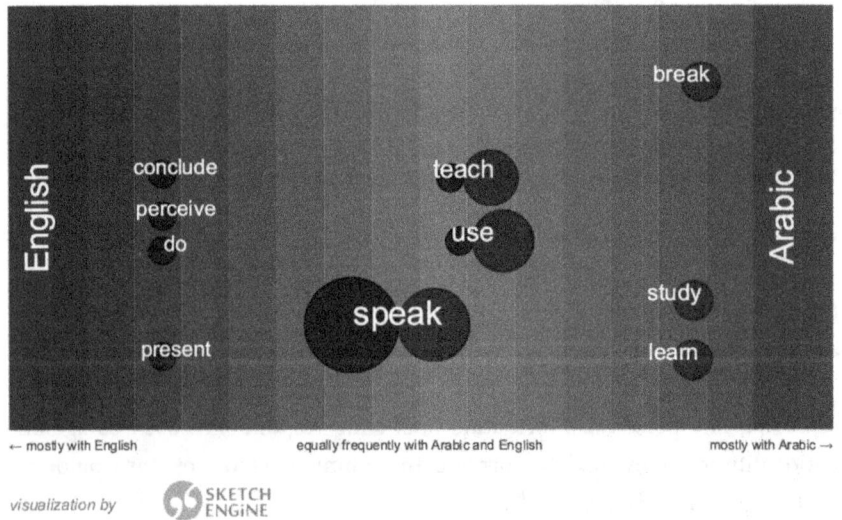

Figure 4.3 Female corpus: Word sketch difference Verbs with Arabic/English as objects.

qualitative analyses unravels the dominant themes and pinpoints the prevalent feelings about EMI among young Kuwaitis. *Sketch Engine* is used to generate keyword lists and elicit the recurrent, general themes and provide sketches (Kilgarriff et al., 2015) of their collocational behaviour (see Figures 4.2 and 4.3).

Analysing non-numeric data by assigning codes to it has been an established practice since the early decades of the twenty-first century. Coding has been praised because it 'compels the researcher to be systematic in handling data (...) and impedes the researcher's impulse to notice only passages that support his or her preliminary hypotheses' (Howard, 2014, p. 79). It refers to allocating a word or phrase to a language stream to signify one or more of its attributes (Geisler, 2018). The twenty-first century witnessed a flourishing in Computer-Assisted Qualitative Data Analysis (CAQDAS) tools. Researchers now utilize CAQDAS tools such as Excel, Dedoose and QDA Miner to unravel the hidden relations between sentences that might otherwise be missed. To avoid any biases, I have decided to code the entire corpus (see Appendix) and then build the interpretation based on the most frequent codes rather than code the sentences that contain the most frequent types.

Findings

Quantitative Analysis

Sketch Engine generated a list of keywords in both male and female corpora and their respective frequency. The most frequent keywords in both were 'Arabic', 'language' and 'English'. To increase the accuracy of the analysis, the frequencies of all tokens of the same type were added together.

Male Corpus. In the male students' writing, the type 'Arab' had the highest frequency, occurring 231 times and was represented by two tokens: 'Arabic' and 'Arab'. This type represents 2.8 per cent of the whole corpus. The token 'Arabic' appears 195 times, while the token 'Arab' appears 36 times.

(1) The Arabic language is in danger.
(2) I decided to read more Arabic books than I used to.
(3) For example, in high school, I studied biology in Arabic and when I joined AUK and took a course in Biology, it was like I was studying Biology for the first time in my life.

'Arab' is used in structures like 'Arab identity' or 'Arab world':

(4) In an attempt to protect the Arab identity, I feel as though local talk shows should be incentivised to use Arabic, in an attempt to promote the Arabic.
(5) And I believe that the linguistic situation in the Arab world in the next century will have more bilingual speakers than monolinguals.

The word 'language' occurs 189 times (2.3 per cent in the whole corpus). It is commonly found in n-grams like 'Arabic language' or 'English language'. The

N-gram 'Arabic language' occurs 26 times, while the N-gram 'English language' occurs 20 times:

(6) Due to the Arabic language complexity and its many various dialects, it has the most complicated diglossia situation.
(7) Moving on, the language I use most often is the English language, followed by a deteriorated equal proficiency in both Kuwaiti colloquial Arabic and Tagalog.

The type 'English' represents 2 per cent of the corpus and occurs 159 times:

(8) Studying science and math in English could be easier because its theories and practical are easy to perform and understand in English.
(9) In my day-to-day life, I primarily speak English while rarely speaking Arabic.

A word sketch difference between Arabic and English reveals that 'Arabic' is the object of verbs like 'prioritize', 'practice', 'learn' and 'know', while verbs like 'get', 'see' and 'believe' are mainly used with 'English'. Interestingly, both 'Arabic' and 'English' have the same frequency as objects of the verb 'speak'. In other words, the participants use both languages equally, but when they think about them consciously, they tend to 'prioritize' Arabic. The following example reflects the participants' awareness that Arabic is part of their identity:

(10) In closing, individuals should prioritize Arabic to protect the Arab identity from being lost.

Female Corpus. The results of the quantitative analysis of the female corpus practically replicate those of the males. The type 'Arab' occurs 279 times (2.66 per cent) and is represented by two tokens: 'Arabic' and 'Arab'. Examples include:

(11) As an Arab, I mostly use Arabic most of the time especially colloquial Arabic, but I also use English when studying.
(12) Another reason is that I feel deeply connected to my identity whenever I read in Arabic.

The second most frequent type is 'language' with a total frequency of 250 (2.5 per cent). Its most common collocations are 'Arabic' and 'English'. The N-gram 'Arabic language' has a total frequency of 26 and the N-gram 'English language' occurs 19 times:

(13) Besides, I think that talk shows should use the Arabic language because most Arabs stick to their Arabic language for communication purposes.

(14) Moreover, in higher education, the English language should be used more often than Arabic because higher learning institutions involved diverse groups of students.

The total frequency of the type 'English' is 231 (2.3 per cent). Examples include:

(15) To add, I sure stated that it would be better if sciences and math were taught in English but that does not mean that the students should only know scientific terminology in English only.
(16) Personally, I read both MSA [*Modern Standard Arabic*] and English books.

A word sketch difference between Arabic and English reveals that 'Arabic' is the object of verbs like 'break', 'study', 'learn' and 'use', while verbs like 'present', 'do' and 'perceive' are mainly used with 'English'. Like in the male corpus, the verb 'speak' is a borderline case, as participants speak both languages interchangeably. Interestingly, 'Arabic' has a higher frequency as the object of the verb 'teach'.

Qualitative Analysis

The prompt has been designed to encourage respondents to share their attitudes regarding the use of English in three interrelated domains: their informal everyday communication, education and leisure time activities. A total of 790 t-units were coded. Each t-unit was assigned a code that reflected its attitude towards any of the three domains, whether positive, negative or neutral (Table 4.1).

Table 4.1 Percentage of codes

Code	Male corpus (%)	Female corpus (%)	Overall (%)
Positive_English_social	17.31	17.30	17.35
English_threat	7.46	9.67	8.73
Positive_English_Education	11.64	13.63	12.78
Negative_English_Education	5.67	3.72	4.55
Positive_English_Entertainment & leisure time activities	5.67	5.57	5.44
Negative_English_Entertainment & leisure time activities	6.58	2.64	4.44
Neutral	45.67	47.47	46.71
Total	100	100	100

Approximately half of the t-units coded in both corpora (46.71 per cent) are neutral and show no significant attitude towards either language. In addition, 47.47 per cent of the females' responses show no specific attitude towards languages, while 45.67 per cent of the male responses do not align with a specific language.

(17) I don't believe English to be a threat to us unless we choose to not to work on our Arabic.
(18) Arabic and English are important these days; however, we can't learn one language and ignore the other.

As far as informal interaction within their community of practice goes, students are asked if using a particular language makes them seem more powerful or more prestigious. Again, 17.30 per cent of the females and 17.31 per cent of the males think that English is a threat.

(19) The Arab identity is considered to be endangered by the infringing influence of foreign languages such as English and French.
(20) To add, I avoid speaking in English with Arabs because I consider it strange to do so.
(21) The listener would perceive me as either an educated person or a 'McChicken'.

While the student in (19) thinks that the Arab identity is endangered, the student in (20) thinks that using English is socially strange. The respondent in (21) describes those who use English as 'McChicken', an expression common among young Kuwaitis to refer to a vain westernized person. This attitude can be detected only in the male responses.

While the percentage of students who think that using English has positive social consequences is significantly low among both genders, females are more likely to embrace English than males. For example, 7.46 per cent of the males would use English in their informal communication compared to 9.67 per cent of the females, who believe that using English makes them 'feel more prestigious'. This connection between language and social prestige is reminiscent of Seth's (1994) perception that English makes you 'king'.

(22) Personally, whenever I speak English in general my accent doesn't seem foreign and people tend to compliment me and ask about my education, which makes me feel more prestigious.
(23) Also, what is common here in Kuwait is, Speaking English gives you more power.

(24) Thus, English is perceived as a more prestigious language than Arabic in Kuwait because many people do not use it.

Both genders think that English should be used in teaching sciences and math. It seems that EMI is largely accepted as most participants acknowledge that English is the language of science. It should be noted that some students come from private schools and have studied these subjects in English.

(25) As in my school, subjects like math and science would be in taught in English.
(26) That's also how I went through my academic life using almost always English because it is the mandatory and dominant language spoken and taught in my school.

In the previous example, the student clearly states that science and math were taught in English; it is even described as 'mandatory'.

Arabic is the preferred language for males in their leisure time activities like reading, watching movies or communicating on social media platforms. For example, 6.58 per cent of their responses select Arabic, while only 2.64 of the female responses favour Arabic over English. Male students interpret this preference because they can relate more to the culture and humour.

(27) Speaking about talk shows, I like the one's in Arabic more I understand the context more and the humor better.
(28) The language that should be used in talk shows is Arabic or KCA [*Kuwaiti Colloquial Arabic*], because that will be even better for anyone living in Kuwait, in order for them to have a deep connection and to enrich their sense of what the Kuwaiti identity is all about.

Discussion

The findings of both quantitative and qualitative analyses point to a growing awareness among young Kuwaitis that both Arabic and English are essential. The almost equal frequency of 'Arabic' and 'English' in both corpora and the high frequency of the code 'neutral' in the qualitative analysis prove that young people now are well aware of the complexity of the linguistic situation in the Arab world, especially the Arabian Gulf. They believe that English language is needed to cope internationally and understand science and technology, thus echoing Alhassan et al. (2021). Moreover, English is a lingua franca that the youth need for professional and academic reasons. However, both genders value Arabic as the language of the Qur'an and their heritage.

(29) We must make a contrast between our practices in the English and Arabic language, just like we are focusing on English when it comes to the academic or professional side of our lives, we are responsible for embracing our native language in our daily life.
(30) Although holding on to Arabic seems to be harder nowadays, I think the more we work on loving it, the more we can go back to it.

Such awareness supports the findings of previous studies calling for dual or bilingual education (Alazemi, 2017; Belhiah & Elhami, 2015; Solloway, 2016; Troudi & Jendli, 2011). Previous studies emphasized the importance of a dual curriculum to help students overcome their challenges and perform better. The current study proves that young people are more aware than ever before of the importance of their linguistic heritage and the necessity of embracing their native tongue as an identity marker. Such neutral attitudes about both languages suggest that Alazemi's (2017) recommendation to integrate both English and Arabic in our educational system would provide young people with the knowledge they need to develop academically and maintain their native cultural identity.

Two less frequent attitudes should also be considered: the first is related to pre-college schooling and the second relates to social image. Concerns about the gap between public and private education, especially in the pre-college stage, and how this affects students echo Ali's (2018) findings. Although a few participants pointed to this gap, the details of this problem are outside this study's scope. The connection between social image and gender differences cannot be disregarded. Females accept English as the 'prestige' language and use English more often in informal communication and leisure time activities (see examples 22–24). On the other hand, males might hesitate to use a foreign language in their daily conversation as it may be construed as less 'macho' (see example 21).

Conclusion and Implications

The spread of English, whether in schools or universities, is a global phenomenon. In the GCC countries, this phenomenon relates to the local demographics. Due to the high percentages of expats, English is spoken everywhere, not just in schools or universities. However, the Z generation is exposed to multiple cultures and is constantly wired. This generation is more aware of linguistic differences than their ancestors were. They understand that English is a need, and Arabic is their identity marker.

Although young Kuwaitis realize that English is the language of academic and professional development, they are also aware of the invaluable role of their native tongue. To assume that English is a threat to the Arab identity is a hasty conclusion that disregards the growing realization among young people that Arabic is an integral part of their identity and who they are. Governments and policymakers should seriously consider either introducing Arabic-English bilingual education or universalizing Arabic-medium instruction while keeping English as an active second language (not a 'matter-of-fact' language taught in ineffective and inefficient courses).

The implications of this study could shape our educational policies. Although EMI is part of the international model of higher education, it is necessary to consider students' cultural backgrounds. More courses about the Arab culture should be introduced. Arabic courses should be part of GenEd requirements. The strict policy mandating English as the only language of communication on some campuses should be revised. Extracurricular events could also focus on the Arab culture and encourage students to reconnect with their heritage.

Limitations of the Study and Future Research

Finally, the findings of this study should be adopted with caution. There are a few limitations related to the respondents that may affect the possibility of generalizing these findings. First, the study was conducted among students who attend(ed) the same private institution. Therefore, it does not account for those attending other institutions or those going to public ones. Furthermore, the background of the participants has not been considered. For example, students coming from public high schools are more likely to face trouble with the international model of higher education because of its emphasis on English as a medium of instruction. Hence their perspectives are different from those who used to attend private schools. Also, the questions were shared out among undergraduates whose major was English, so their responses may have included biases towards English and its use. Students enrolled in other programmes might disagree with the attitudes shared by English majors. Finally, sixty respondents are not enough to generalize a hypothesis or explanation about young people's attitudes in the whole of Kuwait.

Future research should be conducted across multiple higher education institutions in Kuwait to facilitate various comparisons, for example, between public and private institutions. Fourteen private institutions in Kuwait adopt the international model of English-medium higher education, and a series of questions could be asked.

- Do they all apply the same strict policies regarding EMI?
- What is the students' perception of EMI?
- What type of support is offered to struggling students?
- What is the students' educational background and English proficiency level upon admission and afterward?
- How does EMI impact the students' ability to transfer their knowledge gained through English to Arabic environments and to produce new knowledge and applications of it in Arabic?

In short, further research is needed to elucidate these and other questions, especially to investigate the similarities and dissimilarities between language of instruction policies and practices in the sciences and humanities, including their advantages and disadvantages, effectiveness, efficiency and sustainability.

It is also critical to understand that as educators, our efforts should be limited to discussing the challenges students face in class and their views on and attitudes towards their education. The languages used in teaching and learning should be taken into consideration, too. Although students' perspectives are not the only factor in curriculum design and educational policies, they are still important and should shape future educational policies. By conducting surveys like the one in this chapter and gathering similar information, policies and practices can be adapted to students' needs and concerns. Embracing modern approaches to education should not be understood as copying foreign models and pasting them where they may or may not be fully fit for purpose. Instead, as GCC countries develop their educational systems, they should preserve, pass on and enrich their national cultures, both protecting students' heritage and equipping them to engineer better futures.

References

Ahmadi, Q. S. (2017). Unwelcome? English as a medium of instruction (EMI) in the Arabian Gulf. *English Language Teaching, 10*(8), 11.

Alazemi, A. (2017). *Teaching of academic subjects in English and the challenges Kuwaiti students face*. University of Exeter. Retrieved from https://ore.exeter.ac.uk/repository/handle/10871/27997.

Alhassan, A., Ali, N. A., & Ali, H. I. H. (2021). EFL students' challenges in English-medium business programmes: Perspectives from students and content teachers. *Cogent Education*, 8(1), 1888671.

Ali, H. (2018). *Omani engineering students' experiences of learning through the medium of English* (Doctoral, University of Huddersfield). Retrieved from http://eprints.hud.ac.uk/id/eprint/34548/.

Ali, H. (2020). Omani students' coping strategies in an English medium engineering programme. *Arab World English Journal (AWEJ)*, 11. Retrieved from https://papers.ssrn.com/sol3/papers.cfm?abstract_id=3649338.

Altbach, P. G., Reisberg, L., & Rumbley, L. E. (2009). Trends in global higher education: Tracking an academic revolution. A report prepared for the UNESCO 2009 world conference on higher education. Retrieved 17 November 2018, from https://s3.amazonaws.com/academia.edu.documents/30910755/Altbach__Reisberg__Rumbley_Tracking_an_Academic_Revolution__UNESCO_2009.pdf?AWSAccessKeyId=AKIAIWOWYYGZ2Y53UL3A&Expires=1543179662&Signature=RfruIjaEFbWlG7XOGjNaou1%2FzPQ%3D&response-content-disposition=inline%3B%20filename%3DTrends_in_global_higher_education_Tracki.pdf.

Al-Wadi, H. (2016). The role of English as a medium of instruction in reshaping Bahraini senior teachers' perceptions of their roles as middle leadership in their schools. *Journal of Language and Education*, 2(1), 6–15.

Bassiouney, R. (2020). *Arabic sociolinguistics* (2nd ed.). Edinburgh, Scotland: Edinburgh University Press.

Belhiah, H., & Elhami, M. (2015). English as a medium of instruction in the Gulf: When students and teachers speak. *Language Policy*, 14(1), 3–23.

Burden-Leahy, S. M. (2009). Globalisation and education in the postcolonial world: The conundrum of the higher education system of the United Arab Emirates. *Comparative Education Review*, 45(4), 525–544.

Create and Search a Text Corpus. (2016, April 5). Retrieved 14 July 2021, from http://www.sketchengine.eu.

Daniel, C. E., Halimi, F., & Alshammari, I. A. (2018). The impact of motivation and parental encouragement on English language learning: An Arab students' perspective. *The Reading Matrix*, 8(1), 176–194.

Dearden, J. (2014). *English as a medium of instruction – A growing global phenomenon*. British Council.

GCC: Government spending on education as share of total expenditure by country 2020. (2021). Retrieved 3 July 2021, from https://www.statista.com/statistics/720988/gcc-share-of-government-spending-on-education-by-country/.

Geisler, C. (2018). Coding for language complexity: The interplay among methodological commitments, tools, and workflow in writing research. *Written Communication*, 35(2), 215–249.

Kertz-Welzel, A. (2018). *Globalizing music education: A framework*. Bloomington: Indiana University Press.

Graham, K. M., Eslami, Z. R., & Hillman, S. (2021). From English as the medium to English as a medium: Perspectives of EMI students in Qatar. *System, 99*, 102508.

Gregory, D., Johnston, R., Pratt, G., Watts, M., & Whatmore, S. (Eds.). (2009). *The dictionary of human geography*. John Wiley & Sons.

Habbash, M., & Troudi, S. (2015). The discourse of global English and its representation in the Saudi context: A postmodernist critical perspective. In R. Raddawi (Ed.), *Intercultural communication with Arabs: Studies in educational, professional and societal contexts* (pp. 57–75). Singapore: Springer.

Howard, R. M. (2014). Why this humanist codes. *Research in the Teaching of English, 49*(1), 75–81.

Kilgarriff, A., Marcowitz, F., Smith, S., & Thomas, J. (2015). Corpora and language learning with the Sketch Engine and SKELL. *Revue Francaise de Linguistique Appliquee, XX*(1), 61–80.

Kuwait (27 November 2016). Retrieved 3 July 2021, from http://uis.unesco.org/en/country/kw.

Kuwait Population 2021 (Demographics, Maps, Graphs). (2021). Retrieved 3 July 2021, from https://worldpopulationreview.com/countries/kuwait-population.

Mustafawi, E., & Shaaban, K. (2019). Language policies in education in Qatar between 2003 and 2012: From local to global then back to local. *Language Policy, 18*(2), 209–242.

Phillipson, R. (1992). *Linguistic imperialism*. London, England: Oxford University Press.

Kuwait Direct Investment Promotion Authority. (n.d.). *Investing in Kuwait: Aguide for investment opportunities in Kuwait*. Retrieved from Kuwait Direct Investment Promotion Authority website: https://e.kdipa.gov.kw/main/4Education.pdf

Seth, V. (1994). *A suitable boy*. India: Penguin Books.

Solloway, A. J. (2016). *English-medium instruction in higher education in the United Arab Emirates: The perspectives of students*. University of Exeter. Retrieved from https://ore.exeter.ac.uk/repository/handle/10871/26316.

Troudi, S., & Jendli, A. (2011). *Emirati students' experiences of English as a medium of instruction*. Peter Lang Publishers.

Weber, A. S. (2011). Politics of English in the Arabian Gulf. Presented at the 1st International Conference on Foreign Language Teaching and Applied Linguistics, 60–66. Sarajevo. core.ac.uk.

Appendix

The first step in coding a corpus is segmentation. Segmenting verbal data ensures that each unit/segment fits into only one category of the coding scheme. The segmentation unit was usually linguistic; for purposes of this study, the segment was the sentence. Each sentence was a t-unit, that is, a group of words that enabled the writer to make a move. The word count for male submissions was 7,551 words, which were then divided into 335 t-units. Since the number of female participants was higher than that of males, their submissions yielded a longer corpus with a total word count of 9,145 words and 454 t-units. The t-units were then entered into an Excel file for coding.

Before writing the code, it was important to conduct a pilot study to understand the common perceptions represented in the corpora. The prompt elicited perceptions about English and English-medium education were classed into three domains: everyday communication, education and leisure time activities. These perceptions were either positive or negative, or, in many cases, neutral. The two corpora were entered into two separate Excel files for coding. Each file had all the t-units as a column; the code was entered on a separate sheet in the same file. Using the Data Validation feature, codes were entered next to t-units (see Figure 4.4).

Each t-unit was coded qualitatively according to the code explained here. Each code was followed by an example from the corpora used in this study:

- **Positive_English_social**:

The code *Positive_English_social* was used for any t-unit that expressed favourable attitudes towards the use of English in a social context.

e.g. *Thirdly, English made me gain a lot of respect as well as placed me in a prestigious level when I used it in most places.*

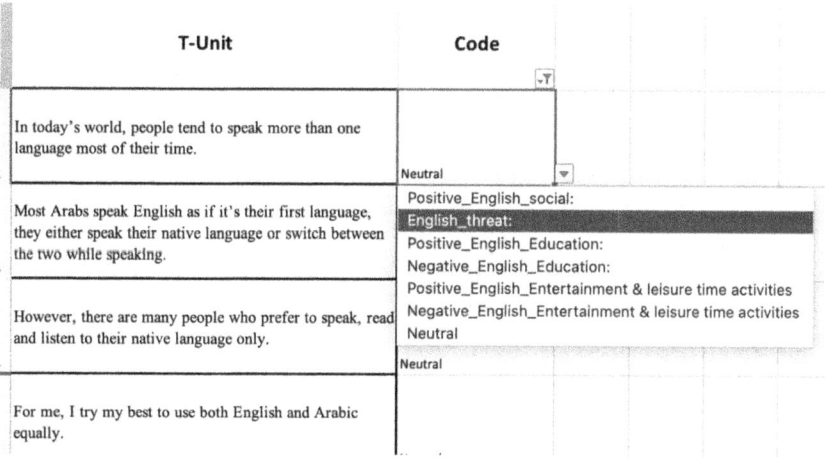

Figure 4.4 Using Excel to code t-units.

- **English_threat:**

The code *English_threat* was used for any t-unit that expressed concerns about the use of English in Arab societies.

e.g. In addition, speaking our language is a way to protect our identity as Arabs.

- **Positive_English_Education:**

The code *Positive_English_Education* was used for any t-unit that expressed favourable attitudes towards the use of English in education.

e.g. I would rather study maths and science in English.

- **Negative_English_Education:**

The code *Negative_English_Education* was used for any t-unit that expressed unfavourable attitudes towards the use of English in education.

e.g. Schools should definitely teach foreign languages, but the core language must be Arabic.

- **Positive_English_Entertainment & leisure time activities:**

The code *Positive_English_Entertainment* was used for any t-unit that expressed favourable attitudes towards the use of English for reading, on social media or other pastime activities such as watching movies or talk shows or listening to music.

e.g. Most of the media content I consume is in English.

- **Negative_English_Entertainment & leisure time activities:**

The code *Negative_English_Entertainment* was used for any t-unit that expressed unfavourable attitudes towards the use of English for reading, on social media or other pastime activities.

e.g. Listening to Arabic music especially Gulf music connected me more to my culture.

- **Neutral:**

The code *Neutral* was used for any t-unit that expressed no attitudes towards language.

e.g. For me, I try my best to use both English and Arabic equally.

5

EMI in Saudi Higher Education

Challenges and Prospects

Abdulwahid Al Zumor and Habib Abdesslem

Introduction

Language policy in Saudi higher education encounters the dilemma of balancing the national desire to maintain the role of Arabic as the medium of teaching science and the pressures of globalization and internationalization to incorporate English-medium instruction to facilitate the Kingdom's progress towards a knowledge-based economy. To address this challenge, the Saudi official policy documents have always maintained that Arabic is the language of instruction at the university level but added that other languages could be used. This policy statement indicates that the government wishes to continue referring to Arabic as the de jure medium of instruction with the possibility of adopting another language if necessary, without explicitly referring to English as an option. However, 'the practice of institutions is to move towards a greater use of English' (Alhawsawi, 2014, p. 36). The loophole that the government policy offers has encouraged Saudi universities to partially or fully teach science subjects in English. This emerging educational paradigm is known as English-medium instruction (henceforth EMI) or English-medium education (EME). Since its inception in the Saudi higher education context in 2004, EMI has not been thoroughly and critically addressed.

In this chapter we report on EMI in Saudi Arabia, a country where English has no official status (Alhamami, 2015, p. 108), a community where English is welcomed and contested (Moskovky & Picard, 2019, p. 82), and an educational system that is not clear on adopting a mono (Arabic only) or dual (English, Arabic) policy (Badry, 2019). We look at the Saudi university as a multilingual ecology where English is used along with other languages, as is the case with non-Anglophone universities around the world.

The medium of instruction in Saudi higher education institutions is not one and the same in all universities and across disciplines. State universities use Arabic in teaching humanities and social sciences, and they use mostly English (or maintain they do) in teaching disciplines such as engineering, medicine and computer science. On the other hand, private universities and colleges mostly adopt EMI in teaching science (Jamjoom, 2012), a global trend in higher education that Macaro et al. (2018) estimate is used by 90 per cent of private universities worldwide. In Saudi Arabia, EMI programmes started in 2004–5 (Barnawi & Al-Hawsawi, 2017) with the exception of King Fahd University of Petroleum and Minerals (KFUPM), which commenced the first intensive preparatory year programme (PYP) leading to EMI in 1964 (McMullen, 2014) due to KFUPM's special connection with Saudi Aramco.

As there is no unequivocal government policy document that stipulates the use of English to teach science subjects at the university, the decision has been left to individual institutions. Nevertheless, it has been difficult to find a comprehensive policy document that details the provisions and conditions of the implementation of this instructional approach in any of the Saudi higher education institutions. Therefore, EMI is not a de jure policy; it can rather be said to be a de facto educational practice that has developed in response to national and global pressures and considerations, given the economic and political roles Saudi Arabia plays regionally and internationally.

In order to explore the current status of EMI in Saudi Arabia's higher education, we have adopted the ROADMAPPING framework developed by Dafouz and Smit (2016, 2020). In spite of some overlapping between its components and its exclusive focus on higher education, the framework is multidimensional. It covers both instruction and learning in tertiary education, which is our main concern in this study, and it takes into account globalization and internationalization forces. Moreover, the framework allows for an approach that is dynamic and fluid and goes as far as acknowledging that a language policy exists, even when it is not made explicit by authority, and can best be inferred from practices and beliefs (Spolsky, 2005, p. 2153). We draw on the literature we consulted and resort to our experience as detached insiders (i) to make up for research areas that 'are either underrepresented in current Saudi EFL research, or are missing altogether' (Moskovsky, 2019, p. 40) and (ii) to avoid citing research that we consider vulnerable to criticism (Moskovsky, 2019, pp. 40–43).

The ROADMAPPING Framework

The ROADMAPPING framework aims at examining English-medium education in multilingual university settings. It comprises six dimensions: roles of English (RO) in relation to other languages, academic disciplines (AD), language management (M), agents (A), practices and processes (PP) and internationalization and glocalization (ING) (Dafouz & Smit, 2016, 2020). The first dimension covers the different *roles of English* in the host community and university. The second dimension explores the types of *academic disciplines* that use EMI in higher education and whether EMI teaching practices and assessment vary across university specialities. *Language management* draws attention to the top-down/bottom-up implicit/explicit language policies and planning measures at national and institutional levels. *Agents* refer to the stakeholders and actors who contribute to the planning, decision-making, implementation and assessment of EME. Agents include policymakers, management and administration, language support teachers, academic content teachers, researchers and students. *Practices and processes* explore the pedagogy of content delivery, students' interactional activities in the classroom and their learning strategies, teachers' beliefs and reflections on EMI processes, and their EMI professional development engagement. *Internationalization and Glocalization* is the sixth dimension in the framework. Internationalization is where a nation benefits from other nations' education experience and glocalization is where a nation's education maintains its local characteristics in the face of globalization (Knight, 2004; Scott, 2011).

Roles of English

Arabic and English are the two major languages that actively function in the Saudi linguistic ecology. Arabic is the official language in the country, and it is the mother tongue of Saudi natives. Saudi Arabia, like all Arab Islamic states, proclaims that Islam is its national religion and Arabic its language (Spolsky, 2004) and that the aim of education is to foster the Islamic faith in its youth and prepare them to serve their community, as stated in decree A/90m, Chapters 1 & 3 of the Basic System of Governance, the equivalent of the constitution, issued on 1 March 1992. Moreover, Arabic enjoys a special religious status in Saudis' consciousness (Findlow, 2006; Liddicoat, 2012).

English, on the other hand, is a foreign language and plays an important role in Saudis' life. In a newspaper article published in the *Saudi Gazette*, Al-Seghayer (2012) states that English 'serves several functions and enjoys an eminent status in various sectors at all levels within the Kingdom'. The extent of its use in the country is widening as a corollary of the globalization and modernization policies the country has been engaged in (Mahboob & Elyas, 2014).

In education, Arabic is the language of instruction in state primary, intermediate and secondary schools, with English taught as a subject from grade 1 (starting from this school year, 2021–2) to grade 12. However, some private schools teach in English with variation in the range of English courses and content. At the tertiary level, the situation is different: humanities and social sciences are taught in Arabic, while technology, science, engineering and medicine faculties adopt, or maintain they do, EMI.

The growth of English in the Kingdom has always been triggered by sociocultural and economic changes in the country. According to Karmani (2005), while other language planning strategies like Arabization or mass translation have faltered because they are complex, unsystematic and time-consuming, English has served, particularly from the 1970s, as a tool of industrialization and modernization, especially in higher education.

All Saudi universities can be considered as multilingual settings because within the premises of every higher education institution more than one language is used, and these languages play different roles. For instance, Modern Standard Arabic (MSA) is the language of official communication, the medium of instruction in the humanities and social sciences, and the primary language of university media. The Saudi regional variety of Arabic is used among students and Saudi academic and non-academic staff. Arab non-Saudi faculty members use their own varieties of Arabic in in-group encounters or what could be termed as an educated spoken variety of Arabic in inter-group communication. Non-Arab faculty members use English, but they often opt for codemixing with students, administrative staff and other fellow faculty. They also use their own native language for in-group communication. English plays multiple roles in this context. It is a lingua franca used by international faculty. It is the primary medium of teaching scientific disciplines and the language of most science textbooks, assessment, research and publication. It is the code of communication with international academic institutions and agencies. English is also taught as a compulsory subject in the first year of all university majors. This multilingual intricacy within higher education institutions impacts the teaching and learning of academic content.

We made attempts to find a policy document that regulates the role of English in Saudi higher education. The only document that explicitly states the role of languages other than Arabic in higher education is the Saudi prime minister's resolution number 60 in the year 1993, which was consolidated by a royal decree that states that Arabic is the medium of instruction in Saudi universities, and if necessary, another language can be used after official approval from the concerned university councils (Al Zumor, 2019a). This language policy statement seems to have brought about legality for English to assume a medium of instruction status and to be currently used to teach most of the scientific disciplines at Saudi universities (Alhamami, 2015; Al-Kahtany et al., 2015; Al Zumor, 2019b).

The functional role of Arabic in the Gulf countries' higher education institutions is changing and its competition with English is in full swing. To illustrate this competitive situation, Findlow (2006) found that Arabic is associated with cultural authenticity, localism, tradition, emotions and religion, whereas English is associated with modernity, internationalism, business, material status and secularism (see also Barnawi & Hasnawi, 2017). This dualism applies to the Saudi higher education situation today (Al-Jarf, 2008). However, the relationship between Arabic and English seems to be moving from a condition of coordination, where Arabic is the medium of instruction for particular subjects and English for others, to a condition of subordination, where English is pushing Arabic to the periphery (Al-Jarf, 2008). Consequently, many researchers have expressed their concern about the future of Arabic (Alhamami, 2015; Al-Kahtany et al., 2015; Barnawi & Al-Hawsawi, 2017; Le Ha & Barnawi, 2015).

Academic Disciplines

Science as organized knowledge construction has often been divided into two major families: hard or natural sciences and soft or human sciences. Disciplines are grouped, according to Becher and Trowler (1989), into four subfamilies: pure hard (e.g. physics), pure soft (e.g. history), hard applied (e.g. engineering) and soft applied (e.g. education) (see also Tri & Moskovsky, 2019, p. 1335). Disciplines have often been defined in strict essentialist terms as having traits that make each of them 'what it is'. But disciplines in today's postmodern age expand, overlap and split (Trowler, 2014, p. 1721) and 'the boundaries between areas of knowledge and expertise are increasingly porous' (Gardner, 2018, p. 13). Saudi universities have maintained the dichotomy of hard versus soft sciences. Their colleges reflect the subfamilies division and the departments within the colleges maintain a rather conservative, essentialist division of disciplines. Interdisciplinary degrees and courses are rare, and elective modules within the same discipline are rarer.

Acculturation within the discipline represents a challenge for students and teachers in Saudi universities, especially in colleges and departments where English is expected to be the dominant or sole medium of communication. EMI is mostly used, not solely though, in pure hard disciplines such as physics, chemistry and biology but less so in mathematics (Shamim et al., 2016, p. 38) where symbols and formulas are universal. EMI is also mostly used in hard applied disciplines such as engineering, medicine, dentistry and pharmacy.

Because all content courses are taught in Arabic and by Saudi nationals at primary, middle and high schools, the majority of newly admitted university students in pure hard and hard applied disciplines experience a crucial rite of passage. English in these disciplines is not taught for a year as a subject along with other subjects, as is the case in pure soft and soft applied disciplines; it is the medium through which students have access to knowledge in their respective specialisms. Unfortunately, this access is often hampered by students' poor or suboptimal command of English (Weber, 2011, p. 64). Even medical schools, which recruit top secondary school graduates, are not spared (Telemsani et al., 2011, p. 707), and Arabic often takes charge to rescue the teaching-learning operation (Gaffas, 2016; Shamim et al., 2016, p. 40).

Language teachers and content teachers come from different cultures. Their command of standard English and Arabic varies, and so do their accents. Their knowledge of content is not the same nor are their teaching and assessing methods. To overcome their differences, so to speak, and accommodate many of their low competencies' students, teachers often opt for surface learning, which, according to Warburton (2004, p. 47), involves repetition, memorization, simple description and step-by-step teaching.

Doing science includes asking questions and making hypotheses, planning investigations, gathering, analysing and interpreting data, drawing conclusions and making predictions (Frad et al., 2001, p. 480). Deep learning is a prerequisite for doing science, achieving discipline acculturation and effecting discipline cross-fertilization and growth. It involves understanding relevant concepts and theories and synthesizing, organizing and structuring knowledge (Gardner, 2018, p. 13). Deep learning necessitates curiosity, engagement, responsibility, personal interest and patience. Saudi students in the hard sciences may receive help to produce practice-based textual artefacts in their respective disciplines, for example short reports, memoranda and prescriptions. But when it comes to the research paper, the core genre in academia, they are left to their own devices. They do not receive English for Academic Purposes courses at the undergraduate level or graduate level. Consequently, the relationship they develop with their respective academic disciplines remains superficial and utilitarian.

One would have expected Saudi academic discipline culture to have been positively affected by its counterpart in the English-speaking world. The King Abdullah Scholarship Program (KASP), which became the King's Scholarship Program (KSP) and lately the Custodian of the Two Holy Mosques Scholarship Program (2019, https://www.my.gov.sa/), has given more than 250,000 students the opportunity to pursue undergraduate and graduate studies in countries such as the United States, Canada, the United Kingdom and Australia (Khayat, 2017). However, the sheer number of newly established universities over the last ten years has attracted many of the Saudi teaching staff to assume highly lucrative management responsibilities and to take on administrative roles for which they, as academics, were not trained. Consequently, a brain drain has been taking place within the confines of Saudi universities. As for the Saudi junior staff members, who are actively engaged in fulfilling their teaching duties, they play a negligible role in improving the discipline culture in their respective departments on account of their status and role. And, most of them are busy applying for acceptance to study abroad, to obtain a scholarship from the government and to follow in the footsteps of their senior Saudi colleagues. Stagnation and rigidity characterize academic disciplines in Saudi universities.

Language Management

Spolsky (2009, p. 4) defines language management as 'efforts by some members of a speech community who have or believe they have authority over other members to modify their language practice'. Spolsky considers individuals and organizations as internal and external forces in managing language change and behaviour.

In this section, we focus on management as performed by institutions in response to language policy statements and declarations. We explore how language policy is conceived and implemented in the Saudi higher education setting. We focus on universities' rules and regulations with regard to teaching and learning through English. We take the PYP as an illustrative example.

Efforts to improve the quality of teaching English in Saudi Arabia are highlighted in developmental documents and national strategic plans. For instance, King Abdullah Public Education Development Project, known as 'Tatweer', emphasizes the importance of enhancing students' English language skills and classifies them under the twenty-first-century skills along with life skills, labour market skills and computer skills. For Tayan (2017), such projects are in line with neoliberalist discourse and correspond to market-driven education. To provide early exposure to English by school students, English was first introduced in the fourth grade in 2014 (Mitchell & Alfuraih, 2017), and, according to *Al-Arabiya News* (2021), it will be taught to first graders starting from the school year, 2021–2. And it is indeed.

In order to prepare high school graduates to join university science programmes taught in English and to bridge the transition gap between Arabic-medium education offered in schools and EMI introduced in higher education, most Saudi universities offer a preparatory year programme as a pre-pathway to studying science disciplines (Gaffas, 2016, p. 30). PYP was first introduced by the Ministry of Education in 2005 (Barnawi & Al-Hawsawi, 2017, p. 200). It is often managed by university language centres or educational companies and seeks to equip students with foundation knowledge in the speciality they intend to take. However, English for General Purposes (EGP) constitutes a large portion of the programmes, and the number of hours assigned is not the same in all universities (Alhawsawi, 2014). The goals of PYP are stated in many universities' websites and PY handbooks. The Dammam University *PY Handbook* (2015), today Imam Abdulrahman bin Faisal University, states that the goal of PYP is to 'Develop the students' English language and improve their communication' and to enhance 'the students' level of general and academic English'. In page 21, the handbook implicates that some teachers do not have a satisfactory command of English, puts the blame on those who overuse Arabic and lays down draconian language management measures. The handbook states:

> Since English is the language of instruction at the University of Dammam, it is imperative for the teaching faculty at all disciplines to be fluent speakers of English – indulging in Arabic explanations of notes and lessons in class is a well-established evidence that the instructor lacks competency in communicative English, and is a good reason for being disqualified from teaching at the University of Dammam.

Although much effort has been expended to enhance students' English language skills, PYP programmes do not sufficiently facilitate students' experience of learning academic disciplines (Al-Shehri, 2017; Gaffas, 2016). Students do not receive enough education in English for Specific Academic Purposes (ESAP). Most instructors are trained to teach English as a Foreign Language (EFL) and what they actually teach is mostly English for General Purposes (EGP) (Ahmed, 2012; Al-Roomy, 2017; Alsharif & Shukri, 2018; Hashmi et al., 2019). However, it is important to note that King Fahd University of Petroleum and Minerals and the Royal Commission of Yanbu Colleges and Institutes have been using EMI for a long time. Success of their graduates in the labour market has encouraged other universities to follow suit.

Agents

In higher education, change is usually driven by multiple forces. These forces can be structures, actors or agency (Saarinen & Ursin, 2012). The structure approach examines the established structures and their role in language policy change. The actors approach explores the individual and institutional players who create and manage higher education language policies. The agency approach focuses on the complementarity and interaction between different actors and domains within structures. Agency, thus, covers the impact of global, national and local forces in shaping changes in higher education (Marginson & Rhoades, 2002).

The most influential agency in Saudi higher education is the government and its neoliberalist market ideology orientation. This orientation was adopted by higher education institutions under the supervision of the Ministry of Education and urged by international calls for Saudi educational reforms after 9/11 (Barnawi & Al-Hawsawi, 2017). A clear manifestation of this orientation is the internationalization of higher education represented by a number of initiatives, including the adoption of EMI. Le Ha and Barnawi (2015) believe that Saudi Arabia and other GCC governments perceive English as their political and economic connection to the rest of the world, which makes them seek to internationalize their higher education by adopting EMI and by importing English products and services to their academic institutions. Their efforts are motivated by the belief that the development of local human capital ensures sustainable economic growth. The Technical and Vocational Colleges of Excellence (TVCE) project, which the government launched in 2011, is an example of this orientation towards the internationalization of Saudi higher education. The project came as a response to the Saudi government's 'concerns regarding its labor workforce's capability and competitiveness in terms of skills, knowledge, and English proficiency' (Le Ha & Barnawi, 2015, p. 550). It sought, on its inception, to offer education and training by international training providers to 400,000 Saudi students in five years.

At the institutional level, the EMI agents are university presidents and councils, deans, heads of departments, content lecturers and English language instructors.

The first three are the people of power, and they enjoy administrative authority and ensure that higher authorities' language policy is enacted. Most of these people of power are Saudis who received their education in Western English-speaking countries. English language instructors and academic content lecturers are the people with expertise and the immediate EMI agents. They design EMI courses, implement them, administer students' assessment and conduct programme evaluation. According to the Ministry of Education statistics of 2017–18, almost 60 per cent of the PhD holders in Saudi universities are non-Saudis, that is Arabic-speaking and non-Arabic-speaking faculty. A fairly large proportion of the local PhD holders are having managerial and administrative roles.

Language instructors and content teachers are important by virtue of their number, but their agency has been a subject of controversy. Al-Kahtany et al. (2015, p. 56) lament that language instructors 'give uncritical support to [EMI], turning a blind eye to the students' incompetence in the foreign language, their unwillingness to use it, and the consequent poor academic performance'. Malik et al. (2018, p. 33) recommend that 'Teacher-student communication [in computer science and IT] must be in English language'. Ali and Hamid (2018, p. 234) contend that EMI has positioned content-area teachers 'either explicitly or implicitly, as language-planning actors who are responsible for promoting students' English proficiency development'.

Saudi students play the role of EMI agents, mainly for instrumental reasons (Al-Jarf, 2008; Shamim et al., 2016). They would favour EMI, or less EMI, depending on their command of the English language, the class activity they engage in, the speciality they are studying for, the labour market demands and their ambition to pursue graduate studies in an English-speaking country or at home.

Employers, alumni and the media play a vital role in EMI adoption. Saudi universities cannot get accreditation from the Saudi Education and Training Evaluation Commission (ETEC) without holding and documenting periodic consultations with programmes alumni and prospective employers. One of the authors of this study had the actual experience of translating for a review panel of ETEC experts in their site visit to the College of Business at King Khalid University and witnessed the actual role of employers and alumni as agents in favour of more effective EMI adoption to enhance graduates' career-oriented attributes. The Saudi media speaking for employers frequently raise the issue of university graduates' insufficient communication skills in English (Barnawi & Al-Hawsawi, 2017).

EMI teachers in Saudi Arabia are faced with the challenging task of harmonizing government, institutional, alumni and employers' demands with (i) their own linguistic and pedagogical skills and (ii) their students' preferences, competencies, expectations and aspirations. The degrees of success or failure of such harmonization are manifest in practices and processes.

Practices and Processes

Reckwitz (2002, p. 250) defined practice as 'a routinized way in which bodies are moved, objects are handled, subjects are treated, things are described and the world is understood', and he considered it as being inherently social. Dafouz and Smit (2020, p. 56) have capitalized on Reckwitz's definition and offered a definition of practice in education as 'a culturally embedded routinized type of behaviour which consists of an irreducible ensemble of physical and mental activities, background knowledge and know-how, states of emotion and motivation'. We adopt these two related definitions and propose that process is to practice as weather is to climate, an analogy Halliday and Matthiessen (2014, pp. 27–28) use to explain the relationship between text and system in language. We suggest that practice has relatively stable traits, and they are recognizable in process.

Education practice in early twentieth-century Arabia and the rest of the Arab world included developing basic literacy and inculcating the principles of Islam (Ochsenwald, 2019). Teachers would make their students learn short, then longer surahs from the Holy Qur'an through repetition leading to exact memorization and accurate recitation (Elyas & Picard, 2010). They would, in parallel, initiate their students to writing and reading the letters of the alphabet and then they would proceed with them towards combining letters into words and words into sentences. Qur'an recitation and basic literacy building would then develop into grammar and exegesis classes. Teachers occupied centre stage in the education process and in society. They were revered by their students and members of the community as being sources of knowledge, wisdom and models for moral conduct.

The downsides of these teaching practices still persist in young Saudis' literacy development path, and they impact their learning and use of English at school and university. The grammar of Modern Standard Arabic and a lot of its vocabulary represent hurdles towards developing sophisticated reading and writing skills (Gherwash, 2017, pp. 72–74). Mastery of these skills becomes all there is in language and language learning. Most school teachers are reluctant to relinquish the authority society bestows on them or to change the traditional method they inherited from their former teachers. Alyami (2014, p. 1522), for instance, reports that many teachers whose school was involved in the King Abdullah Public Education Development Project resisted change, and they relocated to mainstream schools. The students' grammar and vocabulary obsession and phobia, together with their little confidence in reading and writing in Modern Standard Arabic (Gherwash, 2017), seem to accompany their later journey in learning English as a foreign language and to have adverse effects on its mastery (Gaffas, 2016, p. 6) and the mastery of the speciality in which it is expected to be taught.

The studies published in the field of English Language Teaching (ELT) in Saudi Arabia have focused on attitudes and beliefs and relied on the questionnaire and the interview as data collection procedures. What actually takes place in the classroom is not well researched (Moskovsky, 2019, p. 40), save for a few studies that included classroom observation as a subsidiary tool (e.g. Shamim et al., 2016, pp. 38–39). Little research has been conducted on teacher training and on evaluation and testing (Moskovsky, 2019, pp. 19, 40). Paucity in these research areas conceals obsolescent and ingrained practices that extend to PYP and EMI in Saudi Arabian universities.

Most universities offer a PYP or administer an entrance exam for school graduates having a minimum of 75 per cent and wishing to join a hard science specialism or a soft applied discipline, such as business studies, where English is important for their professional careers. The PYP often consists of a General English (GE) course, an English for Specific Purposes (ESP) course and foundation courses relevant to the degree the student wishes to study for. The various findings of the surveys we present here show that PYP has to be reconsidered.

According to a study conducted by Shamim et al. (2016), most of the content courses repeated what the students took at high school and classes often turned into translations of specialized terms and explanations in Arabic. Louber and Troudi (2019, p. 64) found that the assigned English content textbooks were not even used when teachers are Arabic speakers, and most teachers prefer to use Arabic. Al-Shehri (2017, p. 434) expressed his concern about universities relying on private companies that recruit 'low-qualified' native and non-native speakers. Alsamadani (2017, pp. 61, 64) revealed that writing was the least performed class activity, and there was no clear link between content courses and ESP classes. Suliman and Tadros (2010) reported that their female nursing students have a fear of communicating in

English; they have problems of pronunciation and spelling; and they find the classroom atmosphere tense and unengaging. The students in the survey that Gaffas (2016) conducted found the language courses unsatisfactory as far as content, teaching practices and assessment practices are concerned. They felt they needed to develop their reading, writing and speaking skills and to enrich their vocabulary. Shamim et al. (2016, p. 41) found that some teachers would delimit for their students' sections, vocabulary lists and paragraphs to revise from, while other teachers would include in tests and exams items similar to those they taught. Alshahrani (2020, p. 105) noted that it is not uncustomary for teachers to explain the English instructions or test items to their students while the exam is underway. Telemsani et al. (2011, p. 707) expressed their concern about the attrition rate from medical schools and concluded that 'the language of instruction seems to be an important factor'. Shamim et al. (2016, p. 42) issued an even harsher verdict when they said, 'The use of EMI in the PYP has an adverse effect on both the amount and quality of student learning.'

The little success of EMI in PYP is multifaceted and has long-term consequences on students' training and future career. What the students miss out on is developing the ability to read in their specialism and consequently the ability to write essays and research papers. Understanding the meaning of new words in a text through translation is a basic reading strategy, and it reflects a reductionist conception of literacy (Mokhtari & Sheorey, 2002, p. 4). Global reading strategies, such as previewing the text as to its organization, and problem-solving strategies, such as guessing the meaning of a word from context, are hard to come by. Whenever content is new to the students, the teacher is there to explain it for them in Arabic-English.

Arabic-English use is referred to as a manifestation of translanguaging. The term can be defined as the process of making use of the different linguistic resources interlocutors have in order to create meaning (Li, 2018, p. 15). According to its advocates, classroom translanguaging gives learners the opportunity to improve mastery of the languages being used and to gain self-confidence. From what we have seen so far in this chapter, we can claim that the presence of English and Arabic in teacher–student discourse hardly contributes to deep learning, critical thinking or proficiency in either language. As far as we know, post PYP teaching and learning practices and processes have not been studied, and it would be interesting to explore translanguaging at these levels to uncover teachers' and students' reactions to it and the effects it has on students' motivation and achievement.

Internationalization and Glocalization

We adopt Knight's (2004, p. 11) intentional definition of internationalization as 'the process of integrating an international, intercultural or global dimension into the purpose, functions or delivery of post-secondary education' and add that EMI is internationalization's most effective vehicle today. We suggest that the degrees of openness to internationalization and globalization vary from one community to another and that openness is influenced by complex and intricate economic, social, cultural, religious, linguistic, historical and political factors (Spolsky, 2005, p. 2153).

Because life and afterlife are closely related in Saudis' social and discourse practices (Abdesslem & Rouissi, 2010, p. 96), our account on internationalization and glocalization in Saudi Arabia shall be against the backdrop of Islam, the religion of the country, and Arabic, the language of the Holy Qur'an. We shall also refer to two major turning points in the recent history of the country: the 1973 oil embargo and the 9/11, 2001, attacks (Karmani, 2005, p. 739).

As early as 1927, Saudi Arabia started sending male middle school graduates to Egypt, and in 1937 it established its first preparatory school (madrasat taḥḍhīr al-bi'thāt) to help those students it intended to send to Egypt with their science and English subjects (Ochsenwald, 2019, p. 13). Saudi Arabia also invited teachers mainly from Egypt and Syria and adopted Egyptian-inspired school curricula that included secular, often contested, subjects such as English and natural sciences (Ochsenwald, 2019, 2019, p. 19). This 'regionalization abroad', which we coin after Knight's (2004) 'internationalisation abroad', slowed down during the 1950s and 1960s, as the whole region sank into war, turmoil and mistrust.

In 1967, King Saud University established the first College of Medicine in the country under the guidance of the London College of Medicine (Telemsani et al., 2011, p. 704). But it was only in the aftermath of the 1973 oil embargo and the ensuing phenomenal rise in oil production and prices that Saudi Arabia engaged in intensive internationalization abroad. It sent students and trainees to its major economic partners, Britain and the United States, to acquire the skills the country needed for its rapid development. Most scholarships were awarded in the hard sciences and a few in the humanities, mainly to students wishing to specialize in the English language. The students, and the people, were at the time under the spell of Sahwa Islamiya (Islamic Awakening), an ultra-conservative movement, which, according to Lacroix (2010, pp. 2–3), infiltrated the Saudi education system. The students had very little contact with the host, but for them alien, culture. Although the courses they took were in EMI, they did not gain, as far as their competence in English is concerned, more than what they needed for their training. Consequently, the cultural dimension, which is part and parcel of internationalization, did not take effect in the Saudi students' training abroad. Those among them who joined the newly established universities to teach often used more Arabic than English in their classes, as did their many Arabic-speaking colleagues. By doing so, they gained their students' appreciation and respect, for the latter understood content better and related well to their teachers as experts and fellow Muslims. As the country grew into a gigantic development site teeming with expatriates from the Indian subcontinent, some Arab countries, some African countries and a few from the English-speaking world (Barnawi, 2018, p. 47; Khadria, 2008), communication was rather cacophonic and pidginized. English was not considered of paramount necessity in those days.

The 9/11, 2001, attacks on the United States triggered what the Western media referred to as the war on terror. Saudi Arabia received the harshest of criticism and 'realized' that it had to restructure its education system (Barnawi, 2018, pp. 55–56; Le Ha & Barnawi, 2015; Karmani, 2005; Weber, 2011, p. 63). The contents of school books were revised, English was introduced at primary level in government schools and Saudi young learners were allowed to study in the private international schools reserved for the children of expatriates.

Today, Saudi Arabia boasts a very modern infrastructure and has ambitious plans for postmodern mega projects. What it needs most is the development of its human capital to engage effectively in a knowledge-based economy (Le Ha & Barnawi, 2015, p. 550). Like most non-Anglo-Western communities and nations in the world, Saudi Arabia is managing the pressure and attraction of globalization, the outcome of neoliberalism and its driving force. It is steering away from an oil-based economy, a private sector populated by a polyglot expatriate labour force, and an administration overburdened by national employees (Faudot, 2019, p. 95).

Saudi Arabia is actively engaged in reforming its education system to allow its new tech-savvy generation of young Saudis to have access to cutting-edge knowledge. The country has maintained its internationalization-abroad-policy, but it has been rather cautious when it comes to internationalization at home, especially following the limited success of ambitious government initiatives, such as the Colleges of Excellence Project (Le Ha & Barnawi, 2015) and the King Abdullah Project for Development of Public Education, Tatweer, (Tayan, 2017, pp. 65–68).

Saudi Arabia has not attracted many international students, even among its large community of expatriates. EMI, which ensures student mobility across many universities in the world, is not compulsory in many faculties and departments (Al-Shahrani, 2020). To date, Saudi Arabia has not given franchise to overseas universities to open branches on its territory. Its university curricula are not fully internationalized and Arabic language and Islamic studies courses are taught in all disciplines, albeit with a reduced percentage for the latter (Barnawi, 2018, p. 55).

Saudi Arabia is heading towards glocalization, that is tailoring globalization to the local context (Tayan, 2017, p. 68), while trying to restrain and domesticate neoliberalism (Abdesslem, 2020. p. 101). As far as education is concerned, glocalization, which we take to subsume internationalization and transnationalization and cannot be dissociated from EMI, will give Saudi Arabia the opportunity to work out realistic plans that will help its communities of teachers and students to improve their command of English (Le Ha & Barnawi, 2015, pp. 555–557) and allow the country to maintain its national identity, character and unity by preserving its language and Islamic values. This glocalization orientation is reflected in a number of official documents, namely: (i) the Saudi Vision 2030 Human Capital Development Program and National Character Development Program (https://www.vision2030.gov.sa/en); (ii) Objective 4 of the KASP 2015 version (in Khayat, 2017, p. 19); (iii) Objectives 1, 2 and 3 of King Abdullah Public Education Development Project (in Tayan, 2017, p. 62); and (iv) the Ministry of Education Strategic Objectives and the Key Performance Indicators thereof (in Barnawi, 2018, pp. 52–54). They all seek to harmonize the Islamic values of generosity, solidarity and communality with the neoliberalist values of self-interest, competition and exploitation of human and natural resources. Universities, faculties and departments will have to reflect glocalization in their visions, missions, objectives and practices.

Conclusion

The major challenge that Saudi Arabia faces is the development of its local human capital so that it can move from a rentier economy to a knowledge-based economy. To meet this major challenge, it has adopted what politicians call 'the Third Way' in tackling a number of dilemmas. Saudi Arabia, the cradle of the Arabic language and the birthplace of Islam with its values of tolerance, solidarity and spiritual rewards, is trying to manage neoliberalism and its values of individualism, competition, secularism and material profit. It has adopted English as a foreign language and given pride of place to Arabic in its pre-tertiary education. Because content is taught in Arabic at high school and because high school graduates' English is poor, Saudi public universities opted for making students who wish to study science subjects take a PYP in English and then continue their studies in EMI. This policy has not been very successful, so far. English has remained a very foreign language among students and in the community. The country's elite is running the risk of becoming divided into those with an EMI training and those with Arabic as a medium of instruction (AMI) training on account of the strict division between science and humanities disciplines at the university.

English language instructors and content teachers at the university are between the hammer of the people of power who insist that only English be used and the anvil of the students who need Arabic as a lifebuoy. Students' poor command of English and their not so happy experience in learning MSA, together with teachers' varied linguistic, cultural and academic backgrounds, cause surface learning practices and processes to prevail and encourage appearance testing to thrive.

Universities need to provide pre-service and in-service training for language and content school teachers. Teachers of Arabic would have to treat MSA as a modern, living language, not a set of obsolete rules of grammar and an alien vocabulary. Teachers of Arabic and English need to learn to approach the teaching of speaking, listening, reading and writing as ongoing processes, not as products. Translation could be introduced as an autonomous subject and not as a good for everything teaching/learning tool. Decision-makers may consider introducing one or two content courses in English to high school students to make their transition to university education smoother. By doing so, the PYP, normally a requirement for foreign students wishing to join a university in a country other than their own, would turn into a normal first year in the students' undergraduate courses.

Interdisciplinary elective modules and specialities are worth offering in English from the humanities to students in the hard sciences and from the hard sciences to students in the humanities. This could contribute to producing both bilingual and cultured experts, decision-makers, employees and citizens. Universities engaged in opening new programmes or revising their old programmes in accordance with rigorous national and international standards could benefit from these suggestions and recommendations and contribute to the glocalization of education in Saudi Arabia.

References

Abdesslem, H. (2020). Neoliberalism and English language education policies in the Arabian Gulf. *Arab Journal of Applied Linguistics, 5*(1), 100–104.

Abdesslem, H., & Rouissi, I. (2010). Discourses and voices in Saudi students' argumentative-expository essays: An exploratory study. *Lettres de Kairouan*, University of Kairouan, 8, 91–116.

Ahmed, J. (2012). Theoretical framework & growing demand of ESP in Saudi Arabia. *Archives Des Sciences, 65*(5), 114–120.

Alarabyia News (2021). Retrieved from https://english.alarabiya.net/en/News/gulf/2020/09/21/English-classes-to-begin-from-first-grade-in-Saudi-Arabia-in-2021-says-minister.

Alhamami, M. (2015). Teaching science subjects in Arabic: Arab University scientists' perspectives. *Language Learning in Higher Education, 5*(1), 105–123.

Alhawsawi, S. (2014). *Investigating student experiences of learning English as a foreign language in a preparatory programme in a Saudi University*. Brighton: University of Sussex.

Ali, N. L., & Hamid, M. O. (2018). 13 English-medium instruction and teacher agency in higher education: A case study. In P. C. G. Lian, C. Chua, K. Taylor-Leech & C. Williams (Eds.), *Un (Intended) language planning in a globalising world: Multiple levels of players at work*. Warsaw; Boston: De Gruyter.

Al-Jarf, R. (2008). The impact of English as an international language (EIL) upon Arabic in Saudi Arabia. *Asian EFL Journal, 10*(4), 193–210.

Al-Kahtany, A. H., Faruk, S. M. G., & Al Zumor, A. W. Q. (2015). English as the medium of instruction in Saudi higher education: Necessity or hegemony? *Journal of Language Teaching and Research, 7*(1), 49–58.

Al-Roomy, M. (2017). ESP in a Saudi context: Where does it stand? *Journal of Language Teaching and Research, 8*(6), 1109–1115.

Alsamadani, H. A. (2017). Needs analysis in ESP context: Saudi engineering students as a case Study. *Advances in Language and Literary Studies, 8*, 58–68.

Al-Seghayer, K. (2012). Status and functions of English in Saudi Arabia. *Saudi Gazette*. Retrieved from http://saudigazette.com.sa/article/24861.

Al-Shahrani, H. (2020). The language situation in the Saudi medical colleges: The case of King Khalid University and King Abdulaziz University. *Language Planning and Policies, 6*(11), 86–144. (In Arabic). الشهراني، هند. المشهد اللغوي في كليات الطب السعودية (جامعة الملك خالد وجامعة الملك عبد العزيز نموذجا). مجلة : التخطيط والسياسات اللغوية، العدد 11، السنة 6، ص 86-144.

Alsharif, D., & Shukri, N. (2018). Exploring pedagogical challenges of ESP teachers at a Saudi Arabian University. *International Journal of Asian Social Science, 8*(10), 841–855.

Al-Shehri, S. (2017). A developmental paradigm for English language instruction at preparatory year programs. *Arab World English Journal (AWEJ), 8*(3), 432–447.

Alyami, R. H. (2014). Educational reform in the Kingdom of Saudi Arabia: Tatweer schools as a unit of development. *Literacy Information and Computer Education Journal*, 5(2), 1515–1524.

Al Zumor, A. (2019a). Language planning in Saudi Arabia (1927–2019): Arabic and other languages. *Trames*, 23(4), 409–424.

Al Zumor, A. Q. (2019b). Challenges of using EMI in teaching and learning of university scientific disciplines: Student voice. *International Journal of Language Education*, 3(1), 74–90.

Badry, F. (2019). Internationalisation of higher education in the countries of the Gulf Cooperation Council: Impact on the national language. *Arab States 2019 Global Education Monitoring Report*, UNESCO Publication, 1–10.

Barnawi, O. Z. (2018). *Neoliberalism and English language policies in the Arabian Gulf*. Abingdon; New York: Routledge..

Barnawi, O. Z., & Al-Hawsawi, S. (2017). English education policy in Saudi Arabia: English language education policy in the Kingdom of Saudi Arabia: Current trends, issues and challenges. In R. Kirkpatrick (Ed.), *English language education policy in the Middle East and North Africa* (pp. 199–222). Cham, Switzerland: Springer.

Becher, T., & Trowler, P. R. (1989). *Academic tribes and territories: Intellectual enquiry and the culture of disciplines*. The Society for Research into Higher Education & Open University Press.

Custodian of the Two Holy Mosques Scholarship Program (2019). Retrieved from https://www.my.gov.sa/.

Dafouz, E., & Smit, U. (2016). Towards a dynamic conceptual framework for English-medium education in multilingual university settings. *Applied Linguistics*, 37(3), 397–415.

Dafouz, E., & Smit, U. (2020). *Road-mapping education in the internationalised university*. New York: Palgrave Macmillan.

Dammam University, PY Handbook. (2015). Retrieved from https://www.iau.edu.sa/sites/default/ files/resources/prepyearhandbooknewadddes.compressed.pdf.

Elyas, T & Picard, M. (2010). Saudi Arabian educational history: Impacts of English language teaching. *Education, Business and Society: Contemporary Middle Eastern Issues*, 3(2), 136–145.

Faudot, A. (2019). Saudi Arabia and the rentier regime trap: A critical assessment of the plan Vision 2030. *Resources Policy*, 62, 94–101.

Findlow, S. (2006). Higher education and linguistic dualism in the Arab Gulf. *British Journal of Sociology of Education*, 27(1), 19–36. doi:10.1080/01425690500376754.

Fradd, S. H., Lee, O., Sutman, F. X., & Saxton, M. K. (2001). Promoting science literacy with English language learners through instructional materials development: A case study. *Bilingual Research Journal*, 25(4), 475–501.

Gaffas, Z. (2016). *The impact of English language preparatory programmes in a Saudi Arabian University: An investigation of students' perceptions of their language difficulties, experiences and suggestions* (Doctoral dissertation). University of Sheffield.

Gardner, H. (2018). Higher education: A platonic ideal. In O. Zlatkin-Troitschanskaia, G. Wittum & A. Dengel (Eds.), *Positive learning in the age of information: A blessing or a curse?* (pp. 9–21). Wiesbaden: Springer.

Gherwash, G. (2017). Diglossia and literacy: The case of the Arab reader. *Arab Journal of Applied Linguistics, 3*(3), 56–85.

Halliday, M. K., & Matthiessen, C. (2014). *An introduction to functional grammar*. Oxon: Routledge.

Jamjoom, Y. (2012). Understanding private higher education in Saudi Arabia: Emergence, development and perceptions. Retrieved from http://ethos.bl.uk/OrderDetails.do?uin=uk.bl.ethos.573032.

Karmani, S. (2005). Petro-linguistics: The emerging nexus between oil, English, and Islam. *Journal of Language, Identity, and Education, 4*(2), 87–102.

Khadria, B. (2008). India: Skilled migration to developed countries, labour migration to the Gulf. In S. Castles & R. L. Wise (Eds.), *Migration and development: Perspectives from the south*. Geneva: International Organisation for Migration.

Khayat, R. A. (2017).*Toward genuine transformations: The internationalization of higher education in Saudi Arabia* (Doctoral dissertation, University of Toronto (Canada)).

Knight, J. (2004). Internationalization remodeled: Definition, approaches, and rationales. *Journal of Studies in International Education, 8*(1), 5–31.

Lacroix, S. (2010). Islamic dissent in an Islamic state: The case of Saudi Arabia. *AUC Forum*, American University in Cairo, Egypt, 1–6.

Le Ha, P., & Barnawi, O. Z. (2015). Where English, neoliberalism, desire and internationalization are alive and kicking: Higher education in Saudi Arabia today. *Language and Education, 29*(6), 545–565.

Li, W. (2018). Translanguaging as a practical theory of language. *Applied Linguistics, 39*(1), 9–30.

Liddicoat, A. J. (2012). Language planning as an element of religious practice. *Current Issues in Language Planning, 13*(2), 121–144. doi:10.1080/14664208.2012.686437.

Louber, I., & Troudi, S. (2019). 'Most of the teaching is in Arabic anyway', English as a medium of instruction in Saudi Arabia between the facto and official language policy. *International Journal of Bias, Identities and Diversities in Education, 4*(2), 59–73.

Hashmi, U. M., Rajab, H., & Sindi, A. E. (2019). Dental students' perceptions of ESP material and its impact on their language proficiency: A case study of a Saudi Arabian University. *Arab World English Journal, 10* (4), 3–17.

Macaro, E., Curle, S., Pun, J., An, J., & Dearden, J. (2018). A systematic review of English medium instruction in higher education. *Language Teaching, 51*(1), 36–76. doi:10.1017/S0261444817000350.

Mahboob, A., & Elyas, T. (2014). English in the kingdom of Saudi Arabia. *World Englishes, 33*(1), 128–142. doi:10.1111/weng.12073.

Malik, H. A. M., Abid, F., Kalaicelvi, R., & Bhatti, Z. (2018). Challenges of computer science and IT in teaching-learning in Saudi Arabia. *Sukkur IBA Journal of Computing and Mathematical Sciences, 2*(1), 29–35.

Marginson, S., & Rhoades, G. (2002). Beyond national states, markets, and systems of higher education: A glonacal agency heuristic. *Higher Education, 43*(3), 281–309.

McMullen, M. G. (2014). The value and attributes of an effective preparatory English program: Perceptions of Saudi university students. *English Language Teaching (Toronto), 7*(7), 131. doi:10.5539/elt.v7n7p131.

Mitchell, B., & Alfuraih, A. (2017). English language teaching in the Kingdom of Saudi Arabia: Past, present and beyond. *Mediterranean Journal of Social Sciences, 8*(2), 317–317.

Mokhtari, K., & Sheorey, R. (2002). Measuring ESL students' awareness of reading strategies. *Journal of Developmental Education, 25*(3), 1–10.

Moskovsky, C. (2019). EFL teaching and learning in Saudi Arabia, 25 years of research. In C. Moskovsky, & M. Picard (Eds.), *English as a foreign language in Saudi Arabia: New insights into teaching and learning English* (pp. 4–69). London: Routledge.

Moskovky, C., & Picard, M. (2019). *English as a foreign language in Saudi Arabia: New insights into teaching and learning English.* London: Routledge.

Ochsenwald, W. (2019). The transformation of education in the Hijaz, 1925–1945. *Arabian Humanities, 12*, 1–19. doi: 10.4000/cy.4917

Reckwitz, A. (2002). Towards a theory of social practices: A development of culturalist theorizing. *European Journal of Social Theory, 5*(2), 243–263.

Saarinen, T., & Ursin, J. (2012). Dominant and emerging approaches in the study of higher education policy change. *Studies in Higher Education, 37*(2), 143–156.

Saudi Vision. (2030). Retrieved from https://www.vision2030.gov.sa/en.

Scott, P. (2011). The university as a global institution. In R. King, S. Marginson, R. Naidoo (Eds.), *Handbook on globalization and higher education* (pp. 59–75). Cheltenham, UK; Northampton: Edward Elgar.

Shamim, F., Abdelhalim, A., & Hamid, N. (2016). English medium instruction in the transition year: Case from KSA. *Arab World English, 7*(1), 32–47.

Spolsky, B. (2004). *Language policy.* Cambridge; New York: Cambridge University Press.

Spolsky, B. (2005). Language policy. In J. Cohen et al. (Eds.), *Proceedings of the 4th International Symposium on Biligualism* (pp. 2152–2164). Somerville, MA: Cascadilla Press.

Spolsky, B. (2009). *Language management.* Cambridge: Cambridge University Press.

Suliman, W. A., & Tadros, A. (2010). Nursing students coping with English as a foreign language medium of instruction. *Nurse Education Today, 31*(4), 402–407.

Tayan, B. M. (2017). The Saudi Tatweer education reforms: Implications of neoliberal thought to Saudi education policy. *International Education Studies, 10*(5), 61–71.

Telemsani, A., Zaiani, R. G., & Ghazi, O. H. (2011). Medical education in Saudi Arabia: A review of recent developments and future challenges. *Medical Journal for the Middle East, 17*(8), 703–707.

Tri, D., & Moskovsky, C. (2019). English-medium instruction in Vietnamese higher education: A ROAD-MAPPING perspective. *Issues in Educational Research, 29*(4), 1330–1347.

Trowler, P. (2014). Depicting and researching disciplines: Strong and moderate essentialist approaches. *Studies in Higher Education, 39*(10), 1720–1731.

Warburton, K. (2004). Deep learning and education for sustainability. *International Journal for Sustainability in Higher Education, 4*(1), 44–56.

Weber, A. (2011). Politics of English in the Arabian Gulf. *First International Conference on Foreign Language Teaching and Applied Linguistics*, May 5–7, Sarajevo, 60–66.

6

EMI Programmes in Turkey

Evidence of Exponential Growth

Doğan Yuksel, Mehmet Altay and Samantha Curle

Introduction

This chapter explores the exponential growth of the English-medium instruction (EMI) higher education (HE) programmes in Turkey by comparing the number and types of EMI programmes between 1999 and 2019, utilizing document analysis. It aims to provide evidence of the EMI 'boom' (Kalkan, 2019), as discussed not only in Turkey (Aslan, 2018; Karakaş, 2018, 2019; Kırkgöz, 2017, 2019; West, Guven, Parry & Ergenekon, 2015) but across the world (Dearden, 2014, 2015; Kirkpatrick, 2014; Macaro et al., 2018). This evidence is timely as Karakaş (2019, p. 207) notes: 'the exact number of EMI programs and courses are unknown' in the Turkish context. This chapter traces the growth of EMI programmes via official documents published by the Council of Higher Education in Turkey to explain how national-level policy contributes to the expansion of EMI programmes.

Language Policy and Planning in the Turkish EMI Setting

Language policy and planning should be considered in terms of sociopolitical, historical and socio-economic aspects at local, national and global levels (Hornberger, 2006). When it comes to the underlying rationale of the expansion of EMI programmes, globalization and internationalization are considered to be driving forces in many contexts such as China (Zhang, 2018), Malaysia (Ali, 2013), Vietnam (Tran & Nguyen, 2018), Korea (Byun et al., 2010; Green, 2015) and Turkey (Kırkgöz, 2017, 2019). Together with these global forces, local

Turkish policy developments have been examined to trace the growth of EMI programmes at the primary, secondary and HE levels (Kırkgöz, 2009, 2017, 2019). Other studies have examined Turkish institutional policies (Arık & Arık, 2014; Karakaş, 2019). This chapter builds on this previous work by focusing on the growth of EMI programmes only in the HE context within a twenty-year period (1999 to 2019) to illustrate this 'boom' (Kalkan, 2019). It provides the numbers of full and partial EMI programmes in four academic divisions in public as well as foundation universities in Turkey.

A Brief History of EMI in Turkey

Turkey is among a few monolingual countries that have adopted English as the medium of instruction in HE without a colonial past (Curle, Yuksel, Soruc & Altay, 2020). EMI higher education programmes in Turkey began in the 1950s with the founding of the Middle East Technical University in Ankara. By the establishment of Boğaziçi University (formerly known as Robert College) in 1971 in Istanbul and Bilkent University (i.e. the first private foundation-funded university of Turkey) in 1984 in Ankara, a trend of the development of EMI programmes emerged (Selvi, 2014). Considering this historical depth, the issues of implementation, effectiveness, efficiency and success of EMI programmes have long been debated in Turkey. In contrast to other G20 countries, Turkey has focused on the 'quantity' of HE in recent years by significantly expanding the number of its universities (West et al., 2015; Kalkan, 2019). There has been a huge increase in the number of EMI programmes today compared to in the past (Arık & Arık, 2014).

When the growth of EMI programmes has been reviewed globally, rationales for such expansion have included internationalization (O'Dowd, 2015), the need to attract students (both domestic and international; Dafouz, 2018; Doiz, Lasagabaster & Sierra, 2013), a shift in the aims of universities (Welch, 2001), a desire to enhance the quality and prestige of educational programmes (Nguyen, Walkinshaw & Pham, 2017), competition between public and private sectors (Dearden, 2014), university rankings (Rauhvargers, 2013) and holding a reputable place on the international market (Graddol, 2006).

In the Turkish context, external factors such as the internationalization of the HE system in Turkey after joining the Bologna Process in 2001 (Karakaş, 2018) and economic affordability in an increasingly globalized world (Kırkgöz, 2019) have been put forward as reasons for expanding EMI. Moreover, EMI universities have traditionally been 'more favoured and popular for students and parents in comparison to universities without EMI' (Başıbek et al., 2014, p. 1819), as is the case for some public and private elite EMI universities in Turkey. This popularity might be due to 'the increased chances of finding jobs after graduation' (Oz, 2005, p. 341) or a perception of increased social prestige (Atık, 2010). In a similar vein, studying through EMI has been regarded as a vehicle to access better education and get a more respected job with good benefits (Kırkgöz, 2005; Altay & Yuksel, 2021; Altay, 2020; Huang & Curle, 2021), as well as develop intellectual (Turhan & Kırkgöz, 2018) and linguistic (Yuksel, Soruc, Altay & Curle, 2021) capabilities.

Higher Education Regulations on Foreign Language Medium of Instruction in Turkey

In this section, we will focus on three aspects of HE regulations as they relate to the general principles of foreign language medium of instruction (MOI): regulations to open a new foreign language MOI programme, regulations to study in these programmes and regulations to open an intensive language unit (i.e. preparatory school) to support students studying foreign language MOI programmes. We will also explore the relationship between these regulations and the growth of EMI programmes in Turkey, wherever possible.

Turkey has a relatively long-established basis for foreign language MOI even though it is not an ex-colonized country. French was the earliest foreign language MOI in HE as it was initiated for the use of medical students in 1827 (Marmara University, 2018). The main purpose of this radical step was to follow medical innovations, which mostly originated from the West. It was not until the foundation of the first American school outside the United States in 1863 that English was first used as an MOI in Turkey (Minifie, 1998). Boğaziçi University was followed by Middle East Technical University in 1956, and a limited number of further state and foundation universities joined them. The first official regulation regarding foreign language instruction programmes was established in 1984 (Turkish Official Gazette, 1984). Since then, this regulation has been updated four times (in 1994, 1996, 2008 and 2016). Each updated version of this regulation yields common as well as distinct features in terms of objectives, prerequisites to establish a foreign language MOI programme and requirements to study one of these programmes.

The purpose of teaching in a foreign language at the HE level was initially determined as 'equipping students with the power and skills to spectate broadcasts, to contribute to international meetings and discussions in the intended foreign language with the help of scientific and technological advancements' (Turkish Official Gazette, 1984, p. 4). According to Kırkgöz (2009), this regulation 'marks the beginning of the macro policy regulations on the teaching of English at the level of higher education' (p. 671). Later, the purpose changed to enable the students 'to gain foreign language proficiencies related to their fields' (Turkish Official Gazette, 2016, p. 4).

If a university decided to establish a foreign language MOI programme at the associate or bachelor's degree levels, they were required to meet the following criteria:

(a) Having lecturers who bear the fundamental qualities determined by the Council of Higher Education to teach in the foreign language,
(b) Having the foundational literature and teaching materials necessary to teach in the foreign language and providing opportunities for students to utilize them (Turkish Official Gazette, 1984, p. 4, original in Turkish translated by authors).

This regulation is important because even though foreign language HE MOI programmes were established as early as 1956, there were no rules governing or monitoring these programmes before this regulation. With these two basic (and somewhat vague) criteria, universities were given some guidelines to establish foreign language MOI programmes. The 1984 Regulation also included national standards to study through a foreign language by specifying success thresholds, content of tests to be used, as well as course content to be used in preparatory schools.

The 1994 Regulation (Turkish Official Gazette, 1994) had a striking limitation for HE institutions aiming to establish foreign language MOI programmes. The new regulation stated that only universities which had been teaching through a foreign language since it was founded could establish new foreign language MOI programmes. Furthermore, several 'elite' universities, namely Middle East Technical, Boğaziçi, Bilkent, Koc and Galatasaray, were listed as potential universities to teach through a foreign language. For the first time, some courses in graduate programmes were permitted to be given in a foreign language. Another difference in this regulation was the decentralization of the standards to study in a foreign language. It gave the universities the right to determine their own conditions, including preparatory procedures, attendance, and the number of midterm exams and their weighting.

The 1994 Regulation also stipulated criteria for lecturers to work in a foreign language MOI programme. Lecturers were required to hold an undergraduate, graduate or postgraduate degree from a 'native speaker' country of the foreign language that they would teach, or a degree from a university in Turkey where that foreign language is the MOI; or a proficiency certificate from a German, American, French or British culture centre; or a proficiency certificate indicating a successful score from the national foreign language exam. The 1996 Regulation (Turkish Official Gazette, 1996) extended these proficiency certificates to international exams such as TOEFL and IELTS. Also in the 1996 Regulation, some institutions were granted permission to provide some courses (not the whole programme) in a foreign language MOI. This paved the way to the current partial EMI programmes. In 2008 (Turkish Official Gazette, 2008), besides a few minor changes about preparatory schools, the aim of language education was updated and modernized. It aimed to improve the mental lexicon: enabling students to comprehend what they read or heard and be able to express themselves in both writing and speaking in a foreign language. Similarly, the 2016 Regulation (Turkish Official Gazette, 2016) included some updates and regulations about both teaching a foreign language and teaching in a foreign language in terms of intensive language units, qualifications of lecturers and monitoring of these programmes.

Methodology for This Analysis

This chapter adopts document analysis as a method of analysis (Kim, 2017) by utilizing Student Selection and Placement Centre manuals and policy documents of the Council of Higher Education to track the expansion of the EMI programmes in Turkey. Student Selection and Placement Centre administers the recruitment and admissions of incoming students into various HE institutions based on standardized national exams. Every year, they publish manuals containing information about the specific features of the programmes as well as quotas for each programme. The Council of Higher Education is in charge of the planning and execution of HE establishment in Turkey. Two basic sources are used in the enumeration of the EMI programmes in 1999 and 2019 (Student Selection and Placement Centre, 2020a, b), and policy documents prepared by the Council of Higher Education are traced to examine the policy on teaching foreign languages and teaching in a foreign language in Turkey.

EMI programmes in HE institutions are examined at three levels: university, division and academic subject. At all these levels, we based our classification on 'full' and 'partial' EMI to give a more in-depth picture of EMI programmes in Turkey. A 'full EMI programme' refers to an academic study where all courses are offered in English, whereas a 'partial EMI programme' offers at least 30 per cent of all courses in English, and the remaining 70 per cent are delivered in Turkish. In the coding of full EMI programmes in the Student Selection and Placement Centre manuals (2020a, b), first, we checked if English was used in parentheses after the name of the academic subject as in the following case:

Programme Code	Name of the Programme	Special Conditions and Notes
351332	Mechanical Engineering (English)	

We included them in our full EMI programme list if this was the case. However, some programmes were not listed in this way but still offered full EMI. In these programmes, there was a number in the 'Special Conditions and Notes' section, which referred to the MOI of the programme. These numbers changed from university to university and included some extra information about the programme. These programmes, as shown, were also included in the full EMI list.

Programme Code	Name of the Programme	Special Conditions and Notes
261171	Philosophy	97*

*97 Medium of instruction is English.

Partial EMI programmes were similarly identified. In the 'Special Conditions and Notes' section, the number 86 was used for all partial EMI programmes presenting a generic label in both the 1999 and 2019 manuals.

Programme Code	Name of the Programme	Special Conditions and Notes
106910197	Economics	86*

*86 Medium of instruction in this programme is at least 30 per cent English.

The first and second authors coded all these programmes manually, separately. Later, the two coding results were cross-examined, and minor disagreements were discussed, and a consensus reached. The Student Selection and Placement Centre (2020a, b) manuals also included some universities in other countries such as Cyprus, Macedonia and Azerbaijan. All EMI programmes in these counties were excluded from our analysis. 'Soft-EMI' programmes such as

English language teaching, English language and literature and translation were also excluded from the list.

At the university level, Turkish universities can be grouped as 'state' and 'foundation' (also known as 'private') universities. State universities are fully funded by the government, but foundation universities are mainly supported by some kind of charitable foundation and are also partially supported by the government. In research literature, 'private' and 'foundation' universities are used synonymously; however, in Turkey, based on the law of the Council of Higher Education (2000), there is no room for 'private' universities, and all foundation universities are non-profit institutions.

At the second level of analysis, we examined the numbers and types of EMI programmes at the division level. Turkish universities have faculties that offer different programmes in a specialized field (e.g. engineering, medicine, communications); however, we chose the division as the unit of analysis because we observed that some programmes belonged to a different faculty, which caused some confusion and inconsistency in the number of the academic subjects. In terms of classifying division, we referred to the framework for Divisions and Departments as adopted by the University of Oxford (ODDF, University of Oxford, 2020) and grouped each academic subject under one of the four divisions, namely: Social Sciences, Medical Sciences, Humanities and Mathematical, Physical and Life Sciences (MPLS). A full list of academic subjects is listed in Appendix.

Our final analysis focused on EMI programmes at the academic subject level. Here, we focused on EMI subjects that were popular between 1999 and 2019. By providing the academic subjects with the highest numbers, we aim to provide overall trends in the fields where EMI programmes are offered for both partial and full EMI studies.

EMI Programmes in Turkey in 1999

In 1999, according to information provided by the manual prepared by the Student Selection and Placement Centre (2020a), Turkey had seventy-one higher education institutions with fifty-three state universities and eighteen foundation universities. Thirty-three of these HEIs included partial or full EMI programmes, which accounted for 46 per cent of HEIs. When the type of the university is considered, 34 per cent of state universities ($N = 18$) and 83 per cent of foundation universities ($N = 15$) included full or partial EMI programmes. Most universities adopted either a partial or full EMI strategy, and only three universities offered both partial and full EMI programmes at the same time. Turkish universities offered 231 full EMI programmes and 114 partial EMI programmes, with a total number of 345 programmes in 1999. We have provided the list of ten universities with the highest number of full and partial EMI programmes in Table 6.1 in line with the manual as prepared by the Student Selection and Placement Centre (2020a).

When the academic divisions were taken into consideration, we found that all four academic divisions offered both full and partial EMI programmes. MLPS programmes topped the list with 98 full and 80 partial EMI programmes, followed by 144 programmes in the division of Social Sciences (117 full and 27 partial EMI programmes). The list of numbers of full and partial EMI programmes according to academic division is provided in Table 6.2.

Table 6.1 Numbers of full and partial EMI programmes in 1999 according to the universities

Name of the university	Number of full EMI programmes	Number of partial EMI programmes	Number of total EMI programmes
Middle East Technical (S)	36	–	36
Istanbul Technical (S)	–	31	31
Boğaziçi (S)	30	–	30
Hacettepe (S)	9	21	30
Yıldız Technical (S)	–	21	21
Yeditepe (F)	18	–	18
Istanbul Bilgi (F)	17	–	17
Fatih (F)	14	–	14
Anadolu (S)	–	14	14
Bilkent (F)	13	–	13

*S = State university, F = Foundation university

Table 6.2 Numbers of full and partial EMI programmes in 1999 according to academic division

Divisions	Number of full EMI programmes	Number of partial EMI programmes	Number of total EMI programmes
MPLS	98	80	178
Social Sciences	117	27	144
Humanities	10	3	13
Medical Sciences	6	4	10
Total	231	114	345

Table 6.3 Top ten academic subjects with the highest number of full and partial EMI programmes in 1999

Academic programme	Number of full EMI programmes	Number of partial EMI programmes	Number of total EMI programmes
Business Administration	20	2	22
Electrics and Electronics Engineering	12	7	19
International Relations	16	2	18
Computer Engineering	14	4	18
Economics	14	2	16
Mathematics	13	2	15
Physics	9	2	11
Chemistry	8	3	11
Industrial Engineering	7	3	10
Chemical Engineering	5	5	10

We further examined the most popular EMI programmes in 1999. Business Administration (20 full and 2 partial), Electrics and Electronics Engineering (12 full and 7 partial), International Relations (16 full and 2 partial) and Computer Engineering (14 full and four partial) were the EMI programmes with the highest numbers, representing both MLPS and Social Sciences divisions. We have provided the list of the top ten academic subjects with the highest number of full and partial EMI programmes in Table 6.3.

EMI in Turkey in 2019

In 2019, according to information provided by the manual prepared by the Student Selection and Placement Centre (2020b), the number of higher education institutions in Turkey increased to 193, with 125 state and 68 foundation universities. One hundred twenty-seven of these HEIs included partial or full EMI programmes, which accounted for 66 per cent of the HEIs in 2019. When the type of university is considered, 55 per cent of the state universities ($N = 69$) and 85 per cent of the foundation universities ($N = 58$) included full or partial EMI programmes, with sixty of the universities offering both partial and full EMI programmes, which accounts for 47 per cent of the universities having EMI programmes. In 2019, the number of full EMI programmes rose to 1,101. A similar increase was also observed in partial EMI programmes ($N = 351$). The total number of EMI programmes was 1,452. We have provided the list of

Table 6.4 Numbers of full and partial EMI programmes in 2019 according to the universities

Name of the university	Number of full EMI programmes	Number of partial EMI programmes	Number of total EMI programmes
Istanbul Technical (S)	33	27	60
Yeditepe (F)	56	1	57
Middle East Technical (S)	52	–	52
Yıldız Technical (S)	16	27	43
Istanbul Bilgi (F)	38	2	40
Bahçeşehir (F)	39	1	40
Boğaziçi (S)	36	–	36
Izmir Economy (F)	30	1	31
Atılım (F)	29	–	29
Yaşar (F)	27	1	28

Table 6.5 Numbers of full and partial EMI programmes in 2019 according to academic divisions

Divisions	Number of full EMI programmes	Number of partial EMI programmes	Number of total EMI programmes
MPLS	526	213	739
Social Sciences	444	104	548
Humanities	70	16	86
Medical Sciences	61	18	79
Total	1,101	351	1,452

ten universities with the highest number of full and partial EMI programmes in Table 6.4 according to the manual prepared by the Student Selection and Placement Centre (2020b).

In 2019, MPLS divisions had the highest number of full ($N = 526$) and partial ($N = 213$) EMI programmes, followed by Social Sciences (444 full, 104 partial). The numbers in Humanities and Medical Sciences divisions were close: 86 and 79, respectively. Table 6.5 lists the numbers of full and partial EMI programmes according to academic division.

When the academic subjects were examined, it can be seen that International Relations, Electrics and Electronics Engineering, Computer Engineering and Business Administration were the subjects with the highest numbers representing two academic divisions: MPLS and Social Sciences. Table 6.6 provides the list of the top ten academic subjects with the highest number of full and partial EMI programmes.

Table 6.6 Top ten academic subjects with the highest number of full and partial EMI programmes in 2019

Academic programme	Number of full EMI programmes	Number of partial EMI programmes	Number of total EMI programmes
International Relations	63	17	80
Electrics and Electronics Engineering	52	21	73
Computer Engineering	52	15	67
Business Administration	56	11	67
Mechanical Engineering	39	20	59
Economics	44	11	55
Civil Engineering	42	12	54
Industrial Engineering	41	11	51
Architecture	36	10	46
Psychology	32	12	44

A Comparison of the Development of EMI over Twenty Years

This section will review the development and growth of EMI programmes over twenty years in Turkey by comparing the number of the EMI programmes in 1999 and 2019. At the university level, the number of universities offering EMI programmes increased substantially (420 per cent) from 345 (231 full EMI programmes and 114 partial EMI programmes) to 1,452 (1,101 full EMI programmes and 351 partial EMI programmes; see Figure 6.1). In the same period, the number of HEIs in Turkey increased to 192 from 71 (270 per cent), evidence of exponential growth (West et al., 2015) or this significant 'boom' often mentioned in the literature (Kalkan, 2019). As can be seen in Figure 6.1, the number of partial EMI programmes did not increase (307 per cent) as much as that of full EMI programmes (476 per cent), and this can be explained by (among other factors) the greater advantage in getting hired for a good job after graduating from a full EMI programme (Altay & Ercin, 2020).

In 1999, Middle East Technical University offered the highest number of full EMI programmes ($N = 36$), and Istanbul Technical University housed the highest number of partial EMI programmes ($N = 31$). In 2019, the highest number of EMI programmes in a university increased to 60 (Istanbul Technical University with 33 full and 27 partial EMI programmes), and Yeditepe University offered the highest number of full EMI programmes in 2019 ($N = 56$). The number of full EMI programmes offered by Yeditepe University can be explained by the fact that 'private institutions have largely adopted EMI-only policies in an effort to capitalise on English to vie for more fee-paying students' (Karakaş, 2019, p. 207).

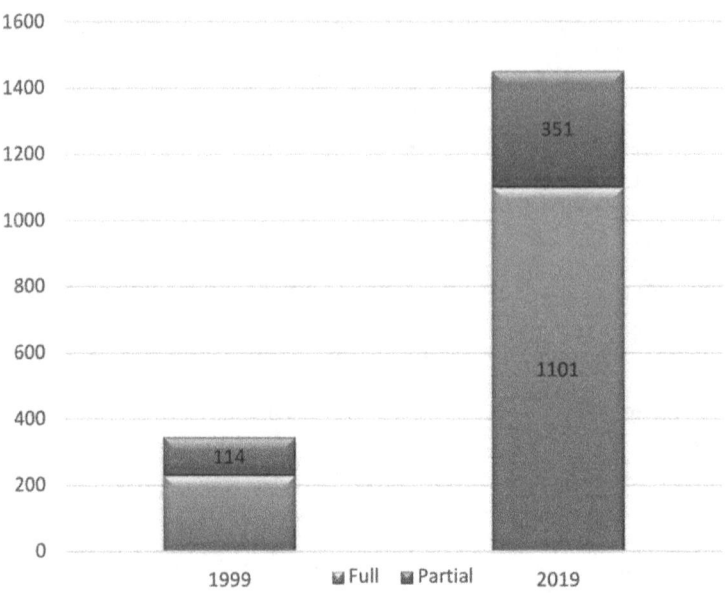

Figure 6.1 A comparison of the full, partial and total number of EMI programmes in 1999 and 2019.

Another important difference between 1999 and 2019 was the increase in the number of universities that offered both full and partial EMI programmes. There were only three universities in 1999; this multiplied by twenty and increased to sixty in 2019.

When the academic divisions are compared, we have seen a similar order of the divisions with increased numbers in 1999 and 2019. MPLS and Social Sciences dominated the list in both years with dramatic increases from 178 to 739 (415 per cent) and 144 to 548 (380 per cent), respectively. Figure 6.2 illustrates the changes in the numbers of academic programmes in different divisions.

When the trends and popularity in academic subjects are compared in 1999 and 2019, we see that the top five academic subjects in 1999 kept their presence in the top ten list in 2019, all increasing in different numbers. Three academic subjects in MPLS, namely Mathematics, Physics and Chemistry, together with Chemical Engineering, dropped off the list and were replaced by Civil Engineering, Mechanical Engineering, Architecture and Psychology. Business Administration ($N=22$) was at the top of the list in 1999 but dropped to third in 2019 even though it increased by 304 per cent ($N=67$). When we closely examine the top ten academic subject list, we see that five (out of ten) of them are engineering programmes. This finding is in line with that of Arık and Arık (2014), who also found that around 50 per cent of EMI programmes investigated

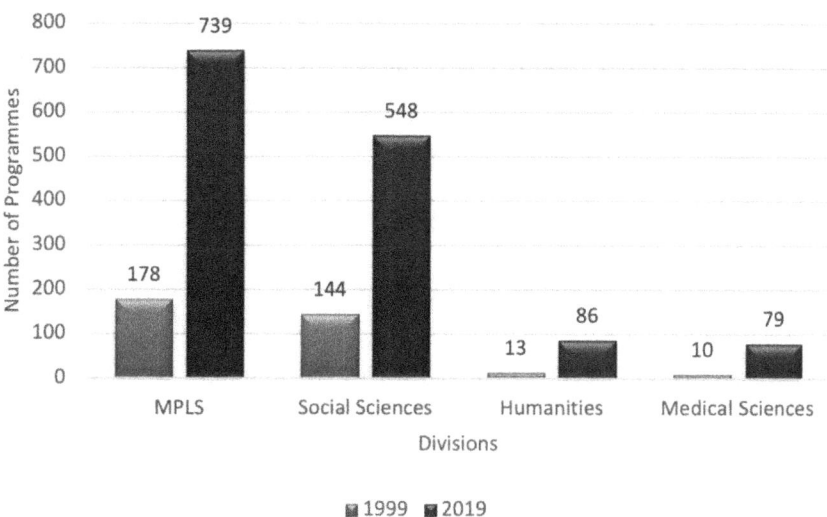

Figure 6.2 Changes in the number of academic programmes in different divisions.

were either engineering or English-related programmes. There were eighteen EMI International Relations programmes in 1999. This increased to eighty (444 per cent) and became the EMI programme with the highest number in 2019. The decrease in the popularity of MPLS subjects (e.g. Mathematics, Physics and Chemistry) may be attributed to the 2008 Council of Higher Education regulation, which lifted the obligation to open a faculty of Arts and Sciences to establish a university in Turkey (Kalkan, 2019).

Conclusion

This chapter focused on the numbers and types of EMI programmes in Turkey between 1999 and 2019. It compared these programmes at three levels: university, division and academic subject. It also reviewed the HE regulations published in the Turkish Official Gazette prepared by the Council of Higher Education about foreign language MOI in terms of requirements for opening new foreign language MOI academic programmes, employing lecturers and admitting students into these programmes. Previous studies have also analysed language policy documents (Kırkgöz, 2009, 2017, 2019) or reported the number of EMI programmes in HE institutions (Arık & Arık, 2014). However, this chapter provides a deeper exploration of the growth of EMI in Turkey by relating the language policy change with the number of EMI programmes. It also provides a time-span comparison of the EMI programmes between 1999 and 2019 to illustrate the growth of EMI that has often been mentioned in the scholarly literature (Karakaş, 2018, 2019; West et al., 2015). Previous studies have provided a general overview of how EMI programmes have recently been on the rise in Turkey (Yuksel & Genc, 2020). However, to the best of our knowledge, no prior study has explored the growth of the EMI programmes in the Turkish HE context by providing the changes in the academic division and subject numbers. Milestones of the development that we have discussed in this chapter are summarized in Figure 6.3.

Our analysis revealed, similar to the increase in the number of universities (West et al., 2015; Kalkan, 2019; Oz, 2005), EMI programmes have also increased exponentially (Arık & Arık, 2014; Yuksel & Genc, 2020). This chapter provides some important information that has not been provided before in terms of the numbers of full and partial EMI programmes between 1999 and 2019 in different state and foundation universities and trends in academic subjects in recent years. It also portrays the rise in the numbers of academic subjects in different divisions between 1999 and 2019. This clearly demonstrates the 'boom' in EMI programmes across twenty years in Turkish HE. This expansion requires further critical research in terms of the consequences for EMI stakeholders to ensure a positive student experience and successful HE teaching and learning outcomes.

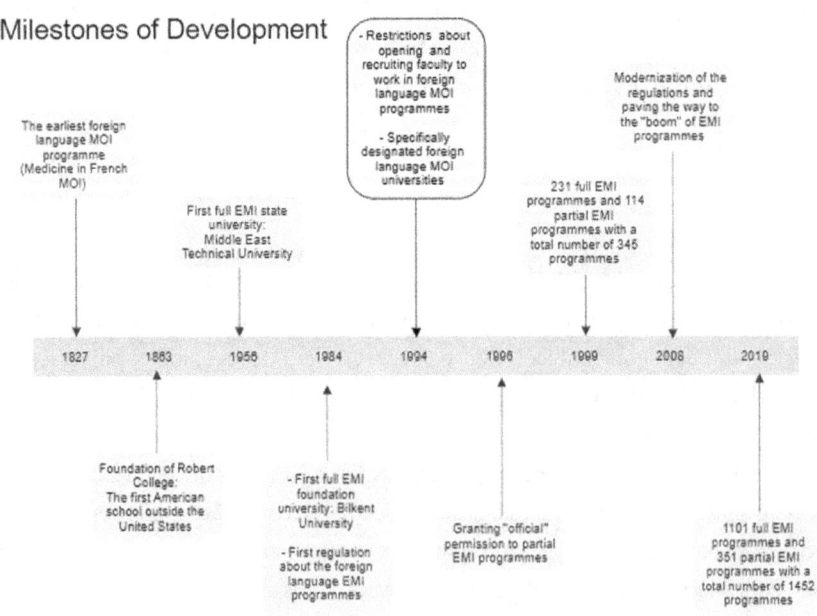

Figure 6.3 Milestones of foreign language MOI development in Turkey.

References

Ali, N. L. (2013). A changing paradigm in language planning: English-medium instruction policy at the tertiary level in Malaysia. *Current Issues in Language Planning, 14*(1), 73–92.

Altay, M. (2020). The implications of EMI education for graduates' employment conditions. *Kocaeli University Journal of Social Sciences Institutes, 2*(40), 109–120.

Altay, M., & Ercin, N. (2020). Uncovering the reflections of English medium instruction in engineering graduates' career. *Sakarya University Journal of Education, 10*(3), 577–588.

Altay, M., & Yuksel, D. (2021). Job prospects of different EMI engineering programmes' graduates. *Participatory Educational Research, 8*(2), 460–475.

Arık, B. T., & Arık, E. (2014). The role and status of English in Turkish higher education. *English Today, 30*(4), 5–10.

Aslan, M. (2018). The debate on English-medium instruction and globalisation in the Turkish context: A sociopolitical perspective. *Journal of Multilingual and Multicultural Development, 39*(7), 602–616.

Atik, E. (2010). *Perceptions of students towards English medium instruction at tertiary level: The case of a Turkish private university* (Unpublished master's thesis). Middle East Technical University, Ankara, Turkey.

Başıbek, N., Dolmacı, M., Cengiz, B. C., Bür, B., Dilek, Y., & Kara, B. (2014). Lecturers' perceptions of English medium instruction at engineering departments of higher education: A study on partial English medium instruction at some state universities in Turkey. *Procedia-Social and Behavioral Sciences, 116*, 1819–1825.

Byun, K., Chu, H., Kim, M., Park, I., Kim, S., & Jung, J. (2010). English-medium teaching in Korean higher education: Policy debates and reality. *Higher Education, 62*(4), 431–449.

Council of Higher Education (2000). *The law on higher education*. Ankara, Turkey: Ankara University Press.

Curle, S., Yuksel, D., Soruc, A., & Altay, M. (2020). Predictors of English medium instruction academic success: English proficiency versus first language medium. *System, 95*, 1–11.

Dafouz, D. (2018). English-medium instruction and teacher education programmes in higher education: Ideological forces and imagined identities at work. *International Journal of Bilingual Education and Bilingualism, 21*(5), 540–552.

Dearden, J. (2014). *English as a medium of instruction – A growing global phenomenon: Phase 1 Interim Report*. Oxford: British Council.

Dearden, J. (2015). *English as a medium of instruction – A growing global phenomenon*. Oxford: University of Oxford.

Doiz, A., Lasagabaster, D., & Sierra, J. M. (2013). *English-medium instruction at universities: Global challenges*. Bristol, England: Multilingual Matters.

Graddol, D. (2006). *English next*. Oxford: British Council.

Green, C. (2015). Internationalisation, deregulation and the expansion of higher education in Korea: An historical overview. *International Journal of Higher Education, 4*(3), 1–13.

Hornberger, N. H. (2006). Frameworks and models in language policy and planning. In T. Ricento (Ed.), *An introduction to language policy: Theory and method* (pp. 24–41). New York: Blackwell Publishing.

Huang, H., & Curle, S. (2021). Higher education medium of instruction and career prospects: An exploration of current and graduated Chinese students' perceptions. *Journal of Education and Work.* DOI: 10.1080/13639080.2021.1922617.

Kalkan, O. (2019). *The transformation of higher education in Turkey between 2002–2018: An analysis of politics and policies of higher education* (Unpublished master's thesis). Middle East Technical University.

Karakaş, A. (2018). Visible language-covert policy: An investigation of language policy documents at EMI universities in Turkey. *International Online Journal of Education and Teaching (IOJET), 5*(4), 788–807.

Karakaş, A. (2019). A critical look at the phenomenon of 'a mixed-up use of Turkish and English in English-medium instruction universities in Turkey. *Journal of Higher Education and Science/Yükseköğretim ve Bilim Dergisi, 9*(2), 205–215.

Kırkgöz, Y. (2005). Motivation and student perception of studying in an English medium university. *Journal of Language and Linguistic Studies, 1*(1), 101–123.

Kırkgöz, Y. (2009). Globalisation and English language policy in Turkey. *Educational Policy, 23*(5), 663–684.

Kırkgöz, Y. (2017). English education policy in Turkey. In R. Kirkpatrick (Ed.), *English education policy in the Middle East and North Africa* (pp. 235–256). Cham, Switzerland: International Publishing AG.

Kırkgöz, Y. (2019). Investigating the growth of English-medium higher education in Turkey and the Middle East region. In D. Staub (Ed.), *Quality assurance and accreditation in foreign language education* (pp. 9–20). Cham: Springer.

Kirkpatrick, A. (2014). The language(s) of HE: EMI and/or ELF and/or multilingualism? *The Asian Journal of Applied Linguistics, 1*(1), 4–15.

Kim, E. G. (2017). English medium instruction in Korean higher education: Challenges and future directions. In Ben Fenton-Smith, Pamela Humphreys, Ian Walkinshaw (Eds.), *English medium instruction in higher education in Asia-Pacific* (pp. 53–69). Cham: Springer.

Macaro, E., Curle, S., Pun, J., An, J., & Dearden, J. (2018). A systematic review of English medium instruction in higher education. *Language Teaching, 51*(1), 36–76.

Marmara University (2018). History of the faculty of medicine. Retrieved 20 June 2018, from https://tip.marmara.edu.tr/fakulte/tarihce.

Minifie, J. (1998). Merhaba. Allaha ısmarladık: A sabbatical year in Turkey. *Journal of College Admission, 158*, 25–29.

O'Dowd, R. (2015). *The training and accreditation of teachers for English-medium instruction: A survey of European universities.* León: Universidad de León.

Oz, H. H. (2005). Accreditation processes in Turkish higher education. *Higher Education in Europe*, *30*(3–4), 335–344.

Nguyen, H. T., Walkinshaw, I., & Pham, H. H. (2017). EMI programs in a Vietnamese university: Language, pedagogy and policy issues. In B. Fenton-Smith, P. Humphreys, & I. Walkinshaw (Eds.), *English medium instruction in higher education in Asia-Pacific. Multilingual Education*, vol 21. Cham: Springer.

Rauhvargers, A. (2013). *Global universities rankings and their impact.* Brussels: European University Association. Report 2. Retrieved from: https://eua.eu/downloads/publications/global%20university%20rankings%20and%20their%20impact%20-%20report%20ii.pdf.

Selvi, A. F. (2014). The medium-of-instruction debate in Turkey: Oscillating between national ideas and bilingual ideals. *Current Issues in Language Planning*, *15*(2), 133–152.

Student Selection and Placement Centre (2020a). *University placement manual.* Retrieved 10 March 2020, from https://www.osym.gov.tr/Eklenti/1557,tablo4pdf.pdf?0.

Student Selection and Placement Centre (2020b). *University placement manual.* Retrieved 10 March 2020, from http://dokuman.osym.gov.tr/pdfdokuman/2019/YKS/tablo4_18072019.xls.

Tran, L. T., & Nguyen, H. T. (2018). Internationalisation of higher education in Vietnam through English medium instruction (EMI): Practices, tensions and implications for local language policies. In I. Liyanage (Eds.), *Multilingual Education Yearbook 2018. Multilingual Education Yearbook*, (pp. 91–106). Cham: Springer.

Turhan, B., & Kırkgöz, Y. (2018). Motivation of engineering students and lecturers toward English medium instruction at tertiary level in Turkey. *Journal of Language and Linguistic Studies*, *14*(1), 261–277.

Turkish Official Gazette (1984). Directive on the principles to be followed in foreign language teaching and foreign language medium of instruction in higher education institutions. 20 April 1984 No: 18378.

Turkish Official Gazette (1994). Directive on the principles to be followed in foreign language teaching and foreign language medium of instruction in higher education institutions. 7 October 1994 No: 22074.

Turkish Official Gazette (1996). Directive on the principles to be followed in foreign language teaching and foreign language medium of instruction in higher education institutions. 1 April 1996 No: 22598.

Turkish Official Gazette (2008). Directive on the principles to be followed in foreign language teaching and foreign language medium of instruction in higher education institutions. 4 December 2008 No: 27074.

Turkish Official Gazette (2016). Directive on the principles to be followed in foreign language teaching and foreign language medium of instruction in higher education institutions. 26 March 2016 No: 29662.

University of Oxford (2020). Divisions and departments. University of Oxford. Retrieved 30 January 2017, from http://www.ox.ac.uk/about/divisions-and-departments.

Welch, A. R. (2001). Globalisation, post-modernity and the state: Comparative education facing the third millennium. *Comparative Education, 37*(4): 475–492.

West, R., Güven, A., Parry, J., & Ergenekon, T. (2015). *The state of English in higher education in Turkey*. Ankara: British Council & TEPAV.

Yuksel, D., & Genc, E. (2020). A statistical review of higher education programs holding EMI in Turkey. *Paper presented at 11th ELT Research Conference*, Çanakkale, Turkey.

Yuksel, D., Soruç, A., Altay, M., & Curle, S. (2021). Does English language proficiency improve when studying through English medium instruction? A longitudinal study in Turkey. *Applied Linguistics Review*, 1–30.

Zhang, Z. (2018). English-medium instruction policies in China: Internationalisation of higher education. *Journal of Multilingual and Multicultural Development, 39*(6), 542–555.

Appendix

The University of Oxford's Divisions and Departments framework

Humanities	Mathematical, Physical and Life Sciences	Social Sciences	Medical Sciences
Classics	Computer Science	Anthropology and Museum Ethnography	Biochemistry
English Language and Literature	Chemistry	Archaeology	Clinical Medicine
History	Earth Sciences	Government	Clinical Neurosciences
History of Art	Engineering Science	Economics	Experimental Psychology
Medieval and Modern Languages	Materials	Education	Medicine
Music	Mathematics	Geography and the Environment	Obstetrics and Gynaecology
Oriental Studies	Physics	Interdisciplinary Area Studies	Oncology
Philosophy	Plant Sciences	International Development	Orthopaedics, Rheumatology and Musculoskeletal Sciences
Theology and Religion	Statistics	Technology and the Internet	Paediatrics
Art	Zoology	Business	Pathology
		Law	Pharmacology

Humanities	Mathematical, Physical and Life Sciences	Social Sciences	Medical Sciences
		Politics and International Relations	Physiology, Anatomy and Genetics
		Social Policy and Intervention	Population Health
		Sociology	Psychiatry
			Surgical Sciences
			Primary Care Health Sciences

Source: University of Oxford (2020). Divisions and Departments, University of Oxford. Retrieved 30 January 2020, from http://www.ox.ac.uk/about/divisions-and-departments.

7

Issues of Educational Language Policy and EMI in North Africa

Salah Troudi

Introduction to the Language of Education in North Africa

Before reviewing the place of EMI in the northern part of Africa, it needs to be stressed that to the people of this region, from Morocco to Egypt, Arabic has historically played an incontestable role as the sole medium of learning. It has been and still is a source of pride, identity and accomplishment to the inhabitants of the five countries where the majority speak Arabic as their mother tongue. The sciences and other fields of academia and scholarship, such as human and social studies, were all conducted in Arabic. Throughout history, the scholars of this part of the world have contributed to developing knowledge and human thought via Arabic. Therefore, a review of and discussion about the role of EMI needs to consider the place and position of Arabic in the national educational systems and the corresponding sociocultural milieus. In the nineteenth and twentieth centuries, the educational landscape in the region experienced the introduction of French and English as a direct result of the presence of the French and British colonialist powers. French and English infiltrated the sociolinguistic scene of the region, especially in the larger cities, resulting in a complex and varied mosaic of a wide range of bilingualism and multilingualism, whereby local varieties of Arabic and varieties of Amazigh, known in English as Berber, came into contact with different levels of French and English. In Tunisia, Algeria and Morocco, French initially started as a foreign language in primary and secondary schools and then gradually gained a firm position as a medium of instruction, mainly for the scientific subjects, especially in higher education. It is only in the last decade or so that scholars and educationalists in these countries have started considering and debating the potential role of English as a language of instruction in higher education. In Libya and Egypt, English is taught as a foreign language in schools and used as a medium of instruction in scientific subjects at universities. Although there are more English-speaking universities in Egypt, now and more people can speak English in the region than ever before, English still does not have the same social and media status in Tunisia, Algeria and Morocco that French has.

EMI in Tunisia: A Distant Possibility

In a British Council publication, Dearden (2015) reported the findings of a survey-based study on EMI as a global phenomenon. The study covered fifty-five countries, and the survey respondents were British Council staff residing in these countries. One of the salient features of the study is the total absence of any of the North African nations. Instead, three Arab countries were represented: Bahrain, Qatar and Saudi Arabia, but no data were provided about whether EMI was allowed in any of the three educational sectors in Bahrain. Nevertheless, the generated data, primarily qualitative, point to an overall awareness in the surveyed countries of the importance of English, and EMI in particular, for economic growth and development, competition in a globalized world for knowledge and international participation through the development of students' language and communication skills. Despite the limitations of the study, which was characterized by inconclusive data and the non-participation of prominent stakeholders (e.g. teachers, students and policymakers), a clear conclusion was that EMI was increasingly on the rise and had conquered a strong position, especially in private institutions in many countries. An interesting finding was that fewer than 50 per cent of the surveyed countries had official statements and documents about EMI and its role in the area of language policy. In addition, most of the excerpts from policy statements provided in the report were general and even vague, stressing the importance of learning English at different levels but lacked a firm commitment to an EMI policy, except for Uzbekistan and Estonia. Uzbekistan supported EMI at all levels and in all institutions, whereas Estonia was for the Estonian language being the medium of instruction in all subjects at all levels. In the Arab world, the absence of clarity and official commitment at the level of official policy has also been highlighted elsewhere (Troudi, 2009; Troudi and Jendli, 2011).

Concerning the language situation in the Tunisian educational system, several scholars, such as Daoud (2001, 2002, 2007), Battenburg (1996) and Labassi (2009), have painted a complex picture characterized by a continuum of unequal coexistence and even competition between two major languages, Arabic and French, with English slowly working its way into schools and universities. Bahloul (2001), like Daoud, acknowledges the ever-growing demand for English in education and calls for a change in language policy. The phrase 'English as a medium of instruction' was not used in these early theoretical and discussion papers. Still, there was a clear recognition of the need to consider a change in language of education policy, especially in the science subjects. The ideology behind a call for English in the sciences is pragmatic, evoking discourses of economic development, modernization and global positioning. There is currently no doubt about the global force of English in education in practically all fields. Therefore, Tunisian scholars' calls for a shift in language policy are a natural and unavoidable result in the face of such a powerful phenomenon.

However, the reality on the Tunisian ground is complex and characterized by some seemingly insurmountable challenges, at least for the time being. The position of French as a language of instruction in the sciences and most academic subjects at universities is deeply rooted. A direct legacy from the French colonial period, French was politically reinforced in the last few decades after the Tunisian independence through strong ties with France and its francophone policies. A francophone Tunisian elite has also long benefited politically and socially from its French-style education and command of French. Arabic, the national and official language of the country, has a strong position in primary and most of secondary education, with scientific subjects being taught in French in the four years of the secondary stage. At the tertiary level, French rules supreme, except in the humanities, law and theological studies. English is taught as a foreign language in the intermediary and secondary stages and for academic purposes in many tertiary disciplines. English is also more notably present in the private sector – a relatively new educational phenomenon in the country. Against such unequal and powerful linguistic dualism, English is likely to struggle for some time before it can find a way into the educational system. Even if the opposing political agendas of liberalism, nationalism, conservatism and socialism are put aside, significant educational challenges for EMI in Tunisia remain at the levels of proficiency, pedagogy and teacher education. With a major economic crisis and political and social upheavals, Tunisia cannot afford to invest in EMI and prioritize it. There are many more dire priorities to tackle in all the educational sectors before the country can address a policy shift in the medium of instruction. In addition, EMI proponents often argue for its benefits on the learners, yet there is increasing research evidence from different countries about the adverse effects of EMI on the quality of learning experience and academic achievement.

Boukadi's (2015) mixed-method study on Tunisian English teachers concludes that the country needs English to compete in the global economy. She argues that Tunisian doctors and engineers are restricted in the international job market due to a lack of English proficiency. The significance of the study lies in its investigation of language policy issues from teachers' perspectives. Their enthusiasm for English and belief in the necessity of a stronger place for it in the curriculum are not matched by supportive and clear language planning. Despite vital needs and calls for professional development in pedagogy and curriculum reforms, the situation remains dire. Discursively and theoretically, there is awareness of the increasing demand for English in academia and the sciences. Yet, at the level of language of instruction policy, the status quo reigns supreme. This post-revolution state of affairs in language policy (Boukadi and Troudi, 2017) continues to pose an intellectual challenge to educationalists and education officials alike.

Badwan's study (2019), also sponsored and published by the British Council, investigated Tunisian students, university teachers and Ministry of Education officials about their views on the country's readiness for EMI and its implementation. The majority of the questionnaire and interview respondents were in favour of EMI, but they were aware of many challenges, some of which do not seem surmountable given the dire economic conditions and political tensions in present-day Tunisia and which do not currently show any signs of improvement. On the one hand, the absence of EMI is very likely to thwart economic growth and international development. On the other hand, the country's resources are minimal and depleting. The current national priorities are economic and social as the levels of unemployment are very high. Therefore, there is no budget for introducing English as a language of instruction. Thus, despite people's political and academic readiness for EMI, Tunisia does not have the means to initiate any language changes.

At face value, the study is shrouded in neutrality vis-à-vis English and EMI. It is informed by a sociocultural conceptualization of reality that sees individuals constructing their realities in specific social contexts. However, the aims of the study, its focus and recommendations cannot hide a clear plan for preparing the ground for a gradual implementation of EMI in Tunisia. The study does acknowledge a variety of challenges, such as university teachers' inability to teach in English, but the proposition and necessity of EMI were not questioned. It is, of course, difficult not to see EMI as a potential threat to Arabic as a language of academia when French is already marginalizing it. The spread of the English paradigm functions in an expansionist linguistic fashion with strong and established methods and strategies using triumphalist discourses. Its agents continue to present EMI as a linguistic capital serving as a condition for economic and societal development for the less-developed parts of the world. This perspective on EMI has informed some theoretical papers and empirical studies in the Arab world and North Africa. There is, of course, an opposing view of EMI warning of the unavoidable and detrimental effects of EMI policies and practices on local and national languages, learners' quality of education and social equality. This view has also informed some papers and studies, and EMI will continue to attract opposing views because of its controversial nature and mercantile and political aspects. Related to the question of EMI is the issue of academic publication for academics. While French is the de facto language of scholarly publication for Tunisian scholars, many are motivated to publish in English journals for more international presence and impact. Ableljaouad and Labassi (2020) investigated the challenges met by scholars whose education and academic preparation were done in French and pointed out the need for English for Research Publication Purpose to support academics in their endeavours to publish in English. Their colleagues across North Africa also experience this challenge.

With international cooperation and with institutions such as the British Council and some US educational agencies, there have been numerous teacher development projects in other North African countries such as Algeria and Morocco. In Tunisia, too, there is a steady increase of private universities and colleges with French as the medium of instruction but with relatively more hours per week dedicated to English for Academic Purposes than in public universities.

EMI in Morocco: A Preferred Future

North African nations as developing countries and economies in transition have been urged to join the EMI trend. With such forces as globalization, neoliberalism and aggressive capitalism overpowering national economic independence and stability, these countries find it impossible to ignore discourses associating learning English with economic development and prosperity. Thus, an indisputable argument has been woven into political, economic and educational discourses and strategies in North Africa and other world regions. This argument is based on the premise that the 'economic capital benefits' (Rassol, 2013, p. 45) of developing nations are inescapably tied up with English proficiency. A significant challenge for Tunisia, Algeria and Morocco is that their educational systems have long been entrenched with and within the French educational system, and French has been the medium of instruction. A structural move to EMI, although not in any near future, would be a massive upheaval to the educational system and students' learning experiences as well as the fundamental principle of equality of access to higher education. Moreover, EMI is likely to widen the gap between social classes and disadvantage those who cannot afford the extra expenses needed for private English tuition and additional learning materials. To benefit from EMI as a symbol of linguistic and cultural power, one needs to have access to material and monetary capital in the first place (Bourdieu, 1991).

In addition to these points, the economics of language does not address the societal, cultural and linguistic impacts of an EMI strategy or policy on the quality of peoples' lives. Additionally, the often-unquestionable premise that English is a condition for economic development has also been questioned. For example, empirical analysis by Arkand and Grin (2013) has demonstrated through econometric evidence that English proficiency is 'in no manner associated with a higher level of economic development, when the latter is measured by its common incarnation of GDP per capita' (p. 262). However, questioning the associations between EMI and economic development has not dampened EMI enthusiasts and protagonists from pushing it forward as an elixir for growth, modernization and global market competition.

Shahu (2016) places the evolution of English in Morocco in the middle of a multilingual continuum marked primarily by the strong presence of French as a symbol of colonial inheritance and Arabic as the official language of the country and a sign of its belonging to the larger Arab nation or pan Arabism. The linguistic diversity in Morocco is also described as a space of cohabitation for several competing languages with different statuses. Tamazight, the first language of a good proportion of Moroccan people, has gained the status of the second official language and is slowly working its way towards the educational system, having secured a place in a few media channels. However, this multilingualism is not seen as a sign of linguistic richness and diversity by many Moroccan intellectuals and linguists. The increasing marginalization of Arabic (due to the presence of French and now English as signs of modernity) and the lack of meaningful language policies have resulted in 'chaotic multilingualism' (Cheddadi, 2011, pp. 56–57). Shahu argues that the linguistic situation is in crisis and that the current language policy in education has further complicated this situation. This is because decisions on the provision of languages, their status and which one would be the primary medium of instruction were based on political exigencies and ideologies instead of on prioritizing social cohesion, development needs and learners' cultural and educational characteristics. French remains powerful as the main medium of instruction for the sciences and technologies, and this is partly due to its protected status in the educational system and society at large. This privileged position is also politically maintained by the francophone elites and the country's strong economic and political ties with France. The rest of the coexisting foreign languages, such as English, Spanish and German, have not necessarily contributed to a richer multilingual scene in education. Therefore, there are calls for a clear language policy based on the country's social and economic needs to establish some sense of linguistic balance.

In addition to Shahu's work, the year 2016 saw the publication of a study by Belhiah and Abdelatif on EMI in Morocco. They focused on doctoral students of sciences and engineering and their perceptions of using English rather than French as a medium of instruction. The study is exploratory in nature using a five-item Likert scale survey with an open-ended question seeking qualitative input from 208 participants doing doctoral studies in information technology, sciences, agriculture and veterinary medicine. The authors argue that English is popular in Morocco as it is not associated with a history of colonialism as French is. People are aware of the English language's international stature as a language of sciences. As part of their theoretical justification for a study on EMI and a need for it in the Moroccan higher education system, the authors adopt Sadiqi's (1991) argument that the educational context in Morocco is ready for EMI. This is explained by pro-English educational policies, the strong position of English as a lingua franca in several domains, Moroccans' positive attitudes towards English and their motivation to learn it, and the fact that English is not linked with discourses of colonialism and territorial occupation. Economically, Morocco needs English, especially in the areas of business and tourism. Its absence in higher education is seen as the cause why Moroccan students are unable to access up-to-date scientific resources and references; thus, these students are out of step with the rest of the world and cannot compete internationally. The study revealed that the majority (75 per cent) did not have access to English classes/lessons in their colleges and that 82 per cent needed to use English in their academic research. An interesting finding is that although the majority admit they do not master English and need assistance, 94 per cent think English should be adopted as the medium of instruction at universities and colleges. To them, English would improve the quality of scientific research and the students' educational experiences. The authors acknowledge that the measures put in place to support English in higher education have been inefficient despite the official discourse about the importance of English for the educational and economic development of the country. Another interesting finding is the shift of attitudes towards French as the medium of instruction, which 'has become a real burden on the Moroccan higher educational system' (2016, p. 221). Recommendations were for offering courses using EMI, but it is not clear whether the authors favour a complete shift to EMI. There was, however, a clear call for the elevation of the status of English in higher education based on cooperation between language planning experts, English language specialists and policymakers. Belhiah and Abdelatif's study has made a clear and significant contribution to the field of EMI in Morocco. It systematically presents the attitudes of students of sciences and technology towards the adoption of EMI in Morocco. The challenges and conditions to be addressed are a change of medium of instruction policy to take place.

A discussion of the status or future potential for EMI in Morocco cannot be fruitful without considering the language of instruction in primary and secondary schools. While some participants in Shahu's study favoured the inclusion of EMI in secondary schools as a better preparation for university subjects, Belhiah and Lamallam's study (2020) revealed that the issue of mother-language instruction in Moroccan primary schools is quite complex. Their mixed-method study showed that while students and teachers showed positive attitudes towards using the two mother languages of Amazigh and Darija, Standard Arabic is firmly seen as the major medium of instruction. Darija is the local variety or dialect of Arabic, which has recently been allowed into primary schools for pedagogical reasons. It was also met with strong resistance from those concerned about its adverse effects on Arab and Islamic identity. Teachers, in particular, were against using Darija and Amazigh in teaching materials for fear of their negative impact on learning Arabic or foreign languages, such as French and English. The authors argue that despite 'the officialization of Amazigh in 2011 and its implementation in school curricula since 2003' (p. 108), parental and teachers' attitudes towards it are still negative as they do not consider it a worthy medium of instruction. The study reports that some Amazigh parents even discourage their children from learning it at school in favour of Arabic or French, which are much more marketable and are likely to help them find jobs.

In addition, Belhiah and Lamallam bemoan the scarcity and insufficiency of financial resources put in place to protect and develop these two mother tongues in Morocco. The situation of Amazigh and Darija is made more complex by the political situation characterized by the power of nationalist ideologies calling for confirmation of Standard Arabic as the medium of instruction and a symbol of linguistic, cultural and religious identity, on the one hand, and by the strong political and historical influence of La Francophonie, on the other. This point confirms Shahu's (2016) argument about the significant role political exigencies play in shaping the language of instruction policies in Morocco.

In particular, language policy and language instruction policy are political acts even in countries where there is only one dominant mother tongue. In North Africa and the western part of North Africa, that is, Tunisia, Algeria and Morocco, the linguistic scene is multi-layered, complex and vibrant.

EMI in Algeria: A Hypothetical Status

The linguistic scene in Algeria is not less complex than that of Morocco. Several Algerian scholars and linguists have been intensively debating and researching this complexity for at least twenty years. Describing it as sensitive, Milani (2000) places the discussion of the use of national and foreign languages in Algeria among the 'thorny domains' (p. 13). Algerian debates over language use and supremacy are held within a political context characterized by ideological competition between the proponents of Francophonie and the advocates of Arabic as a symbol of social, linguistic and religious identity. Milani argues that with the increasing decline of the status of French in society and education, English is seen as a solution to the educational, technological and economic problems of the country. He also laments the interference of political agendas in matters of language policy and the lack of well-thought-of and designed strategies. English was hastily introduced into the primary schools to weaken the position of French in education and sociality at large. Milani is very critical of the marginalization of language experts and pedagogues from decision-making in language policy. He argues that the Algerian language situation is made more complex by what he calls the asphyxia and ostracism of the two main languages in use: dialectical Arabic and Berber. This is very similar to the situation in Morocco as described by Belhiah and Lamallam. According to Milani, the two vernaculars are considered by politicians as of lower status and have been disparaged in favour of classical Arabic. Berber, however, has more recently experienced more political recognition and a surge in status. With classical Arabic being the medium of instruction, Milani speaks of linguistic schizophrenia among Algerian children at school in that they have to study in a language 'with which there is no personal resonance' (p. 16).

English in Algeria has, therefore, to be considered in relation to this complex and sensitive linguistic situation of multilingualism with several languages of different social and official status competing for more influential positions in society and education in particular. Introducing English into schools is partly seen as a political attempt to sideline French and provide students with the learning and communication means to compete at a global level in the sciences and technologies. However, there were warnings that the introduction of English would exacerbate an already sensitive and fragile linguistic situation characterized by social tensions and identity crises. The main argument, similar to the case of imposing Arabic as the primary medium of instruction, is that language policy did not consider the sociocultural fabric of the Algerian society. English, however, is heralded as a neutral, not implicated with a history of colonialism in Algeria, and a popular language. Nevertheless, it is experiencing some major challenges in education, mainly due to sociocultural and pedagogical reasons. English learners in Algeria do not have the same social and contextual support they can depend on when learning French. French still exists on many levels and in many domains in Algeria, though learners' access might vary according to class and region. This is not the situation for English, which remains a foreign language. Pedagogically, English is being stripped of its cultural elements in favour of a utilitarian approach. With this lack of educational support for English and the lack of clear policy, Milani recommends going back to French as the primary foreign language and protecting Arabic and the vernacular languages.

Against this varied linguistic background in Algeria, Chemami's study investigates sixteen-year-old school pupils' daily use of languages and their attitudes towards them. Literary Arabic, Algerian Arabic, also known as Darija, Tamazight, French and English were the five choices presented to the participants in a bilingual questionnaire. The first four languages create the multilingual or plurilingual landscape of Algeria. At 68 per cent, Algerian Arabic was reposted to be the most frequently used language, French being a distant second with 20 per cent. Literary Arabic, which is the standard form of Arabic used at school and official media, was equal to Tamazight in the persistent option for research instruments. English received 0 per cent as 70 per cent admitted to rarely or very rarely using English. French was a frequently used language, with 65 per cent of participants opting for it.

These are not surprising findings about the linguistic practices of young people given the linguistic history of Algeria and the language of education policies followed by the state since the country's independence in 1962. Chemami refers to the phenomenon of diglossia to explain the historical emergence and development of the Algerian Arabic or Darija, which originally branched out of an early form of Standard or Literary Arabic. With almost 80 per cent of the Algerian people using Darija as their first means of communication, most Algerians will identify with it as their mother tongue. A significant level of code switching also characterizes this form of Arabic with French, Tamazight and occasionally English. Chemami reports that French still enjoys a solid status in the educational system and society, with some recent changes in attitudes towards it. The study also shows that there is a promising future for English in schools and universities. The cooperation with the United States and Canada in teacher training, curriculum development and materials production in English language teaching (ELT) has provided some structural support for English teachers in Algerian schools. School children in Chemami's study showed readiness to learn English and made several suggestions to improve their language skills, especially in reading and writing. The author suggests that the country moves beyond a language of education policy that favours French and English as prestigious languages of sciences and technology and Arabic as a language of tradition. The call is for a plurilingual policy to usher in 'a solidarity which would have a democratic impact on the redefinition of the Algerian identity' (p. 232). However, it is not clear how this solidarity is likely to materialize and what political and educational conditions need to be put in place before a cohesive and egalitarian language policy can be created and enacted.

The most recent research study on EMI in Algeria is by Medfouni (2020). She investigated discourses and attitudes towards implementing EMI in three Algerian universities and the ways language is used in scientific courses. The main findings show a clear preference on the part of students and teachers for English as the medium of instruction. While only three institutions were involved in the study, the findings are significant and represent an increasing Algerian trend. French is no longer in favour even though it is still the official and practically the only medium of instruction for scientific disciplines. Students associate it with colonialism and the turbulent and violent history of the French invasion of their country. On the other hand, English is associated with globalization, internationalization, economic development and opportunities for the future. Above all English is not linked to colonialism and does not remind Algerians of foreign intervention in their country. These findings echo those of Shahu's study

(2016) in Morocco which shares a similar modern colonial history with Algeria. From Tunisia to Morocco, university students seem to be increasingly interested in EMI as they see it as their passage to the world of global economy, research and especially international employment opportunities. However, the studies reviewed in this chapter, including Medfouni's point out to major obstacles that need to be surmounted before EMI can gain a solid place in North African universities. The reality on the ground reflects a lack of political will to adopt EMI which is accompanied by lack of curricular, pedagogical and logistical support. The situation is also made more difficult by students' low English proficiency levels and skills and the reluctance of many university lecturers to switch to English. This is logical and understandable given that most North African university lecturers of scientific subjects have done their university and postgraduate studies in French with very little exposure to English. In fact, Medfouni talks of translanguaging in the university classes where students and teachers interacted in French and Arabic, with more French used by lecturers in some highly ranked departments such as medicine and pharmacy in central universities. In peripheral universities there was more use of Arabic by teachers and students, which is a reflection of their Arabophone background. This was also stated by an earlier study conducted by Seddiki (2015), where observed biology classes revealed a substantial use of Arabic by teachers. English was very rarely used except in occasions when students or lecturers referred to some academic references. Students used Arabic, and a strict French-only medium was not adhered to. There was also a gender difference with females preferring French to English as medium of instruction as French still enjoys a prestigious status. An important implication from Medfouni's research is that currently EMI has a hypothetical status in Algeria and students and teachers' attitudes and their preferences of English are not based on educational realities. Their positive attitudes towards English are aspirational and characterized by unrealistic expectations about the reality of implementing EMI in Algeria. Even French, long established as a de facto medium of instruction for the sciences, does not have exclusive use in the classroom. This raises the issue of language policy and the unavoidability of reconsidering the role of mother tongues in education.

EMI in Libya: Preference for Arabic-English Bilingualism

The linguistic landscape in Libya and its educational system are more straightforward than its three neighbours to the West. The period of the Italian colonization did not last as long as that of the French in Tunisia, Algeria and Morocco. It did not leave a similar linguistic and cultural legacy. Arabic rules supreme in Libya, especially with a national policy in education that has reflected a strong penchant for Arab nationalism for a long time and then a turn to pan-Africanism and a rejection of any form of foreign intervention in Libya, and any form of cultural imperialism. The literature search yielded very few publications on language education and EMI in Libya. In a paper about the quality of higher education in Libya and its challenges, Tamtam et al. (2010, 2011) argue that political nuances and administrative complexities have negatively affected the quality of education at universities. In addition to managerial, structural, logistical, planning, leadership and networking problems, universities have not been working for the employability of their graduates. Undergraduate and graduate programmes are not well linked to the labour market.

In a review of an official document on the objectives and structures of education in Libya, the role of Arabic is clearly emphasized. The educational system aims to maintain Arabic as a language of instruction and a symbol of religious and cultural belonging and identity. There is a mention of the importance of learning a foreign language to communicate with the outside world, but there is also a striking absence of any mention of English, whether as a foreign language or a medium of instruction at the university level.

The same authors, Tamtam et al. (2013), conducted an interesting comparative study between two science and engineering departments in Libya. One uses EMI, while the other uses Arabic as the medium of instruction. In both cases, five teachers from each university were conveniently selected and interviewed. The study's main aim was to investigate faculty members' views about the impact of EMI or Arabic as the medium of instruction (AMI) on the quality of the students' learning experiences in the sciences and engineering. They were also asked about Arabic-English bilingualism as a medium of education. The main findings show that the students in the two cases had some challenges. Those in the EMI departments like using English for reasons such as employment opportunities and global communication, despite their poor performance in English and the difficulties they experience in answering test questions. EMI did affect their overall academic performance, but they were in favour of it. Students in the AMI departments were reported to like learning through Arabic as this does not pose technical and lexical comprehension challenges to them. They did not like studying via English, but they were also aware that AMI restricted their employment opportunities and did not prepare for global communication. Both cases also showed positive attitudes towards learning via Arabic and did prefer a policy of Arabic-English bilingualism to EMI or AMI alone. The students' English proficiency and the cultural context do not prepare them for EMI, and their academic performance at university is very likely to be negatively affected. The study participants called for the introduction of EMI at the secondary and even the primary stages of education for better preparation and transition to EMI university courses.

This study is unique in EMI literature as it offers a direct comparison between two languages of instruction policies. The data would have been more informative and significant had the authors included students from the two universities to learn directly from them about their experiences with EMI and AMI. In North Africa, comparative studies are rare and most likely not feasible because there are practically no universities that use AMI in sciences and engineering departments. Some universities use a bilingual approach in human sciences, such as in psychology, where certain subjects are taught in Arabic while others in French or English.

EMI in Egypt: Preparing at Pre-university Stage

Placing Egypt within Kachru's (1986) outer circle, El-Fiki (2012) makes a strong connection between a need to improve proficiency in English and the country's major objectives of modernization through more vital global contribution, economic and business development, and technical and scientific research. Like in the rest of the North African nations, the premise is that English is key to a more decisive role in the international community. Her multi-method study investigated EFL and English medium subject teachers' (EMS) perceptions of a pedagogical reform introduced by the government. This is mainly characterized by the adoption of a communicative approach to teaching. A unique phenomenon in North Africa is the Egyptian experimental language schools, where the scientific subjects, natural sciences, mathematics and computer skills are taught in English with French being a foreign language. These schools are a clear sign that the country is investing in preparing a large number of Egyptian primary and secondary students for EMI at the higher education stage. The intention is to make the students' transition to EMI departments at universities smooth and free of the common language proficiency challenges met by EMI students in the Arab world. However, experimental language schools are not free of charge like the rest of the government schools where the curriculum is taught in Arabic. Parents pay what seems to be a small fee, but it is not affordable for all

Egyptian families where the standard of living is low, thus creating even more social inequalities. The main findings of El-Fiki's study are centred on the role of contextual factors in shaping the nature and process of change in teachers' practices.

The stress on English as a conduit to Egypt's economic development is discussed by McIlwraith and Fortune (2016), who states that the Ministry of Education is serious about promoting ELT in pre-university education right from the first year of the primary stage. They refer to the *Pre-university Education Reform 2014-2030* and *The National Curriculum Framework for English as a Foreign Language*, which aim to enable children to participate actively in a global society. McIlwraith and Fortune identify a long list of challenges affecting ELT in Egypt, mainly teacher education and the inequity between rural and urban areas. Children from low-income families do not have the means to compete and pay for private tuition in English, and fewer will make it to higher education. Employers complain about the low English proficiency of their Egyptian employees whose teachers were blamed for their low levels. The authors recommend that British Council English courses and supervisor training be part of the Egyptian ELT training plan.

In a literature-based study in the area of ELT, Abdel Latif (2018) provides a thorough analysis of a total of 142 published studies. The corpus of empirical research, which was primarily experimental and quantitative, revealed a focus on the mainstream areas of ELT, such as teacher education and language skills with reading. The data points to the dearth of evidence on published work on EMI. There was no mention of EMI as a separate research topic, and it is possible that any study with an EMI content was considered under the curriculum/programme evaluation category, which represented only 7 per cent of the published research studies. Abdel Latif identifies a clear methodological research gap marked by a strong dominance of the experimental and quantitative trend to research and a stark paucity of interpretive and qualitative studies. These are needed to understand teachers and learners' experiences in the various areas of ELT. In a chapter on English language policy at the pre-university stages in Egypt, Abdel Latif (2017) confirms that despite the number of reforms and changes to the ELT curricula, which were mainly at the level of official and standardized school textbooks, several areas are still in need of improvement. Public schools need to be supported with professional development for English teachers, especially in language skills, if the gap with the private sector is to be reduced. He warns that an impoverished ELT in the public sector will lead to further social inequalities and divisions. Students who can afford private education will continue to benefit from a stronger ELT and have easier access to the job market locally and internationally.

Conclusion

Research and publications on EMI in North Africa are still in an early stage despite a steady increase of attempts to study and investigate the status and future of EMI in this region of the world. The studies and papers reviewed in this chapter represent a broad spectrum of EMI policies and practices. In Libya and especially in Egypt, EMI is more established at the tertiary level than in Tunisia, Algeria and Morocco, where French is the official medium of instruction. This situation is not likely to change soon despite a widespread recognition and consensus that EMI is needed if these nations are to play more substantial roles in international affairs, global economy and scientific research. Political, educational, economic and sociolinguistic considerations will keep EMI at bay for the time being. Although some tertiary institutions are showing interest in EMI (e.g. in Tunisia, there is now a state university with an EMI policy), it will be a long time before we can see a shift to an EMI policy in public education.

References

Abdel Latif, M. A. (2017). English language policy at the pre-university stages in Egypt: Past, present and future directions. In R. Kirkpatrick (Ed.), *English language education policy in the Middle East and North Africa* (pp. 33–45). Cham, Switzerland: Springer.

Abdel Latif, M. A. (2018). English language teaching research in Egypt: Trends and challenges. *Journal of Multilingual and Multicultural Development, 39*(9), 818–829.

Abdlejaouad, M., & Labassi, T. (2020). English as the lingua franca of academic publishing in Tunisia. *World Englishes*,40(2), 1–14.

Arkand, J. L., & Gein, F. (2013). Language in economic development: Is English special and is linguistic fragmentation bad? In E. J. Erling and P. Seargent (Eds.), *English and development: Policy, pedagogy and globalisation* (pp. 243–266). Multilingual Matters.

Badwan, K. (2019). *Exploring the potential of English as a medium of instruction in higher education in Tunisia.* British Council.

Bahloul, M. (2001). English in Carthage or the 'Tenth Crusade'. Retrieved 1 May 2011, from http://www.postcolonialweb.org/poldiscourse/casablanca/bahloul2.html.

Battenburg, J. (1996). English in the Maghreb. *English Today, 48,* 3–12.

Belhiah, H., & Lamallam, M. (2020). Mother tongue medium of instruction in Morocco: Students' and teachers' perceptions. *Journal of Applied Language and Culture Studies, 3,* 91–111.

Boukadi, S. (26 December 2015). Teachers' perceptions about the future of English language learning and teaching in Tunisia after the 2011 revolution. *Arab World English Journal* (AWJE) Theses / Dissertations. ISSN: 2229-9327.

Boukadi, S., & Troudi, S. (2017). English education policy in Tunisia: Issues of language policy in post-revolution Tunisia. In R. Kirkpatrick (Ed.), *English language education policy in the Middle East and North Africa* (pp. 257–278). Springer.

Bourdieu, P. (1991). *Language and symbolic power* (G. Raymond and M. Adamson, trans.). Polity Press.

Cheddadi, A. (2011). Le paysage linguistique marocain entre heritage du passe et exigences du present. The Moroccan linguistic scene between heritage and the exigencies of the present. *Al Madrassa Al Maghribiya, 3*.

Daoud, M. (2001). The linguistic situation in Tunisia: Current issues in language planning. *English for Specific Purposes World, 2*(1), 1–52.

Daoud, M. (2002). Language policy and planning in Tunisia: Accommodating language rivalry. In S. J. Baker (Ed.), *Language policy: Lessons from global models* (pp. 206–224). Monterey Institute of International Studies.

Daoud, M. (2007). The language situation in Tunisia. In R. K. Baldauf (Ed.), *Language planning and policy in Africa* (pp. 256–277). Multilingual Matters.

Dearden, J. (2015). *English as a medium of instruction – A growing global phenomenon*. British Council.

El-Feki, H. (2012). *Teaching English as a foreign language and using English as a medium of instruction in Egypt: Teachers' perceptions of teaching approaches and sources of change* (Unpublished PhD thesis), University of Toronto.

Kachru, B. B. (1986). The power and politics of English. *World Englishes, 5*(2), 121–140.

Labassi, T. (2009). Periphery non-anglophone scholarship in English-only journals: Conditions of a better visibility. *Changing English, 16*, 247–254.

McIlwraith, H., & Fortune, A. (2016). *English language teaching and learning in Egypt: An insight*. British Council.

Medfouni, I. (2020). *International aspirations, French legacies and translingual practices: Exploring the potential implementation of EMI in Algerian universities* (Unpublished PhD thesis), University of Portsmouth.

Miliani, M. (2000). Teaching English in a multilingual context: The Algerian case. *Mediterranean Journal of Educational Studies, 6*(1), 13–29.

Rassol, N. (2013). The political economy of English language and development: English vs national and local languages in developing countries. In E. J. Erling and P. Seargent (Eds.), *English and development: Policy, pedagogy and globalisation* (pp. 45–67). Multilingual Matters.

Sadiqi, F. (1991). The spread of English in Morocco. *International Journal of the Sociology of Language, 87*, 99–114.

Seddiki, Z. (2015). L'enseignement de la biologie en français en contexte plurilingue algérien: Quelles langues? Pour quelles fonctions? [Teaching biology in French in the pluralistic context of Algeria: Which languages? For what functions?]. *Contextes et Didactiques, 6,* 9–18. doi:10.4000/ced.465.

Shahu, K. (2016). The status of English in language policy models proposed for the Moroccan multilingual context. *Arab World English Journal* (December 2016), 20–31.

Tamtam, A., Gallagher, F., Olabi, G. A., & Naher, S. (2010). Implementing English Medium Instruction (EMI) for engineering education in Arab world and twenty first century challenges. International Symposium for Engineering Education. University College Cork, Ireland.

Tamtam, A., Gallagher, F., Olabi, G. A., & Naher, S. (2011). Higher education in Libya: System under stress. *Procedia – Social and Behavioral Sciences, 29,* 742–751.

Tamtam, A., Gallagher, F., Olabi, G. A., & Naher, S. (2013). The impact of language of instruction on quality of science and engineering education in Libya: Qualitative study of faculty members. *European Scientific Journal, 9*(31), 19–36.

Troudi, S. (2009). The effects of English as a medium of instruction on Arabic as a language of science and academia. In P. Wachob (Ed.), *Power in the EFL classroom: Critical pedagogy in the Middle East* (pp. 199–216). Cambridge Scholars Publishing.

Troudi, S., & Jendli, A. (2011). Emirati students' experiences of English as a medium of instruction research. In A. Al-Isaa & L.S.Dahan (Eds.), *Global English and Arabic: Issues of language, culture, and identity* (pp. 23–48). Peter Lang.

8

EMI in Morocco

Attitudes, Merits, Challenges, Strategies, and Implementation

Hassan Belhiah

The Growing Status of English in Morocco

Morocco's first significant encounter with the British can be traced back to the thirteenth century when King John of England requested Sultan Mohamed Ennassir's support against France (Belhiah et al., 2020). Three centuries later, the diplomatic ties culminated in decrees issued by Sultan Abd al-Malik allowing English merchants to engage in commercial activities with their Moroccan counterparts. On the other hand, Morocco's relations with the United States were first established in the eighteenth century when Sultan Sidi Muhammad Ben Abdullah indicated a willingness to forge economic and diplomatic ties with the United States (Belhiah et al., 2020). In 1797, the US consulate was established in Morocco, paving the ground for military and economic relationships, leading up to an amity treaty for fifty years. This agreement was unprecedented as it was the first of its kind between the United States and an Arab, Muslim or African state. In the twentieth century, American military bases were established in Tangier and Kenitra to stall a potential conquest of Morocco by the Axis powers during the Second World War. The need to communicate with American military officers motivated Moroccan clerks and military officers to learn English, and thus English language centres started to flourish.

The status of English in Morocco has grown steadily ever since and so too the demand for English classes. Errihani (2017) identifies seven agents that contribute to the successful promotion of English language teaching and learning in Morocco: (i) the Ministry of Education, (ii) the Moroccan Association of English Teachers (MATE), (iii) the British Council, (iv) the Regional English

Language Office (RELO), (v) the American Language Centers, (vi) AMIDEAST and (vii) private Moroccan English language schools.

ELT promotion and dissemination transpire in various forms, including teacher professional development workshops, teacher participation in regional, national and international ELT conferences, financial and material support from the British Council and RELO, and ESL teaching in language centres.

Belhiah (2020, p. 46) argues that English is the most sought-after major in arts and humanities colleges in Morocco. He identifies several factors that account for students' inclination for English instead of French or Arabic studies at the university:

> positive attitudes toward English, interest in the culture of English-speaking countries, the perception that English will be vital in students' future lives, the importance of English as a high-value commodity, students' interest in reaching out to people worldwide, the perception that English is linguistically easier than French and Arabic, the status of English as a lingua franca, early age acquisition coupled with parental encouragement, effective teaching methods, and students' keen interest in learning foreign languages.

Moroccan secondary school students' attitudes have also been found to be highly favourable towards English. Nifaoui (2021) compared secondary school students' attitudes towards English and French. Her findings show that students are generally more motivated to learn English than French. Although students hold typically favourable attitudes towards French as reflected in their positive views towards French people and francophone communities, English is perceived as more vital, especially in their professional lives and the ideal L2 self. English, rather than French, can potentially enable students to improve their socio-economic status and establish connections with the outside world. These aspects are unrelated to the linguistic features of the English language per se, she explains, but are engendered by the forces of globalization that render English the lingua franca of international business, telecommunications and travel.

Until recently, the government has been promoting French as the first foreign language of the state, thanks to the French government's strong support for Morocco's claim to the Sahara region. However, by recognizing Morocco's sovereignty over the Sahara region in December 2020, the US government has probably laid the foundations for accelerating the growth of English in the country. Needless to say, 'tourism, social media, the internet, science and technology, along with the internationalization of higher education' will also play a crucial role in this growth (Belhiah, 2020, p. 39).

EMI in Morocco

In K-12 state education, Arabic and French are the primary media of instruction. Arabic had been the language of science and math instruction since 1990. However, in the 2019–20 academic year, French became the language of science and math content. There are English-medium schools in the private sector that follow an American or British curriculum in Casablanca, Rabat, Tangier and Marrakesh. These schools cater to the needs of affluent families who prefer their children to be schooled in English rather than French and, thus, act as competitors to the prestigious francophone schools patronized by the French government and the Organisation Internationale de la Francophonie (OIF). The International Baccalaureate (IB), available in English, Spanish and French, was launched in 1968 and is available in nine private schools, only three of which offer instruction through the English medium. Currently, no state school offers the IB in English, whereby the growth of the IB curriculum in Morocco is kept limited. Bunnell (2016) notes that IB programmes generally have a scant presence in North Africa due to French dominance. As Peterson (1987, p. 63) explains: 'As soon as the IB spread to North America, Asia, and Anglophone Africa, the language problem became more difficult.'

The government launched the English Baccalaureate in 2014, in which English instruction was to be allocated more time, and science courses were to be taught through the English medium. However, the programme was destined to flounder since its inception. The British Council was tasked with developing it and overseeing its implementation as an initial step in three high schools in Rabat, Casablanca and Tangier. However, since the British Council had neither full-time staff nor a reputable task force based in the country, it lacked deep knowledge of the Moroccan educational system, its values and its vagaries. Instead, it relied primarily on what Alderson and Scott (1992) call 'JIJOESs' (Jet In Jet Out Experts) flown from the UK. Moroccan education experts and applied linguists were not at the forefront of this initiative. Their views were only solicited as commentary on the manuscripts prepared by the British Council and its foreign experts.

The English Baccalaureate programme failed to fulfil its promise due to several factors. First, the instructors did not receive adequate training in EMI pedagogy. They were selected voluntarily, and many of them did not master English and could not teach in English. Second, the instructors had to use the same syllabi developed for the Arabic and French curricula. Third, there were no textbooks in English, and the instructors had to translate the existing Arabic and French ones.

Fourth, students and instructors lacked additional resources, whereby they had to navigate the English curriculum and its intricacies on their own. Finally, upon graduating, some outstanding students were denied admission to some university majors under the pretext that they lacked a demonstrable mastery of French as they had studied subject content in English. Therefore, it is hardly surprising that the English Baccalaureate was suspended three years after it had been launched.

In higher education, while most public institutions teach through the Arabic and French mediums, there is a growing trend to teach science and engineering courses in English due to the demand to publish in international journals and, thus, increase universities' ranking. Furthermore, the number of private universities offering partial or complete instruction through the English medium has been growing steadily. These include Al-Akhawayn University in Ifrane, International Institute for Higher Education in Rabat, Private International Institute of Management and Technology in Rabat and Casablanca, and the International University of Rabat. One British and one American university also offer degree and/or semester abroad programmes, namely the University of Sunderland and Cardiff Metropolitan University in Casablanca, Rabat and Tangier, and the University of New England in Tangier. In the next academic year, Morocco plans to supplant the current European three-year degree, known as licence, with an American-inspired four-year bachelor's degree. This change is viewed as an opportunity to prepare Moroccans for the demands of the global economy, where English serves as a lingua franca. This new programme would seek to equip students with the necessary soft skills to succeed in the job market and enable them to learn foreign languages effectively and master information technology. It is worth noting that the USAID is closely involved in the design of the new programme; the foundation year's curriculum has been developed by the USAID Morocco Career Center (CC) and will be implemented throughout universities in Morocco. English as a language of higher education will most likely be boosted if the plan is implemented as new entrants will take English classes, irrespective of their major. They will also study one or more courses in their major in English. In the long run, many of these BA graduates will pursue MA or PhD degrees in EMI contexts overseas, not necessarily in a Western European country, and will be able to teach subject content in English as they return to their homeland. These developments will significantly contribute to the expansion of EMI in the country.

To date, only two studies have examined the phenomenon of EMI in Morocco empirically, both focusing on university students' and instructors' attitudes and perceptions. Belhiah and Abdellatif (2016) investigated science and engineering doctoral students' attitudes and perceptions of the role of English in higher education based on a sample of 208 students. Their findings showed that English is perceived as a vital language due to its pivotal role in conducting scientific research, pursuing graduate studies overseas, and ensuring better employment opportunities. English is seen as fundamental to improving both the quality of scientific research and students' overall educational experience. Therefore, most students consented to the need to mandate EMI in schools of science and engineering, where French is currently in use as the language of instruction. Nadri and Haoucha (2020) studied instructors' perceptions and attitudes towards EMI in one Moroccan university. Overall, while participants in their study conveyed positive attitudes towards EMI, they also expressed an ambivalent stance concerning its implementation, mainly attributable to the absence of programmes that provide either pre-service or in-service training in EMI pedagogy. The study recommended developing 'frameworks of pedagogical standards for training university teachers to ensure that they are prepared for new challenges facing them in an EMI context' (91).

This Study

The present study seeks to broaden our understanding of the growing role of EMI in Morocco by exploring the merits, challenges, strategies and implementation issues related to the EMI policy in Moroccan secondary and tertiary education. The data come from interviews with high school and university students, lecturers and administrators. The study is motivated by the following questions:

1. What are students' and teachers' attitudes towards EMI?
2. What are the perceived merits (advantages and benefits) of EMI?
3. What are its disadvantages and challenges?
4. Which learning and teaching strategies are employed to address language and subject-related issues?
5. How can the EMI policy be implemented effectively in Morocco?

Method and Procedures

Context and Participants

Eighty-four respondents affiliated with two high schools and three universities offering courses taught in English participated in this study: sixty-eight students, twelve professors and four administrators. All the participants were Moroccan nationals. Students submitted their answers anonymously, while the professors and administrators provided their email addresses for follow-up questions or requests for clarification.

Instrument

Interviews are among the most commonly used instruments in qualitative research because they can help obtain 'in-depth responses about people's experiences, perceptions, opinions, feelings, and knowledge'. In such cases, the data 'consists of verbatim quotations and sufficient content/context to be interpretable' (Patton, 2002, p. 4). Three interview questionnaires were developed and emailed to the participating students, professors and administrators. They were first disseminated among two colleagues, both applied linguists, and revisions were made based on their feedback to validate the instruments.

The respondents could choose to provide their answers in English, French or Arabic. All but four respondents wrote their responses in English. Follow-up discussions were carried out with three professors and one administrator focusing on aspects of the interview that needed further elaboration.

Data Collection

The study was conducted over three months (October 2020–December 2020). The email interview form was filled out electronically. The respondents were informed that they were participating in a research project and that their answers, school affiliation and identity would remain confidential. They were also told that their participation was voluntary and that they were free to discontinue their participation.

Findings

Student Interviews

Attitudes towards EMI

Students' attitudes towards EMI are highly positive. Some students reported that English seems to be a straightforward language and that its grammar is relatively easier than French grammar. Others explained that they are excited about starting to learn through the English medium since they had always studied in French, and it was time for a new language:

> I feel great when I study in English. Its sentences are straight to the point.
>
> I like and prefer learning subjects in English because it is much simpler than French.
>
> I feel good because I have always wanted to improve my English.
>
> I prefer learning subject content in English because I've always done it in French and I think that changing the language motivates me to study more.

Students also expressed positive feelings about their classroom experience. They indicated that they felt confident, accomplished, skilled, proud and content. No feelings of anxiety, strain or low self-esteem were voiced:

> Accomplished, I feel that I am actually doing a great job as a student of EMI-based courses.
>
> I'll consider myself as self-confident because really I am, I love what I'm doing and I'm supported by my surroundings, friends, classmates, family.
>
> In EMI classes, I always feel skilled because each time I learn new knowledge and discoveries allow me to develop easily.
>
> Accomplished, and certainly proud as I believe the fact that I am fluent in English boosts my confidence in learning.

Basic Advantages and Disadvantages of EMI

Two basic advantages of EMI were elicited. First, EMI is viewed as a means to access the world, due to the role of English as an international lingua franca and its dominant status as a language of science and technology. Second, EMI is considered an effective strategy for the acquisition of English while studying subject content:

> English is more international. Moreover, for my major, computer science, English is an absolute must.
>
> Advantage is that a lot of research and resources are available in English.
>
> One advantage is you open to the global world.
>
> The key advantage of using English as a medium of instruction is: improved access to English materials as well as better curricula.

As for the major disadvantages, the students pointed out that mastering the requisite academic skills for the university was time-consuming despite their adequate oral English skills. They also stated that not everybody in Morocco is fluent enough to study (and teach) through the English medium, which might dissuade students from enrolling in EMI schools. Finally, some students warned that EMI restricts their use of other spoken languages in Morocco, including their mother tongues, since English is mandated as the sole language of instruction:

> A disadvantage will be that a lot more kids will become discouraged to go to school since they aren't able to understand the language better.
>
> Disadvantages include coming short in communicating with my native language.
>
> I think one of the hurdles of EMI is the difference in language proficiency among students.
>
> The most disadvantage is that sometimes I find it hard to express myself in English when I write a paper or in the exam since I've always been taught in French, so I always have to translate my ideas from French to English.

EMI Benefits and Challenges

A range of perceived benefits of mastering English was reported. When asked about how EMI affects their improvement in English language skills (positively or negatively), all students stated that the effect was positive. They mentioned a range of positive outcomes that pertain to all the four language skills, namely reading, writing, speaking and listening:

> Positive of course. I get stronger at written and spoken English every day.
>
> EMI had a positive impact on improving my English language skills as it allowed me to enrich my current and familiar vocabulary, train my ear and improve my pronunciation while also allowing me to train my listening and my degrees of understanding.
>
> EMI improves my English language skills in a positive way as I tend to read, write and communicate more with professors and students with English.
>
> Since the learning system will change into an English one, students will have the chance to attain more knowledge and vocabulary, which will definitely improve their English level in a positive way.

When queried about the effects of EMI on their improvement in business or engineering content knowledge, the majority affirmed that EMI positively impacted their learning. Specifically, they stated that EMI had helped them feel more comfortable speaking and writing about issues related to their field inside and outside the classroom. They also reported that they could now read online content about business and engineering, which can further expand their knowledge of the subject matter:

> EMI has helped me in computer science: most forums, documentation, websites, courses, discussions, and job descriptions are in English or require good English.
>
> EMI positively affected my improvement in knowledge of business or technical content because nowadays by making it possible to communicate almost everywhere on the planet. Also, with new technology, most websites, applications and machines are in English.
>
> Without fluency in English, we, IT engineering students may find it difficult to understand the concept being conveyed by the authors. Also, many modules in IT engineering require writing academic reports. So, a good fluency in English language is necessary. Hence, EMI affects our content knowledge positively.

Also, EMI was seen as creating opportunities for communicating with various people and learning about their cultures. They explained that EMI enabled them to appreciate different perceptions of the world, as well as become adept at conveying and processing verbal and non-verbal messages in the target language.

> EMI will open a lot opportunities for me to communicate with other culturally different students that are also studying in English. It will be a unique chance for me to get to know different cultures and civilizations.
>
> English makes things easier and I can communicate with foreigners easily, understand their gestures and body language, and exchange knowledge about our culture and theirs.
>
> EMI makes you contact foreign people using their language and slang. It helps you understand them and how they see matters from their perspective better.

A third benefit is instrumental and pertinent to the impact of EMI on students' future careers. EMI is seen as being conducive to students' employment in either Morocco or abroad. Students reported that locally, some companies prefer applicants who are bilingual in English and French. Students also see EMI as essential for overseas employment since English is the international language of commerce and business. Others pointed out that they are entertaining the possibility of pursuing their graduate studies abroad, and EMI avails them of a broader range of options that they would have otherwise been deprived of had they studied exclusively through the French medium:

> EMI will open a whole new world of opportunities for me when it comes to my future career, it will help me to obtain jobs in the most well-known companies around the world and not only inside their country.
>
> I will pursue a Master's (and maybe even a PhD) and there's no question they will both be in English. My English-based Bachelor will lay the foundation of that.

> More imminently, I am pursuing internships and jobs in well-known English based companies, so I need it to communicate with people in the field.
>
> In the professional world, knowing how to speak English is no longer an option or a privilege. It has become essential for everyone to know at least how to read and write in English. With the expansion of international business and the globalization of culture, English has become increasingly present in non-English speaking countries.

Concerning the challenges, students indicated two areas that they struggled with the most. First, some freshmen explained that they had to switch rather quickly from an Arabic/French medium to EMI, which was not straightforward considering their limited exposure to English in high school. Second, several students expressed their concern over instructors' limited proficiency in English, which stands in direct opposition to EMI's rationale for improving students' English proficiency through effective instruction via the English medium:

> The most challenging aspect of EMI is communication because sometimes it is hard to express my ideas when speaking in class or writing.
>
> I think the most challenging aspect of EMI is that it is very hard to find a lot of English-speaking teachers in some countries where the vast majority does not speak English, nor understand it.
>
> One of my teachers makes a lot of mistakes and she gets angry when we tell her that.

Learning Strategies

Students identified three learning strategies to enhance their grasp of the subject content delivered in English. First, some students explained that they translate presentation slides into French, usually during lectures, to be sure that they understand the lessons. Second, some students use YouTube videos, in either French or English, that elaborate on the concepts discussed in class. Finally, three students stated that they are being tutored, in either English or the subject content:

> I summarize more and use google translation with ppt slides.
>
> Since all subjects are meant to be taught in English, I meet a tutor every week for two hours and she helps me improve my English in order to get good marks in the exams.
>
> There are many video lectures and examples in youtube that help me understand what I studied in class better.

Language of Instruction Preference

All students indicated their desire to continue studying through the English medium because, according to them, it is a lingua franca and is considered the international language of business, commerce and science. However, some students stated that alongside English, they would like to be taught in French or Spanish on account of their importance in the Moroccan linguistic marketplace and also in Chinese because of China's growing role in global trade:

> I would prefer to study subject content in English because it is one of the most used languages in the world. It is also the primary language of business as well as sciences.
>
> For the content of the subjects, I prefer it to be in English and French or Spanish because these two languages are universal and open, and important for our country. I prefer English as it's easy. I would like to get into Chinese later but it seems much harder than all other languages.
>
> Since I'm studying business, I think Chinese would be a great option.

Faculty Interviews

Attitudes towards EMI

All instructors expressed enjoyment and contentment with the delivery of subject content in English. They felt this way partly because their previous education had been in English, and they were confident in their ability to express themselves in this language in front of students. In addition, some instructors had been undergraduate students in English-medium programmes in Morocco, while others had pursued their postgraduate studies in an English-speaking country.

> I feel great teaching in English. I was mostly educated in English and it is natural for me to teach in English.
>
> I love it because I express my ideas better in this language.
>
> Enjoyable! All my grad studies were in English so the language I am most comfortable teaching in is English.
>
> It is my comfort zone and I feel very creative. I am very proud and I thank dad who insisted so much on me getting an English education.

Primary Advantages and Disadvantages of EMI

One of the primary advantages of EMI identified by professors was ease. Respondents reported that English is an easy language that allows them to express themselves with a high degree of clarity and accuracy by focusing more on content and less on form. EMI instruction, in their view, also provides the opportunity to access a wide selection of research materials and resources since English is the dominant language of science and technology:

> Simple language; focus on content rather than form; most relevant research is conducted in English.
>
> Easy to convey your message in a concise manner; international language hence very diverse audience.
>
> Students acquire the knowledge in English. Most research is done in English.
>
> International language, availability of research material, accessibility of information.

On the flip side, the respondents underlined two significant difficulties. First, students who have not benefited from EMI instruction in secondary education are at a disadvantage: their low level of English proficiency impedes effective communication and mastery of subject content. Second, French is viewed as more impactful in terms of employment prospects. French continues to be the de facto official language of crucial employment sectors in Morocco, such as administration, business and banking. English, in this regard, is considered an asset only insofar as a mastery of French has already been ensured:

> Freshmen are not ready to communicate and study in the English language.
>
> Many students are in their early stages of learning and lack fluency in English.
>
> The employment market in Morocco is limited for the English speakers if they don't master French.
>
> French is still very important in business in Morocco.

Benefits and Challenges of EMI

One of the primary benefits of EMI elicited in the interviews is that it enhances the ability to communicate with others who speak neither Arabic nor French. In other words, English mastery is a tool for cross-cultural and international communication. In turn, it also increases instructors' value in the global job market and allows them to hone their skills regularly so that they always have an edge:

> English is the universal language (i.e., number one international language). Tools to translate are widely available (books and internet).
>
> EMI is an opportunity to deliver to a multicultural audience.

Great tool for communication with diverse people. EMI brings all people of the world closer and allows all to get to know each other rapidly.

Mastering English allows our youth to compete internationally for those key jobs. English allows candidates to upskill, reskill and learn new ones easily.

A frequently shared view among the participants was that EMI brings benefits to their professional careers. For example, professors become equipped with the necessary tools to publish their research findings in prestigious international journals and, thus, win academic recognition and increase chances for promotion. In some other cases, their ability to freely communicate in English makes them internationally more attractive for consultancy schemes with NGOs and other universities:

I teach and conduct research in English at an international level. English is a must in my case.

More opportunities and clients. I provide consultancies internationally.

Opening up doors to many opportunities with other universities all over the world

Accessibility to information, my services are in high demand especially when there are more students wanting to learn more and more subject matters. Promotion to higher positions.

Concerning the challenges, participants were asked whether it was language or subject-related issues that required a more strenuous effort on students' part. Professors indicated that the difficulties with mastering the subject matter could be ascribed to both language- and subject-related issues. Since only a few K-12 institutions offer EMI, it was natural that students should encounter language challenges upon being submerged into an EMI context. Often, difficulties become paramount in writing and can harm students' performance. According to the respondents, some students also face problems with subject content even after taking ESL courses at the language centre. Even after these courses, some students are still not ready for their chosen field of study:

Most students (especially in Morocco) do not have a good command of the English language.

Writing in particular can be very challenging. Most students have issues with that and therefore making evaluation is difficult.

In the context of Morocco, students do not master the language and do not usually have the technical background.

Since students go through a language center prior to business courses, I would rather say that subject-related issues would be more challenging.

Teaching Strategies

Professors have reported several teaching strategies to mitigate language and subject-related difficulties encountered in the classroom. For example, some professors alternate between French and English during the freshman year since not all students possess adequate proficiency in English. Others provide additional tools to supplement their lectures, such as podcasts and video links, which students might find more appealing than textbooks. One business professor explained that she dwells less on theory and devotes more time to case studies since they result in a higher sense of engagement:

> I switch between French and English when necessary especially with freshmen students, but I encourage students to communicate as much as they can in English.
>
> I use the technological tools available like podcasts.
>
> I find interesting videos about the concepts and issues we discussed and post them on the university digital platform.
>
> I focus less time on theory and more on case studies since students like them more.

Language of Instruction Preference

Nine out of ten professors indicated that English is their preferred language of instruction. First, this is because they were educated through the English medium in their undergraduate or graduate programmes. Second, more teaching materials and resources are available in English than French or Arabic. While one professor explained that he would prefer to teach in French since he obtained his doctorate from France, for another one, English would be his first choice, followed by French. Interestingly, none of the respondents indicated a preference for Arabic, not even as a second or third choice, despite its status as the primary language of schooling and literacy in K-12 education.

> English because I was educated in English and feel at ease.
>
> English because we have many materials to choose from unlike French or Arabic.
>
> English then French but would find it challenging to teach in Arabic.
>
> Materials in my field are mostly in English.

Administrator Interviews

Fundamental Advantages and Disadvantages of EMI

The two administrators interviewed identified no fundamental disadvantages linked to EMI. Inversely, three advantages were reported. First, EMI provides students with the opportunity to read primary sources and first-hand materials in their original form. Second, students can avail themselves of a bigger pool of case studies, especially in business and computer science. Third, EMI permits exposure to an extensive array of research and scientific publications, particularly in science and technology.

> EMI allows the usage of sources in their original language and the abundance of case studies (business and computer science fields).
>
> Advantage: Research options are limitless and much more updated than French ones.
>
> English is the world's language of science and not of just one country; it allows freedom of barriers.

Benefits and Challenges of EMI

The two respondents explained that EMI represents clear benefits for the students' capabilities to communicate with others. As a result, they are likely to become more sensitive, tolerant and open-minded towards people with different backgrounds. The respondents also indicated that EMI is beneficial to students' careers since it enables them to gain access to a bigger segment of the international job market and increases their chances for professional mobility.

> As English is a universal language, using it will help students communicate easier and connect better whether in-class or online (from different countries).
>
> There are no more barriers of language. Students are left with an open mind toward cultures.
>
> EMI opens up doors to international employment and professional mobility because it gives students the power to adapt (language-wise) to any environment.

As for the challenges, it was reported that Moroccan faculty who master English are not always available, which has prompted them to recruit internationally. However, they prefer Moroccan nationals since hiring expatriates is not financially viable. This leaves them with little choice but to hire local instructors despite their limited English proficiency. The interviewees also pointed the linguistic deficiencies of incoming students, who need to improve their academic skills in English in order to guarantee a successful and enjoyable college experience.

> It's hard to find instructors of technical subjects that master the English language.
>
> One challenge for teachers is having the same level of English proficiency as their students.
>
> In Morocco, a big portion of students have a beginner level of English so it takes more work to prepare them to study in English.
>
> Writing professionally and academically seem to be the hardest part as many students learn to speak English only.

Strategies to Ease Students' Transition into EMI

The interviewees explained that their institutions have English support schemes for incoming students to help the applicants meet the academic requirements and enrol despite their language deficiencies. In one school, free tutoring and ESL courses are offered each semester to students who are willing to improve their English. Students can take full-time ESL courses for up to one year before taking classes for credit in one university. ESL courses are delivered at the language centre, which has full-time tenured faculty. The same university has a writing centre that caters to students' writing needs and helps them edit, revise and proofread texts. However, none of the three administrators reported the existence of programmes to improve the faculty's English skills.

> We offer intensive language sessions (in-class and online).
>
> We provide tutoring to raise students' English level.
>
> We have a language center where students can study English full time during their first semester at the university.
>
> We have a great writing center that is popular among students.

Summary and Discussion

Like many studies carried out on other polities, this study has demonstrated that students and instructors alike generally hold positive attitudes towards EMI (e.g. Al-Masheikhi et al., 2014; Dearden and Macaro, 2016; Yeh, 2014). Common sense would suggest that students should have had feelings of apprehension, anxiety or low self-esteem towards EMI since most had not been taught in English previously. Instead, EMI was viewed as a welcome policy among the students, and English was considered an easier language to use than French. By the same token, professors, most of whom had studied in English in their undergraduate and graduate years, expressed feelings of confidence, contentment and enjoyment towards EMI. The study has also identified several merits of EMI. For example, it enables students to improve their English language skills and access a wide array of online learning and study resources, increases their readiness to pursue graduate studies abroad, maximizes their employment opportunities and boosts their cross-cultural competence. Additionally, EMI avails professors of the opportunity to access cutting-edge research in their disciplines and publish in international journals, potentially leading to academic recognition and promotion. EMI also boosts their careers in the global market as they increase their cross-cultural and international communicative skills in English. These findings are in line with previous research (e.g. Dang et al., 2013; Hamid et al., 2013) that had highlighted the role of globalization in the dissemination of EMI and the strengthening of one's English-speaking capabilities.

Perceiving EMI in a positive light and recognizing its beneficial effects on one's personal development and socio-economic status are one thing, while EMI effectiveness and implementation as a policy are another. Several challenges to effective EMI implementation have been reported: students' low-level academic skills, a limited pool of qualified English-speaking instructors, lack of training in EMI pedagogy, inadequate teacher support, dwindling enrolment due to lack of proficiency in English and the ascendancy of French in the Moroccan linguistic marketplace. These problems combined can force parents to opt for French-medium schools and colleges, mainly because their children are already proficient in the language and will have better job prospects since French remains the dominant language of business and commerce in Morocco.

Hence, universities have adopted several learning and teaching strategies and measures to offset the language- and subject-related difficulties. For example, they have translated course materials from English into French, offered individualized tutoring paid for by students or their parents, used instructional videos available on the Web, alternated between English and French, provided students with supplementals, such as video links and podcast, and created support centres and programmes (e.g. language centres, peer mentoring and tutoring programmes, and writing centres).

Conclusion

This chapter has sought to shed light upon the EMI phenomenon in Morocco. Since independence, Arabic and French have been the two mediums of instruction in public education in the kingdom. However, EMI will be making inroads into public education as the country is becoming more aware of the role of this language as a lingua franca and the main language of science and technology. A case in point is the plan to revert from the current European three-year degree, known as licence, to an American-inspired four-year bachelor's degree. This reform has been spearheaded by the USAID and, if implemented, will likely see English play a pivotal role in the education and training of newcomers. It is envisioned to offer more English instruction and promote the study of subject content in this language.

This study has also found that EMI is viewed positively by both students and instructors. Despite some language and content-related difficulties, EMI is associated with feelings of enjoyment, contentment, achievement and self-fulfilment. It is perceived as a desirable commodity. EMI avails students of the opportunity to improve their English proficiency, pursue studies overseas, enhance employment prospects and facilitate cross-cultural competence. For instructors, EMI gives them an edge compared to their francophone counterparts. They gain access to more recent research and teaching materials, obtain more recognition for their research and acquire more opportunities for international consultancies and professional mobility.

These signs bode well for the future of EMI in Morocco. Nonetheless, EMI implementation will hit a snag without adequate planning, and schools will fail to realize the expectations. If history is any guide, French and Arabic-medium instruction has not led to equipping students with adequate linguistic and literacy skills, as demonstrated by the 2018 report on the Program for International Student Assessment (PISA). Morocco was ranked 75th out of 79 countries in reading, mathematics and science (https://www.oecd.org/pisa/publications/pisa-2018-results.htm). In other words, the issue is not only linguistic; it also relates to the extent to which all the necessary conditions are available to turn any language education policy into success. Failing to plan effectively will throw the education system into another quagmire in which Arabic, French and English are being used without a well-defined, long-term purpose or vision: English may be used as a medium of instruction one year, as a first or foreign language another, only to be abandoned a year later and replaced with French, therefore going back to square one. Developing a clear, long-term vision and committing to it is a must.

This study recommends the following practices for the effective development and implementation of an EMI policy. First, the policy development should be undertaken by a committee composed of local linguists and language policy experts, who have an intimate and acute understanding of the sociolinguistic situation in the country. This committee should steer clear of ideological and political motivations by focusing primordially on how EMI can be integrated into the Moroccan education system while preserving the country's indigenous and national languages. EMI should be viewed not as an adversary to the existing languages but as an asset that can enrich the educational environment and sociolinguistic landscape if implemented effectively. Pedagogical and educational concerns should take precedence over political fervour and ideological indoctrination. Second, adequate teacher training is necessary. Most of the instructors, especially in science and engineering, have been educated in Europe or Morocco through the French medium; hence, it will not be easy to convince them to switch to EMI overnight. There is nothing more embarrassing to an EMI instructor than seeing a student emit a condescending sneer or giggle in response to what is perceived as fragmented English. Instructors should be empowered by providing them with pre-service and in-service training in English and EMI methodology.

In like manner, students ought to have at their disposal all the necessary resources to overcome the language barrier. The necessary support can be in the form of a language centre that offers courses in reading, writing, speaking and listening, and/or English for Specific Purposes (ESP); a tutoring programme in which new students are paired with senior ones as EMI coaches; and a writing centre that caters to students' writing needs. Another support strategy that could benefit the students is hiring instructors fluent in students' mother tongues to involve the vernacular whenever necessary and, thus, assuage language and subject-related difficulties. If and when these resources are made available, students will likely be disinclined to abandon the EMI programme, which will, in turn, enhance student success and boost retention rates, paving the ground for an effective implementation of the EMI policy.

References

Al-Masheikhi, F., Al-Mahrooqi, R., & Denman, C. J. (2014). Investigating college of science student attitudes towards using English as a medium of instruction. *The 2014 WEI International Academic Conference Proceedings*, New Orleans.

Alderson, J. C., & Scott, M. (1992). Insiders, outsiders and participatory evaluation. In J. C. Alderson, & A. Beretta (Eds.), *Evaluating second language education* (pp. 78–139). Cambridge: Cambridge University Press.

Belhiah, H. (2020). English as a global language in Morocco: A qualitative study of students' motivations for studying English. In H. Belhiah, I. Zeddari, N. Amrous, J. Bahmad, & N. Bejjit (Eds.), *English language teaching in Moroccan higher education* (pp. 33–48). Singapore: Springer.

Belhiah, H., & Abdellatif, A. (2016). English as a medium of instruction in Moroccan higher education. *Arab World English Journal, 7*(3): 227–238.

Belhiah, H., Bejjit, N., Bahmad, J., Zeddari, I., & Amrous, N. (2020). English language teaching in Moroccan higher education: An introduction. In H. Belhiah, I. Zeddari, N. Amrous, J. Bahmad, & N. Bejjit (Eds.), *English language teaching in Moroccan higher education* (pp. 1–10). Singapore: Springer.

Bunnell, T. (2016). The dearth of International Baccalaureate schools across Africa. *Africa Education Review, 13*(2), 181–195.

Dang, T. K. A., Nguyen, H. T. M., & Le, T. T. T. (2013). The impacts of globalisation on EFL teacher education through English as a medium of instruction: An example from Vietnam. *Current Issues in Language Planning, 14*(1), 52–72.

Dearden, J., & Macaro, E. (2016). Higher education teachers' attitudes towards English medium instruction: A three-country comparison. *Studies in Second Language Learning and Teaching, 6*(3), 455–486.

Errihani, M. (2017). English education policy and practice in Morocco. In R. Kirkpatrick (Ed.), *English language education policy in the Middle East and North Africa* (pp. 115–131). Berlin, Basel: Springer.

Hamid, M. O., Nguyen, H. T. M., & Baldauf Jr R. B. (2013). Medium of instruction in Asia: Context, processes and outcomes. *Current Issues in Language Planning, 14*(1), 1–15.

Nadri, Y., & Haoucha, M. (2020). University teachers' perspectives on adopting EMI in Morocco. In H. Belhiah, I. Zeddari, N. Amrous, J. Bahmad, & N. Bejjit (Eds.), *English language teaching in Moroccan higher education* (pp. 83–93). Singapore: Springer.

Nifaoui, A. (2021). Le Statut du Français au Maroc Face à l'Hégémonie de l'Anglais: Attitudes des Apprenants envers le Français et l'Anglais. *Journal of Applied Language and Culture Studies, 4,* 121–142.

The Organisation for Economic Co-operation and Development (OECD) (2018). PISA 2018 results. Retrieved 10 February 2021, from https://www.oecd.org/pisa/publications/pisa-2018-results.htm.

Patton, M. Q. (2002), *Qualitative research and evaluation methods*. Thousand Oaks: Sage Publications Ltd.

Peterson, A. (1987), *Schools across frontiers: The story of the International Baccalaureate and the United World Colleges*. Chicago: Open Court.

Yeh, C. C. (2014). Taiwanese students' experiences and attitudes towards English-medium courses in tertiary education. *RELC Journal, 45*(3): 305–319.

EMI in Sudanese Higher Education

Opportunities and Challenges

Awad Alhassan

Introduction

English has been increasingly used as a language of instruction in many higher education institutions (HEIs) globally, with a growing number in the EMI programmes of study being offered in various disciplines of knowledge. The much-cited driving forces for EMI in higher education include, among others, internationalization of higher education, staff and students' mobility, improvement of the university visibility and rankings (Drljača Margić & Vodopija-Krstanović, 2018; Wächter & Maiworm, 2014). However, the increase in EMI adoption in ESL/EFL higher education contexts often seems to be decided as a top-down policy without adequate consultation with the main stakeholders. This situation appears to have created a range of implementation challenges, including but not limited to the linguistic and pedagogical challenges for both students and content teachers (see, e.g., Albakri, 2017; Alhassan et al., 2021; Airey & Linder, 2006; Chang, 2010; Holi, 2020; Zacharias, 2013). Sudanese HEIs are not an exception to such an expansion in EMI and the associated opportunities and challenges. The overarching objective of this chapter is to investigate the views and perceptions of Sudanese EMI stakeholders, namely, EMI content teachers, concerning EMI benefits and challenges in Sudanese HEIs with the view to informing EMI policy and pedagogy in Sudan. The significance of the study reported in this chapter stems from the fact that EMI research in Sudan is very scarce, and to the best of my knowledge, this study is the first of its kind in the context set out to specifically investigate EMI in Sudanese HEIs from the perspectives of the key stakeholders. Therefore, the findings and insights gained from the study can indeed better inform EMI policy and pedagogy in the context and beyond. They can also open up more research avenues by motivating applied linguistics researchers and practitioners to engage in more EMI empirical studies in Sudan.

Context

The Republic of Sudan (henceforth Sudan) is an African sub-Saharan country situated in the north-east of Africa and bordered by nine countries (Ethiopia and Eritrea in the east, Kenya in the south-east, Uganda in the south, Egypt in the north, Libya in the north-west, Chad and the Central African Republic in the west, and the Democratic Republic of the Congo in the south-west). According to the last census conducted in 2010, Sudan's population was estimated at 39 million-plus, including South Sudan (8.26 million, about 21 per cent of the total population). Before South Sudan became a separate state in July 2011, Sudan was by far the largest country in Africa and the Arab world, with an area of one million square miles (about 2.5 million square kilometres). Historically, Sudan was subject to British colonization from 1899 to 1956. Being an Afro-Arab country, after independence, Sudan joined both the Arab League and the African Unity Organisation (currently the African Union). Sudan is home to a sizeable linguistic diversity, with 134 living languages listed (UNESCO, 2008). Standard Arabic is the official language in the country, and English is the second official language.

Educational System in Sudan

The Sudanese educational system is composed of both pre-university and university education. The current structure of the pre-university educational system is generally divided into three levels: the pre-school/kindergarten level, which begins at the age of four and lasts two years; the primary or basic educational level, which begins at the age of six and lasts eight years; and the secondary educational level, which is generally divided into two types: academic and technical or vocational education. The former starts at the age of thirteen or fourteen and extends for three years, after which pupils sit for the Sudanese Secondary School National Examinations (academic track), which qualify them for admission into higher education institutions. The latter also lasts for three years, at the end of which pupils sit for the same examinations (vocational track) to qualify for admission into a technical/vocational higher education institution or leave school to join the labour market with a secondary vocational qualification. Arabic is predominantly used as the main medium of instruction and assessment during all these stages of pre-university education, and English is only taught as a subject starting from grade six of the basic educational level. University education has four types of higher education institutions in Sudan: state universities, private and native universities, private[1] and public colleges and institutes, and state technical colleges. These institutions represent both academic and technical types of education in Sudan. In the 2020 academic year, there was a total of 39 public and 106 native/private HEIs in Sudan (http://daleel.admission.gov.sd/). These institutions are generally overseen by the Sudan Ministry of Higher Education and Scientific Research. The qualifying criterion for admissions into all these types of higher education institutions is the Sudanese Secondary School National Examinations taken at the end of both academic and vocational secondary education. Like the case with pre-university education, the medium of instruction in most of these HEIs is predominantly Arabic on both undergraduate and postgraduate programmes of study.

An Historical Sketch of EMI in Sudanese Higher Education

English is a foreign language in Sudan, but it is used as a second official language after Arabic in the official transactions of governmental institutions. It is also taught as a subject in schools and universities and is used in some higher education institutions as the medium of instruction and assessment. English was somewhat used as the medium of instruction in the leading Sudanese higher education institutions, particularly in Khartoum University, the country's oldest university. In 1990, some ideologically driven policies of '*Arabicization*'[2] were introduced whereby Arabic replaced English as a medium of instruction in higher education. These policies stipulated that the higher education curricula must be taught and/or translated into Arabic, and Arabic must be used as a medium of instruction and assessment instead of English in all undergraduate and postgraduate programmes in higher education institutions. However, English seemed to have survived and has remained the medium of instruction and assessment in several postgraduate programmes in some Sudanese HE institutions, particularly in STEM areas (Pitia, 2003). The proponents of Arabicization policies believe that Arabic as a medium of instruction in HE would ensure easy learning and understanding since it is the students' first language. On the other hand, the opponents of the policies, however, argue that Arabic instead of English would undermine the employability and mobility of Sudanese graduates in both national and international labour markets (Braima, 2004). Moreover, students themselves reportedly wish to study in English because they believe this would make them more competitive in foreign/multinational labour markets (Alhassan, 2019; Dafallah, 2007).

Research on the use of English as a medium of instruction in Sudanese higher education is scarce, and the existing body of the research trend seems to predominately focus on researching English as a subject taught to university students as a university requirement or as common core EAP language support programmes (e.g. Braima, 2004; Fathaleem, 2016; Hashim, 2010; Yassin, 1999). Although these studies supposedly treated the provision of English in HE as ESP/EAP, English, however, does not seem to have had a specific academic purpose, nor is it realistically associated with straightforward and fully fledged EMI programmes. This is because EMI itself is not well-grounded in Sudanese HE. Its use has only been sporadic in some programmes, especially in medicine and some STEM fields, and some postgraduate programmes in humanities and social sciences in a few universities. EMI seems to be patchy and is adopted without clear guiding policies. However, educators have expressed their desire and aspiration for the systematic and steady expansion in EMI. They believe that the ideologically and politically driven Arabicization policies of higher education have failed. In fact, these policies have been rather detrimental for both teachers and students.

Language Support for EMI in Sudan

The provision of fully fledged EAP programmes, specifically designed and intended for student support in EMI programmes in Sudanese HE institutions does not seem to be established yet. The history of ESP/EAP in Sudan can be traced back to the early 1970s. At the time, the first English language servicing unit (ELSU) was established at the University of Khartoum to help students cope with their English-medium university programmes (Swales, 2009). However, with the introduction of Arabicization policies, such systematic units and support programmes disappeared and, at best, were downgraded to units where English is a required language subject taught across the disciplines. No explicit, generic or discipline-specific, EAP programmes seem to have survived Arabicization.

EMI during the Colonial and Postcolonial Sudan

The British colonial administration adopted two different approaches to language and educational policies in Sudan. Unlike the northern part of the country, South Sudan was closed, and the education was left entirely to the Christian missionaries, who adopted English and some indigenous languages (Sandell, 1982). In postcolonial Sudan, the civil war and conflict erupted in South Sudan as early as 1955 with the calls and demands for autonomous federal governance for the south within a united Sudan. In the proper sense of the concept, EMI did not appear in South Sudan before the autonomous governance was secured following the signing of the Addis Ababa peace agreement between the government of Sudan and the Southern Sudan Liberation Movement in 1972. Thanks to that agreement, South Sudan witnessed some stability, and the University of Juba was established in 1975 as the first hub of EMI higher education in South Sudan. English took on a prominent role in education there until 1983, when the civil conflict reignited and the situation deteriorated. In 1990, a new regime seized power in Sudan through a military coup. As a result, the civil conflict in South Sudan became worse, and unilateral, ideologically motivated Arabicization policies were adopted in both the north and south of the country, with some new universities being proposed for South Sudan. Due to the war and conflict, Juba University was moved and housed in northern Sudan, and new universities were established in South Sudan. EMI continued to be used at Juba University but at a reduced level next to Arabic, which was the state-imposed and supported language of instruction. The comprehensive peace agreement signed in 2005 ended the conflict in South Sudan. The subsequent language policies (e.g. Abelhay et al., 2011a) gave rise to English as a language of instruction in higher education in South and North Sudan, with greater emphasis and density for the former. South Sudan seceded from the north in 2011 as a separate and independent state, and all southern HEIs were relocated to the newly born state. English continued to be used as a language of instruction, and its use has been steadily growing since then. Against this backdrop, EMI became an interesting research topic for researchers and practitioners to pursue in South Sudan.

EMI-related Research in Sudan

Generally speaking, there are few EMI studies, let alone EAP-oriented studies, in the Sudanese HE context. Perhaps, Liza Sandell's study in 1982 was the only comprehensive attempt at systematically documenting English education in Sudan from political and historical perspectives. Although her work is relatively dated, it remains a reasonably relevant source to provide some backdrop to present-day issues concerning the use of English in Sudanese HE. Broadly and historically speaking, EMI in Sudan has gone through two phases. The colonial phase in the early twentieth century when modern education was introduced into Sudan and the foundations for HE were laid down with the establishment of Gordon Memorial College and the Kitchener School of Medicine (the present-day Khartoum University). At the time, English was used as a language of instruction side by side with Arabic. The postcolonial phase started in 1956, following the Sudanese independence from Britain. English continued to be the language of instruction in both schools and HE until 1965, when the first attempt to Arabicize the educational system was made at the pre-university education level (see, e.g., Sandell, 1982). These ups and downs in postcolonial Sudan EMI were often ascribed to and motivated by the political and civil conflicts, attitudes and actions rather than by purely educational needs and realities (Abdelhay et al., 2011b., Sandell, 1982, p. 92).

However, as mentioned earlier, EMI survived until the 1990s, when policies of massive expansion in the number HEIs and the Arabicization of the education system were ideologically and politically imposed and accelerated in general and higher education. According to reports by UNESCO (2008, 2018), the General Education Organization Act (1992), for instance, designated Arabic as the official language of instruction, and the Higher Education Act of 1990 specified the aims and goals of HE as well as the curricula and types of HEIs and their objectives. It also recognized Arabic as the official language of instruction. English in HE was downgraded to a mere subject taught as a general university requirement. Since then, EMI in Sudanese HE has been significantly weakened and interrupted, and it has been used only sporadically in some study programmes, particularly in STEM and medicine in some private and public HEIs.

The Current Situation and Future Prospects of EMI in Sudan

As discussed, there is an apparent lack of clear and consistent policies on EMI in Sudan. There seems to be a pressing need for HE reforms to maintain quality, accreditation and internationalization. Indeed, EMI, among other things, could play a more significant role in this perspective. In fact, this need has been gaining momentum, especially since the political regime change in Sudan in 2019 after a nationwide uprising. The current Sudanese transitional government has promised reforms in general and higher education, and EMI is expected to gain prominence in HE. The present study is timely, and its findings and implications are primarily hoped to better inform EMI stakeholders on effective implementation methods if EMI is to be maintained and sustained in Sudanese HEIs. Indeed, the current political atmosphere in the country would provide more opportunities to view EMI as a means of internationalization of Sudanese HE. However, this would require unambiguous and results-oriented HE policies that are well informed by research and the best EMI practices in HEIs regionally and globally.

This study attempts to address the following three research questions: (1) How does or can the use of EMI benefit Sudanese HEIs? (2) What challenges are involved in EMI in Sudanese HEIs? (3) What should be done for EMI to be effectively maintained and sustained in Sudanese HEIs?

Methodology and Design

The study has adopted a qualitative methodology to understand teachers' views and perceptions of EMI in Sudanese HEIs and its opportunities and challenges. This approach makes it easier to address the research questions from an insider's emic perspective.

Participants

Thirteen content teachers took part in the investigation. The participants were invited to the study and reassured that their participation would be completely voluntary and the data collected would be used only for research purposes. They were also given the freedom to withdraw from the study at any time without having to explain why. Participants were all Sudanese nationals affiliated to various HEIs from the humanities and social and applied sciences. Their teaching experience in HE ranged from ten to twenty years. They had been teaching in both English and Arabic to varying degrees.

Methods of Data Collection

The study used an open-ended survey to collect the data needed to address the research questions. The survey was designed in function of the research questions and in light of the researcher's experience and the relevant literature.

Purposive sampling (Denscombe, 2010) was used in this study to gain an in-depth description of the issues under investigation in the research context.

This methodology allowed the researcher to include experienced and expert participants who could provide well-informed and valuable insights.

The survey was administered via a Google Form in an English and Arabic version, and the participants were given the option to fill out either version. Thirteen completed response forms were obtained: eight in English and five in Arabic. The Arabic responses were subsequently translated into English by the researcher himself.

Data Coding and Analytical Procedures

Data were collected using an open-ended survey. The thirteen written responses of the survey were coded thematically and inductively. An exploratory and open strategy to coding was adopted whereby everything was coded to allow as many potential issues as possible to emerge and be discovered from the data. A thematic, cross-sectional qualitative coding approach was used to generate themes from the data and the representative quotes to reproduce in the analysis (Coffey & Atkinson, 1996; Mason, 2002; Miles & Huberman, 1994). By using such an analytical framework, the investigation followed a three-phase cycle. The first phase was the coding and labelling of the whole set of data to organize the data chunks into themes/categories. The second phase was descriptive, whereby the data was presented through words in tables and networks. The third phase explained the linkages and connections through comparisons and/or contrasts between the themes generated in the first phase. This procedure enriched the analysis and the explanatory commentaries on the themes.

This framework was suited to the present study data because the data was mainly written or 'text-based', and the goal was to gain a 'systematic overview of the data' to 'locate and retrieve issues, topics, information, examples, and themes which do not appear in an orderly or sequential manner in the data', resulting in greater levels of data versatility for comparisons or connections (Mason, 2002, p. 152).

Results

The findings were based on the salient themes that emerged from the coding and analysis. They were reported and organized under the study research questions.

How Does the Use of EMI Benefit Sudanese HEIs?

Participants reported several benefits to EMI in Sudanese HEIs. They unanimously viewed EMI as an opportunity for internationalization in many ways through academic accreditation, greater visibility and better university rankings.

> Using English language as a medium of instruction would be beneficial to the university. It will gain internationalisation and the opportunity of getting accredited by the concerned organisations. This will enhance a better ranking and status. (P2)

In a similar vein, besides academic accreditation and rankings, EMI was seen as beneficial to develop and engage in international collaboration and academic exchange programmes with international HEIs.

> In my opinion, the benefits that could be gained from the use of the English language as a medium of instruction include: attracting international students, getting the required approval from the accreditation institutions, enhancing the regional and international ranking of our faculties and universities as well as improving the exchange programs between our universities and regional and international universities and institutions. (P8)

Moreover, the slow introduction of EMI, or lack of it, in Sudanese HEIs was reportedly viewed as having detrimental consequences for their visibility, rankings, staff and student mobility, international academic collaboration, accreditation and reputation both regionally and internationally.

> So any higher institution must adopt English as a medium of instruction. If English is absent, the higher institution will be invisible internationally, and hence lose the following: (1) It will not be internationally known or linked to any other higher or academic institutions in the region or the world. (2) It will not be able to compete, since it doesn't cope with the scientific movement, updates and new scientific and academic research. (3) It will lose the opportunity of exchanging experience with other international institutions. Its staff members and students cannot be able to travel or connect to any other institutions to exchange experience and gain more knowledge. (P7)

Internationalization, in particular, was reported as a means for students' mobility and employability.

> Studying in English increases your chances of getting a good job in a multinational company within your home country or finding work abroad. It's

also the language of international communication, the media and the internet which also is important for entertainment as well as work. (P6)

Additionally, besides mobility and employability, participants also believed that EMI would open up new global educational opportunities for students.

> Studying in English provides students with the opportunities to join international universities in Europe and the USA. (P13)

> Since English is spoken in so many different countries there are thousands of schools and universities around the world that offer programmes in English. If you speak good academic English, there're lots of opportunities for you to find an appropriate school and course to suit your needs. Find out about going to university in an English speaking country. (P6)

> The English language enables students to join international universities and colleges and strengthen their knowledge and experience. (P3)

Moreover, EMI was reportedly believed to provide students, particularly at the postgraduate level, with research, publication, scholarly and professional development opportunities.

> In addition to learning an international language, the students' benefits include development of research capabilities, and access to greater chances for international higher education. (P2)

> EMI would increase the opportunities of our students to write and publish articles in internal journals. (P8)

The participants also reported the benefits of EMI with regard to staff mobility, employability, research and professional development.

> I think EMI would make it easy for faculty to have access to and publish in English-medium international journals. It will also help them to communicate and establish networks with peers abroad for collaborative research and training projects. (P9)

> The use of EMI in Sudanese HEIs would make it easy for both academic staff and students to move and compete globally in the job market. (P10)

What Challenges Are involved in the Use of EMI in Sudanese HEIs?

Despite the reported benefits, EMI is believed to present challenges and difficulties. The challenges ranged from the lack of clear EMI policies in Sudanese

HEIs to students' and teachers' language difficulties and the lack of EMI teacher training and professional development.

Students' Challenges

The participants reported linguistic challenges on the side of students, believing that EMI would make it difficult for the latter to effectively cope with their programmes of study.

> I think the main challenge is the low level of English competence among Sudanese students. Most students are not prepared to study a subject in English at the university level. (P4)

Furthermore, the participants attributed low language proficiency to the problems associated with the pre-university English education in Sudan.

> Their [students] basis in the English language from primary and secondary school is too weak in all four language skills. (P4)

> This is an accumulated low language proficiency from the pre-university level of education. (P9)

Lack of interaction was also reported as a challenge associated with students' low language proficiency.

> I think the lack of interaction in the EMI classroom is due to the low language proficiency among students. (P9)

In the same vein, large classes were reported to negatively impact lecture comprehension and teacher–student interaction in EMI classrooms.

> A huge number of students enrolled in courses cause problems of interaction between teachers and students. (P8)

> Another challenge is the large number of students in each class, about 100 students in one class in some universities. Too many to teach a new subject in English and at the same time to try to improve their English or find ways to make the students understand the lectures. (P4)

Additionally, the difference in the language of instruction between students' undergraduate programmes (Arabic) and their subsequent EMI postgraduate ones (English) has made it harder for students to cope with EMI.

> Most of the students enrolling in these English-medium postgraduate programmes have obtained their first degrees for universities where the main medium of instruction was Arabic. (P8)

Teachers' Challenges

In addition to the challenges experienced by students, participants also reported a range of challenges experienced by EMI content teachers. Linguistic challenges were reported as a salient theme in the data:

> Teachers lack the adequate language proficiency and competence to teach through the English medium due to the Arabicisation policy. Adopting such a policy failed to produce the desired effects in the higher education graduates. (P5)

Interestingly, the reported low language proficiency level among EMI teachers was attributed to the Arabic educational background:

> Most of the HE teachers experience several challenges when teaching in English because in fact they did most of their study in Arabic. (P12)

Additionally, lack of teacher linguistic and pedagogical training was also reported as a challenge in EMI classrooms:

> Teachers are not well trained to teach in English. (P9)

> I think the only problem is the lack of qualified and well-trained teachers to teach in English. (P10)

Yet, interestingly, the use of L1 by teachers in EMI classrooms was reportedly seen by participants as a detrimental challenge that can negatively affect students' EMI study:

> Many students were complaining that instructors use the Arabic language heavily in teaching. (P8)

> The teacher uses Arabic in the classrooms. (P9)

What Can Be Done If the Use of EMI Is to be Effectively Maintained and Sustained in Sudanese HEIs?

Having reported both the benefits and challenges of EMI in Sudanese HEIs, this section reports the findings related to the study's third research question. The participants reported several suggestions on how EMI could be effectively maintained and sustained in Sudanese HEIs. One theme that recurrently emerged in the data was the need for content teacher training and professional development. Such training can reportedly be conducted in various ways, and, as the participants indicated, it could enhance EMI delivery and success. One way to achieve this is through research engagement and scholarly publication.

> EMI teachers should engage in research and publication and HEIs should encourage staff to publish extensively in peer-reviewed journals and present widely at both national and international conferences. (P11)

Similarly, EMI content teacher networking, academic exchange and collaboration with peers in EMI international universities were also reported as a means for enhancing such professional development.

> Teachers need to be trained to teach in English. We could make use of the experience of other countries that have successfully adopted EMI in HE. (P12)
>
> We need academic exchange programmes with international universities to help train both staff and students for EMI study. (P13)
>
> In my opinion, we need to increase the exchange programmes with international HEIs to help develop EMI programmes in Sudan. We can organise annual conferences and set up centres for research and curriculum development and innovation. (P11)

Additionally, the participants believed that EMI content teachers need language testing, certification and licensing as part of EMI teaching job requirements. This scheme would arguably improve EMI teaching and learning.

> Teachers at university must all be able to teach in English, this must be a requirement of job recruitment. (P7)

In the same vein, it was believed that HEIs should play a role in EMI teacher education and continuing professional development (CPD), particularly regarding linguistic issues in EMI.

> The ministry of higher education needs to coach teachers on structuring and presenting content in ways that will help with language development. In other words, academic development programmes such as teachers' training and workshops should be offered on what to expect in terms of language ability of the student and in- service training to help teachers support students to cope with their English-medium study. (P5)

In addition to linguistic training, the participants highlighted the importance of pedagogical and methodological training for EMI content teachers.

> Teachers should adapt their methodology to support meaning, by using a lot of visual information and non-verbal communication to support meaning. (P6)

As part of sustaining EMI in Sudanese HEIs, the participants called for increasing, expanding and supporting EMI use across these HEIs.

Sudanese higher education institutions should make EMI a priority. (P9)

Moreover, the participants called for the adoption of *English-only* instruction and less use of L1 in the EMI classrooms.

> The learning process is to be completely in English unless extra information and explanations are needed. (P1)

Similarly, an expansion in EMI with caution was also proposed.

> Institutions that use English as a medium of instruction should be increased and the level of students should be considered when adopting EMI. (P3)

However, the participants highlighted the need for consistency in the use of English in EMI classrooms.

> The English medium of instruction should be consistently used by the teachers to teach their subjects from the beginning of the course to the end as the main language of instruction in class. (P6)

Furthermore, it was reported by the participants that an English-only policy for communication on campus should be introduced.

> Instructors and students need to use the English language in communication in and out of the class. (P8)

As part of effective EMI implementation, participants also spoke of the need to enhance and modernize the EMI classroom teaching and learning environment by providing resources through subscription to research and scholarly databases.

> Having subscriptions to e-books, e-journals databases, and other e-resources and having classrooms well equipped with facilities that help engaging lectures. (P2)
>
> Resources in English, such as internet/Wi-Fi and electronic libraries should be made available to the students. (P4)
>
> University must provide good resources of textbooks, in addition to well-reputed periodicals. (P7)

In addition to EMI content teacher education and professional development, the participants drew attention to the need for language preparation and support programmes for EMI students. Moreover, students with low language proficiency should be supported in their EMI courses.

> First, there should be specified additional classes for the students who aren't fluent in English. (P1)

> At university, there should be extra courses in English for those who study a subject in English, but do not have sufficient English language knowledge. (P4)
>
> Providing preparatory English learning programs to enhance the presentation skills of students. (P2)

HEIs should prepare and support students to thrive on EMI programmes.

> University must help raise the capacity of students in using English as an academic language. This can be done through academic activities where students can compete in proposing or writing an academic paper or research. (P7)

Additionally, participants called for enhancing entry language tests for students before enrolling in EMI programmes.

> We need to be strict to the criteria of having the minimum score in IELTS or TOEFL English tests, as well as passing the interview conducted by the relevant HE institution in question. (P8)

Furthermore, as part of language support and proficiency improvement for students on EMI programmes, participants also called for reforming the English education at the pre-university levels to help students effectively thrive in the subsequent future EMI study at the university level of education:

> English education in primary and secondary school has to improve. It has to ensure that the pupils know English at a sufficient level for university studies. (P4)
>
> We should adopt a bottom-up method, i.e. starting solving problems of low English proficiency in the pre-university stages. As a result, students will come to the university with good command of English that help them starting and leading a successful university study life. (P7)

Discussion

The findings on the benefits of EMI corroborate previous research (e.g. Macaro et al., 2018; Macaro, 2018; Wächter & Maiworm, 2014) in that the internationalization of HE has been the much-cited driving force for many HEIs in the world to adopt EMI as the primary language of teaching and assessment. The findings suggest the need for better coordinated and more clearly stated HE policies to effectively accelerate and materialize internationalization at its various aspects, EMI being at the forefront of the process. The findings also indicate that internationalization in the present study was viewed in a broader sense. It was particularly desired to help enhance and sustain EMI by providing both academic staff and students with training and preparation opportunities to help them thrive in EMI programmes.

Unsurprisingly, the findings about EMI-related challenges echo many previous EMI studies (e.g. Albakri, 2017; Alhassan et al., 2021; Airey & Linder, 2006; Chang, 2010; Coleman, 2006; Dearden, 2015; Zacharias, 2013). EMI is associated with a range of linguistic and pedagogical challenges among content teachers and students alike. EMI adoption by HEIs only for the sake of the perceived benefits without considering and addressing the potential challenges inherent to it can result in sporadic, less effective and unsustainable EMI education. The findings also seem to suggest that there is a need for more context-bound studies. EMI-specific challenges must be ascertained in different educational contexts and considering the particular EMI types and the degree of their impact on success. EMI challenges and difficulties would entail some action on the part of the stakeholders.

The present study's findings resonate with a range of similar conclusions in previous EMI research (see, e.g., Alhassan, 2019; Holi, 2020). Moreover, these findings also lend support to previous studies (e.g. Albakri, 2017; Airey, 2020; Banks, 2018; Borg, 2016; Dearden, 2015; Costa, 2015; Klaassen, 2001) in reporting that EMI teachers need both linguistic and pedagogical training to effectively function in EMI programmes. They need to learn how to make their content delivery accessible to students. The findings also suggest that such training could help enhance and sustain EMI in HEIs. However, it is worth stressing here that training should be based on needs analysis, and the needs may vary from one discipline of knowledge to another and from one context to another.

The findings related to the study's third research question suggest that there is a need for EMI content teacher education and professional development. Moreover, the participants made several suggestions for it.

The findings also emphasized the calls (Cots, 2013; O'Dowd, 2018) to pay more attention to the EMI content teachers' methodological and pedagogical competences for EMI. They should know how to reinforce the teaching and learning process through engaging, scaffolding and socializing students into the subject content. This seems to suggest the need for collaboration between EMI content and EAP teachers, with the latter commenting on and guiding the former on the EMI content preparation and delivery (see, e.g., Alhassan, 2019; Alhassan et al., 2021; Macaro & Tian, 2020). Indeed, EMI content teacher education and professional development are new and still shaping up in the EMI field of research. The findings on EMI teacher research and scholarly engagement connect EMI to the ELT tradition of teacher research engagement (see, e.g., Borg, 2007, 2010; Cain, 2015; Sato & Loewen; 2018; Zamorski & Bulmer, 2002), with potential benefits for the emerging sector of EMI content teacher education and professional development. EMI teacher trainers and educators can use the established ELT tradition, particularly in the pedagogical part of EMI teacher training and professional development, as borne out by other researchers (e.g. Dang et al., 2021; Guarda & Helm, 2017). However, establishing EMI training and professional development programmes is not an easy task as it involves a range of contextual and institutional factors. Hence, there is a need for more discipline-specific, context-bound and needs-based research and experimentation in professional development for EMI subject teachers considering the perspectives of the faculty teaching disciplinary and language courses as insider EMI stakeholders.

Conclusions, Implications and Recommendations

The study reported in this chapter is small scale and qualitative and meant to investigate the affordances and challenges of EMI in Sudanese HEIs. The participants, belonging to various Sudanese higher education institutions, represented the humanities and social and applied sciences. The overarching aim was to explore EMI in Sudanese HE and generate context-specific data to support educators, researchers, university managers, policymakers and other stakeholders as they plan, implement, evaluate and broaden EMI incidence in Sudanese HE. Several EMI benefits along with the potential challenges at the sides of both teachers and students were reported.

The study achieved its objectives by exploring this less researched topic in Sudan and allowing the stakeholders to discuss their views of and experiences with the current EMI situation and make recommendations for further research and educational policymaking.

However, some limitations should be acknowledged. First, the study included only thirteen participants with only one method of data collection. Therefore, its findings do not necessarily represent all Sudanese stakeholders, nor are they intended to be generalized to other contexts. Second, other stakeholders, such as students, university managers and higher education policymakers, were not represented. Their inclusion, if made, could have provided more data and elucidated more perspectives to expand the scope and enrich the study findings. Third, using more than one data collection method (e.g. classroom observations and artefacts) could have helped better triangulate the data methodologically and analytically. Future research in Sudan could widen the scope and set up a more active EMI research agenda in light of these limitations. Future studies should explore, compare and contrast EMI implementation in Sudanese private and state universities. Research could also be expanded to cover the use of EMI in applied sciences compared to humanities and social sciences. More studies on the perspectives of content teachers and other EMI stakeholders are also needed, and they can be conducted about EMI content teacher education and continuing professional development, which are both emerging areas in EMI research. Critical EMI language policy and attitudinal studies can also be conducted to question the rationale and problematize the feasibility and benefits of EMI implementation in Sudanese HEIs. More micro-EMI pedagogical research should also be undertaken to explore EMI lectures, their discourses and the EMI classroom practices and management. Future studies could also pursue EMI research projects in South Sudan, including comparative studies with the northern part of Sudan and other similar post-conflict contexts.

Despite these acknowledged limitations, the study provided a range of findings about and insights into EMI in Sudan that can be transferable to other similar contexts and could motivate future research and inform policy, pedagogy and practice in the ecological context of the study and beyond. In light of the study findings, the following recommendations can be made:

1. There should be clear and consistent policies on the use of EMI in both private and state HEIs in Sudan, clear and accurate statistics and databases should be created for EMI in HEIs, and regular updates should be provided.
2. More EMI programmes should be established in Sudanese HEIs but with clear and research-informed policies on EMI teaching, learning and assessment. EMI content teachers should be provided with adequate and sustainable education and opportunities for professional development. EMI students also need language and learning support to effectively cope with their courses taught in English. More funding and resources should also made available for Sudanese HEIs to boost EMI teaching, learning and research.
3. Sudanese HEIs should establish, develop and sustain international EMI research, teaching and learning collaboration programmes

and partnerships with EMI international universities, particularly in Northern and Western Europe and South East Asia, to use these institutions' EMI established experiences. Such collaboration could help foster academic exchange for both students and academic staff. It could also particularly contribute to the design, development, delivery and evaluation of EMI teacher educational and professional development programmes.

4. Policymakers, educational managers, researchers and practitioners should coordinate among themselves to better connect EMI research with policy and practice.
5. There should be research-informed teacher education schemes and CPD programmes to help subject teachers deliver their English-medium subject contents effectively, both linguistically and pedagogically.
6. English-medium content teachers should be encouraged to engage in research as a means for continuing professional development. They should also be encouraged to establish communication and networks with peers in international EMI universities to enhance research and professional development.
7. There should be a clear and well-defined professional certification system for teachers to develop their linguistic and pedagogical competencies for EMI programmes of study. Likewise, appropriate language entry tests should be developed and administered to students as part of the admission criteria for enrolling in English-medium programmes.
8. The EMI teaching and learning environment should be improved and better supported. More resources and databases should be made available in libraries and teaching and learning centres. More interactive teaching should be maintained, and classes of manageable size should be the norm.
9. An English-only policy should be adopted by Sudanese HEIs, allowing for L1 use and translanguaging strategies in the English-medium classroom to ease and support teaching, learning and the acquisition of disciplinary knowledge.
10. The establishment of both in- and pre-sessional EAP and language support programmes should be ensured to help students cope effectively with their respective EMI study. Most importantly, contextual needs analyses should be conducted to inform and ensure that EAP provision is geared towards the students' actual teaching and learning needs and requirements on various EMI programmes.

11. English language education should be reformed at the pre-university level of education to better prepare students for future English-medium tertiary education.
12. Finally, Sudan needs to invest in the necessary mechanisms to guarantee national and international academic accreditation and ensure quality in its HEIs. Accreditation should be at both the general institutional level and the level of specific English-medium programmes.

Notes

1 These types of universities were established and run by general public's initiatives and donations. They charge fees slightly higher than the fees of public universities and far much less than those of the private universities.
2 Arabicization is the use of Arabic as a sole medium of instruction in the higher education institutions. The policies were introduced in the 1970s but practically came into effect in the 1990s.

References

Abdelhay, A. K., Makoni, B., & Makoni, S. B. (2011a). The Naivasha language policy: The language of politics and the politics of language in the Sudan. *Language Policy, 10*, 1–18. doi:10.1007/s10993-011-9192-9.

Abdelhay, A. K., Makoni, B., Makoni, S., & Mugaddam, A. (2011b). The sociolinguistics of nationalism in the Sudan: The politicization of Arabic and the Arabicisation of politics. *Current Issues in Language Planning, 12*(4), 457–501. doi:10.1080/14664208.2011.628079.

Albakri, S. (2017). *Effects of English medium instruction on students' learning experiences and quality of education in content courses in a public college in Oman* (Unpublished doctoral thesis). University of Exeter.

Alhassan, A. (2019). Investigating business EFL postgraduate student writing in a UK university: A qualitative study. *Cogent Education, 6*(1), 1–14. doi:10.1080/2331186X.2019.1699741.

Alhassan, A., Ali, N. A., & Holi, I. H. (2021). EFL students' challenges in English-medium business programmes: Perspectives from students and content teachers. *Cogent Education, 8*(1), 1–15. doi:10.1080/2331186X.2021.1888671.

Airey, J. (2020). The content lecturer and English-Medium Instruction (EMI): Epilogue to the special issue on EMI in higher education. *International Journal of Bilingual Education and Bilingualism, 23*(3), 340–346. doi:10.1080/13670050.2020.1732290.

Airey, J., & Linder, C. (2006). Language and the experience of learning university physics in Sweden. *European Journal of Physics, 27*(3), 553–560. doi:10.1088/0143-0807/27/3/009.

Banks, M. (2018). Exploring EMI lecturers' attitudes and needs. *EPiC Series in Language and Linguistics, 3*(1), 19–26. doi:10.29007/gjc1.

Borg, S. (2007). Research engagement in English language teaching. *Teaching and Teacher Education, 23*, 731–747. doi:10.1016/j.tate.2006.03.012.

Borg, S. (2010). Language teacher research engagement. *Language Teaching Journal, 43*(4), 391–429. doi:10.1017/S0261444810000170.

Borg, S. (2016). *English medium instruction in Iraqi Kurdistan*. Perspectives from lecturers at State University. British Council. Retrieved from https://englishagenda.britishcouncil.org/sites/default/files/attachments/teaching_english_publication_en_web_version_v1.pdf

Braima, M. A. (2004). *Situation of English language in Sudan post-Arabicisation* (Unpublished doctoral Thesis). University of Malaya.

Cain, T. (2015). Teacher's engagement with published research: Addressing the knowledge problem. *The Curriculum Journal, 26*(3), 488–509. doi:10.1080/09585176.2015.1020820.

Chang, Y. Y. (2010). English-medium instruction for subject courses in tertiary education: Reactions from Taiwanese undergraduate students. *Taiwan International ESP Journal, 2*(1), 55–84. 10.6706/TIESPJ.2010.2.1.3.

Coffey, A., & Atkinson, P. (1996). *Making sense of qualitative data*. SAGE Publications.

Coleman, J. A. (2006). English-medium teaching in European higher education. *Language Teaching, 39*(1), 1–14. doi:10.1017/S026144480600320X.

Costa, F. (2015). English Medium Instruction (EMI) teacher training courses in Europe. *RiCognizioni. Rivista di Lingue e Letterature Straniere e Culture Moderne, 4*(2), 127–135. doi:10.13135/2384-8987/1102.

Cots, J. M. (2013). Introducing English-medium instruction at the University of Lleida, Spain: Intervention, beliefs and practices. In A. Doiz, D. Lasagabaster, & J. M. Sierra (Eds.), *English-Medium Instruction at universities* (pp. 28–44). Multilingual Matters.

Dafalla, F. (2007). *ESP learners' needs: A case study of medicine students at some Sudanese universities* (Unpublished master's dissertation). Sudan University of Science and Technology.

Dang, T., Bonar, G., & Yao, J. (2021). Professional learning for educators teaching in English-medium instruction in higher education: A systematic review. *Teaching in Higher Education, 7*, 1–19. doi:10.1080/13562517.2020.1863350.

Dearden, J. (2015). *English as a medium of instruction – A growing global phenomenon*. London: The British Council. Retrieved 20 May 2020, from https://ora.ox.ac.uk/objects/uuid:4f72cdf8-b2eb-4d41-a785-4a283bf6caaa.

Denscombe, M. (2010). *The good research guide for small-scale research projects* (4th ed.). McGraw-Hill.

Drljača Margić, B., & Vodopija-Krstanović, I. (2018). Language development for English-medium instruction: Teachers' perceptions, reflections and learning. *Journal of English for Academic Purposes, 35*, 31–41. doi:10.1016/j.jeap.2018.06.005.

Fathalalem, K. E. (2016). *Problems of teaching English for Specific Purposes in the Sudanese universities: A case study of four Sudanese universities* (Unpublished doctoral thesis). University of Khartoum, Sudan.

Guarda, M., & Helm, F. (2017). 'I have discovered new teaching pathways': The link between language shift and teaching practice. *International Journal of Bilingual Education and Bilingualism, 20* (7), 897–913. doi:10.1080/13670050.2015.1125848.

Hashim, H. K. (2010). *The relevance of academic business English textbooks to students' studying needs* (Unpublished master's dissertation). University of Khartoum.

Holi, I. H. (2020). Lecture comprehension difficulties experienced by Omani students in an English-medium engineering programme. *Cogent Arts & Humanities, 7*(1), 1–17. doi:10.1080/23311983.2020.1741986.

Klaassen, R. C. (2001). *The international university curriculum: Challenges in English-medium engineering education* (Unpublished doctoral thesis). Delft University of Technology.

Macaro, E. (2018). *English medium instruction: Content and language in policy and practice*. Oxford University Press.

Macaro, E., Curle, S., Pun, J., & An, J. (2018). A systematic review of English medium instruction in higher education. *Language Teaching, 51*(1), 36–76. doi:10.1017/S0261444817000350.

Macaro, E., & Tian, L. (2020). Developing EMI teachers through a collaborative research. *Journal of Multilingual and Multicultural Development*. doi:10.1080/01434632.2020.1862131.

Mason, J. (2002). *Qualitative researching* (2nd ed.). SAGE Publications.

Miles, M. B., & Huberman, A. M. (1994) *Qualitative data analysis: An expanded sourcebook* (2nd ed.). SAGE publications.

O'Dowd, R. (2018). The training and accreditation of teachers for English medium instruction: An overview of practice in European Universities. *International Journal of Bilingual Education and Bilingualism, 21*(5), 553–563. doi:10.1080/13670050.2018.1491945.

Pitia, L. (2003). *Author comments in science textbooks* (Unpublished doctoral thesis). University of Khartoum.

Sandell, Liza. (1982). *English language in Sudan: A history of its teaching and politics*. Ithaca Press.

Sato, M., & Loewen, S. (2018). Do teachers care about research? The research-pedagogy dialogue. *ELT Journal, 73*(1), 1–10. doi:10.1093/elt/ccy048.

Swales, J. M. (2009). *Incidents in an educational life: A memoir (of sorts)*. Michigan University Press.

UNESCO. (2008). UNESCO national education support strategy (UNESS) for Sudan (LB/2008/ED/PI/21). https://unesdoc.unesco.org/ark:/48223/pf0000177703_ara.

UNESCO. (2018). Sudan education policy review: Paving the road to 2030 (ED-2018/WS/9). https://unesdoc.unesco.org/ark:/48223/pf0000265447.

Wächter, B., & Maiworm, F. (2014). *English-taught programmes in European higher education: The state of play*. Lemmens.

Yassin, A. M. (1999). *The need for ESP/EAP teacher training in Sudanese tertiary institutions post- Arabicization* (Unpublished doctoral thesis). University of Khartoum.

Zacharias, N. T. (2013). Navigating through the English-medium-of-instruction (EMI) policy: Voices from the field. Current Issues in Language Planning, *14*(1), 93–108. doi:10.1080/14664208.2013.782797.

Zamorski, B., & Bulmer, M. (2002). Engaging teachers in research: Teacher engagement in research as professional development. *Pedagogy, Culture & Society*, *10*(2), 279–291. doi:10.1080/14681360200200144.

Index

1984 Regulation of Turkey   112
1994 Regulation of Turkey   112–13
1996 Regulation of Turkey   113
2016 Regulation of Turkey   113

Abdellatif, A.   150
Abdlejaouad, M.   133
academic disciplines, Saudi Arabia   91–2
additive multilingualism   21, 22
Alavi, S. Z.   28
Alazemi, A.   71, 80
Alderson, J. C.   149
Algeria   134
   EMI in, hypothetical status   137–40
   French in   137–40
   language of education policy   137–40
   multilingualism   138
Alhassan, A.   71, 79
Ali, H.   80
Ali, N. L.   96
Al-Issa, A.   14
Al-Jadidi, H.   51
Al-Kahtany, A. H.   96
Alsamadani, H. A.   98
Al-Seghayer, K.   89
Al-Shahrani, H.   99
Al-Shehri, S.   98
Altbach, P. G.   71
Alyami, R. H.   98
Amazigh   136–7
Arabian Gulf, EMI in   68–71
Arabic   8–9, 13, 18–22, 70, 89–92, 94, 103, 129, 149, 169
   in Algeria   137–40
   in Kuwait   75–81
   as language of instruction   87, 90
   in Libya   141–2
   medium   150, 156
   in Morocco   134, 136, 137
   in Tunisia   131, 133
Arabic as the medium of instruction (AMI)   141–2

Arabic-English bilingualism   140–2
Arabicization/Arabization   8–9, 11, 18, 22, 169, 170, 172, 178
Arabic-medium instruction   70, 81
Arab identity   3, 75, 76, 78, 81
Arab nationalism   141
Arkand, J. L.   134
attitudes
   instructors   150–1, 157–60, 162–3
   students   150–7, 162–3

Badwan, K.   132
Bahloul, M.   131
Bahrain   17, 130
Barnawi, O. Z.   15, 19, 48, 95
Battenburg, J.   131
Becher, T.   91
Belhiah, H.   71, 135–7, 148, 150
Berber   137
bilingualism   129
   Arabic-English   71, 80, 81, 140–2
Boukadi, S.   132
Brandenburg, U.   49
Brooks, R.   51
Bunnell, T.   149
Burden-Leahy, S. M.   71
Byun, K.   27

Canagarajah, A. S.   9, 20
chaotic multilingualism   135
Cole, F. L.   31
colonial languages   12
colonial Sudan, EMI in   170–1
colonization/colonialism   8–9, 20
communicative competence   55–6
content analysis   31–2, 37
continuing professional development (CPD)   179, 185
Council of Higher Education, Turkey   113, 115, 121
CPD. *See* continuing professional development (CPD)
Curle, S.   10, 12

Dafouz, E. 88, 97
Dahan, L. S. 14
Daniel, C. E. 71
Daoud, M. 131
Darija 136–9
data
    analysis 31–2, 174
    coding 174
Dearden, J. 71, 130
decolonization 19–21
deductive content analysis 31, 38
deep learning 92
de Wit, H. 46, 49
dual curriculum 80

educational expenditure 68–9
Education and Training Evaluation
    Commission (ETEC) 96
education practices and processes in
    Saudi 97–9
EFL. *See* English as a Foreign Language
    (EFL)
EGP. *See* English for General Purposes
    (EGP)
Egypt
    ELT in 143
    EMI in 142–3
    language of education policy 142–3
El-Feki, H. 142, 143
Elhami, M. 71
ELT. *See* English Language Teaching
    (ELT)
EMI. *See* English-medium instruction
    (EMI)
EMI programmes, in Turkey. *See* Turkey:
    EMI programmes
employment 34, 37, 50, 51
EMS teacher. *See* English medium subject
    (EMS) teachers
English 90–1, 103, 129–31, 134, 169
    competencies 55–6
    comprehension 56–7
    dominance of 18
    education 181
    as foreign language 10–11
    gender difference in the use of 3, 78
    growth in Morocco 147–8
    importance of 150
    investment in 14–15
    in Kuwait 69, 75–81
    as language of instruction 94
    language skills 154
    as lingua franca 3, 10–11, 18, 22, 51,
        52, 59, 79, 90, 150
    mastery 158
    as a medium of instruction 2, 11–13,
        15–20, 22, 54, 131, 149, 150,
        157, 160, 169–70, 175
    positive attitudes 148
    proficiency 14–17, 22, 33–8, 55–8,
        60, 132, 134, 140, 143, 158, 177,
        178, 180
    replacement of Arabic by 15, 17, 22
    as second language 10–11, 19
English as a Foreign Language (EFL) 94,
    142
English Baccalaureate programme
    149–50
English for Academic Purposes
    (EAP) 170, 185
English for General Purposes (EGP) 94
English for Specific Academic Purposes
    (ESAP) 94
English for Specific Purposes (ESP)
    course 98, 170
English Language Teaching (ELT) 98,
    139, 143, 148, 183
English-medium content teachers 185
English-medium instruction (EMI)
    5–6, 25
    advantages 55–6, 60
    in Algeria 137–40
    Arabian Gulf 68–71
    challenges for Omani HEIs 56–7, 60
    defined 1
    in Egypt 142–3
    faculty members perspectives 53–5
    in Iran 2, 26
    advantages/opportunities of 27–8,
        32–4, 37–9
    data collection and procedure
        30–2
    disadvantages/challenges of 27–8,
        34–6, 38–9
    implementation 26–7
    improvement 36–7
    proficiency of instructors 35, 38
    proficiency of students 35–8

Kuwait 68-70
  data collection: procedures 72-3
  future research 82
  language of instruction policies and practices 82
  limitations of the study 81
  literature review 71
  qualitative analysis, Arabic-English usage 73-4, 77-9
  quantitative analysis, Arabic-English usage 73-7, 79
  t-units analysis 77-9
in Libya 140-2
literature review 26-8
in Morocco 5, 133-7, 149-51
  advantages and disadvantages of 153-4, 157-8, 161
  benefits 154-5, 158-9, 161, 163
  business or engineering, improvement in 154-5
  career benefits 159, 161, 163
  challenges 156, 159-62
  English language skills, improvement in 154, 163
  future 164
  instructors' attitudes towards 150-1, 157-60, 162-3
  opportunities for communication 155
  strategies to ease students' transition into 162
  students' attitudes towards 150-7, 162-3
  for students' employment 155-6, 163
North Africa and educational language policy 4-15
  Algeria 137-140
  Egypt 142-143
  Libya 140-142
  Morocco 133-137
  Tunisia 130-133
in Oman 51-2
  internationalization of HEIs 53-60
  methodology and design 52-3
  participants for methodology 28-30, 39

in Saudi's higher education 87-8
  government's role 95
  internationalization of 95
  ROADMAPPING Framework (*see* ROADMAPPING Framework in Saudi Arabia)
in Sudan
  colonial and postcolonial 170-1
  content teachers' methodological and pedagogical competences 182-3
  current situation and future prospects 172-3
  HEIs 177-81
  history 169-70
  international research 184-5
  language support for 170
  qualitative methodology 173-4
  recommendations 184-5
  teaching and learning 185
  training 176-9, 182-3
in Tunisia 130-3
English medium subject (EMS) teachers 142
English-only policy 180, 185
Errihani, M. 147
ESAP. *See* English for Specific Academic Purposes (ESAP)
ESP course. *See* English for Specific Purposes (ESP) course
Estonia 130

Findlow, S. 91
fluency 14, 57
Fortune, A. 143
foundation universities, Turkey 115, 117
France 18
French 129, 134, 142, 148, 149, 151, 158
  Algeria 137-40
  medium 150, 156
  in Morocco 134-6
  in Tunisia 131, 133
full EMI programme 114-19

Gaffas, Z. 98
GCC. *See* Gulf Cooperation Council (GCC)

GE course. *See* General English (GE) course
Gein, F. 134
General Education Organization Act (1992), Sudan 172
General English (GE) course 98
General Foundation Programmes (GFPs) 52, 57, 58
GFPs. *See* General Foundation Programmes (GFPs)
Gholami, K. 27
glocalization/globalization 4, 9–11, 18, 20, 90, 100–2
Gordon Memorial College 172
Gulf Cooperation Council (GCC) 11, 12, 18–22
   Bahrain 17
   educational expenditure 68–9
   illiteracy rate 68
   Kuwait 16
   Oman 15–16
   Qatar 15
   Saudi Arabia 13–14
   UAE 14

Ha, P. L. 48
Halliday, M. K. 97
Hamid, M. O. 96
Haoucha, M. 151
Hejazi, Y. 28, 38
higher education (HE)
   history of EMI in Sudanese 169–70
   internationalization of 2–3
   in Turkey 115
      institutions 115, 117
      internationalization of 110
      regulations 111–13
Higher Education Act of 1990, Sudan 172
higher education institutions (HEIs) 11
   EMI in Sudan 5–6
      benefit 175–6, 182
      effective maintenance and sustainability 178–81
      English as a medium of instruction 169, 170, 175
      international research 184–5
      recommendations 184–5
      students' challenges 177
      teachers' challenges 178
      teaching and learning 185
   internationalization of 45–9, 60
      EMI and 53–8
      Kuwait 70
      in Oman 51–2, 60
      ranking 45, 59
      Saudi Arabia
         government's role 95
         medium of instruction in 87
         multilingual intricacy 90
         role of Arabic in 91
Hopkyns, S. 14
humanities 88, 90, 103

IELTS, internationalization of 49–50
illiteracy rate 68
inductive content analysis 31
inequality gap 70
instructors
   attitudes towards EMI 150–1, 157–60
   language of instruction preference 160
   teacher training for 165
   teaching strategies 160
   training in English for 165
international accreditation 49, 54, 55, 60
International Baccalaureate (IB) 149
internationalization 11, 18–19, 69
   abroad policy 100, 101
   defined 100
   of higher education 71
      Saudi Arabia 95
      in Turkey 110
internationalization and glocalization (ING) 100–2
internationalization of HEIs 2–3, 45–9
   defined 45
   of IELTS 49–50
   myths about 49
   in Oman 51–2
      EMI and 53–60
international rankings 45, 49, 60
investments 14–15
   in education 69
Iran
   EMI in
      advantages/opportunities of 27–8, 32–4, 37–9

data collection and procedure 30–2
disadvantages/challenges of 27–8, 34–6, 38–9
implementation 26–7
improvement 36–7
proficiency of instructors 35, 38
proficiency of students 35–8

Jones, E. 46

Kachru, B. B. 142
Karmani, S. 90
KASP. *See* King Abdullah Scholarship Program (KASP)
Khartoum University 169
King Abdullah Public Education Development Project 93–4, 98
King Abdullah Scholarship Program (KASP) 93
King Saud University 100
Kırkgoz, Y. 112
Kitchener School of Medicine 172
Knight, J. 100
Kuwait 16
 Arabic-English bilingual education 71, 80, 81
 Arabic usage in 75–81
 educational expenditure 68–9
 EMI (*see* English-medium instruction (EMI): Kuwait)
 English usage in 69, 75–81
 internationalization of English 69
 linguistic imperialism 69–70
 private institutions in 82
 students' attitudes towards EMI 3
 as threat to Arab identity 72, 78, 81
 university's language policy 72

Labassi, T. 131, 133
Lacroix, S. 100
Lamallam, M. 137
language
 challenges 159
 of education policy
  Algeria 137–40
  Egypt 142–3
  Lybya 140–2
  Morocco 133–7
  Tunisia 130–3
 of instruction 177
 preference 157, 160
 management, Saudi 93–5
 prestige 3, 78, 80
language policy
 and planning, Turkey 109–10
 Saudi 87, 91, 93–5
language support programmes 185
Latif, A. 135, 136, 143
learning strategies 156, 163
Le Ha, P. 95
Libya
 Arabic-English bilingualism 140–2
 EMI in 140–2
 language of education policy 140–2
lingua franca English 3, 10–11, 18, 22, 51, 52, 59, 69, 79, 90, 135, 150
linguistic
 challenges 177, 178, 182
 diversity in Morocco 134
 dualism 131
 imperialism 69–70
 training 179, 182
Louber, I. 98
low English proficiency 56–8, 132, 140, 143, 158, 177, 178, 180

Macaro, E. 88
Malik, H. A. M. 96
Maringe, F. 46
Matthiessen, C. 97
McIlwraith, H. 143
Medfouni, I. 139, 140
medium of instruction (MOI) 111–14, 121
Middle East Technical University 119
Miliani, M. 137–8
mixed-method study 132, 136
modernization 90
Modern Standard Arabic (MSA) 90, 97, 98, 103
MOI. *See* medium of instruction (MOI)
Morocco
 Amazigh in 136
 Arabic in 134, 136, 137
 EMI in 133–7 (*see* English-medium instruction (EMI): in Morocco)

French in   134–6
growth of English in   147–8
language of education policy   133–7
mother-language instruction   136–7
multilingualism   134
MSA. *See* Modern Standard Arabic (MSA)
multilingualism   129
  Algeria   138
  Morocco   134

Nadri, Y.   151
Nassaji, H.   28
The National Curriculum Framework for English as a Foreign Language   143
neoliberalism   4, 94, 95, 101, 102
N-gram Arabic language   75–6
N-gram English language   75–6
Nguyen, T. T.   27, 37, 38
Nifaoui, A.   148
North Africa
  EMI and educational language policy   4–15
    Algeria   137–40
    Egypt   142–3
    Libya   140–2
    Morocco   133–7
    Tunisia   130–3
  language of education in   129–30

Oman   15–16
  English-medium instruction (EMI)   51–2
  IELTS   50
  internationalization of HEIs   50–1, 59–60
  EMI and   53–60
  role of English in education   50–1
open-ended questionnaire   30, 38, 39
open-ended survey   173–4

partial EMI programme   114–19
pedagogical training/challenge   178, 182
Peterson, A.   149
Phillipson, R.   7, 21, 69–70
Phuong, Y. H.   27, 37, 38
plurilingualism   138
postcolonial Sudan, EMI in   170–1

preparatory year programme (PYP)   4, 88, 93–4, 98–9, 103
pre-university educational system, Sudan   169–70
Pre-university Education Reform 2014-2030   143
private education   15–16
private universities, Turkish   115
professional certification system for teachers   185
professional development   176–80, 182, 183
proficiency   55–8, 132, 140, 143, 158, 177, 178, 180
public and private education gap   80
purposive sampling   29, 53, 173
PYP. *See* preparatory year programme (PYP)

Qatar   15, 70, 130
qualitative data analysis   31–2, 39
  Arabic-English usage in Kuwait   73–4, 77–9
qualitative methodology   52–3
  EMI in Sudan   173–4
quality education   55
quantitative analysis, Arabic-English usage in Kuwait   73–7, 79

Reckwitz, A.   97
resource availability   33
ROADMAPPING Framework in Saudi Arabia   4, 88–9
  academic disciplines   91–2
  agents   95–7
  internationalization and glocalization (ING)   100–2
  language management   93–5
  roles of English   89–91
  teaching practices and processes   97–9

Sadiqi, F.   135
Sandell, L.   171
Saudi Arabia   13–14, 18, 130
  Arabic-English use   99
  content courses   92
  educational reforms   101

EMI in higher education 87–8
  Arabic-English use 89–91, 99
  internationalization of 95
  ROADMAPPING Framework (*see*
    ROADMAPPING Framework
    in Saudi Arabia)
  role of government in 95
  English Language Teaching (ELT) 98
  language courses 98–9
  language of instruction 99
  language policy 87, 93, 95
  medium of instruction in HEIs 87
  PhD holders 96
  role of employers, alumni and
    students 96
  universities 87, 90, 91–4, 96
science disciplines, Saudi
    universities 91–2, 103
Scott, M. 149
Seddiki, Z. 140
semi-structured interviews 30–1, 38, 39
Seth, V. 78
Shahu, K. 134–7, 139–40
Shamim, F. 98, 99
Sketch Engine 73–4
Skutnabb-Kangas, T. 7, 21
Smit, U. 88, 97
social prestige 78
social sciences 88, 90
Soe, T. 27
soft-EMI programmes 114–15
Solloway, A. J. 71
Spolsky, B. 93
State universities, Turkey 115, 117
students
  attitudes towards EMI 150–7
  comprehension 56–7
  language of instruction
    preference 157
  learning strategies 156
  mobility and employability 175–6
Student Selection and Placement Centre
    manuals 113–15, 117
subtractive education 22
Sudan
  Arabicization 169, 170, 172
  context 168
  current situation and future prospects
    of EMI in 172–3

educational system in 168–9
EMI in
  benefits in HEIs 175–6, 182
  challenges in HEIs 176–8
  in colonial and postcolonial
    170–1
  content teachers' methodological
    and pedagogical
    competences 182–3
  effective maintenance and
    sustainability 178–81
  history of 169–70
  international research 184–5
  language support for 170
  qualitative methodology 173–4
  recommendations 184–5
  teaching and learning 185
internationalization of higher
    education 172–3, 175, 181–2
Suliman, W. A. 98

Tadros, A. 98
Tamazight 134, 138–9
Tamtam, A. G. 37, 141
Tatweer. *See* King Abdullah Public
    Education Development
    Project
Tayan, B. M. 94
teacher education 179, 180, 182
teacher research 183
teacher-student interaction 177
teaching strategies 160, 163
Technical and Vocational Colleges
    of Excellence (TVCE)
    project 95
Telemsani, A. 99
Ter-Vardanyan, Z. 39
translation 98–9, 103
Troudi, S. 98
Trowler, P. R. 91
Tunisia 134
  Arabic in 131, 133
  EMI in 130–3
  French in 131, 133
  language of education policy 130–3
t-units analysis 77–9, 84–6
Turkey
  Council of Higher Education 113,
    115, 121

EMI programmes 4
   academic division level 115, 116, 118, 120
   academic subject 115, 117–21
   brief history of 110–11
   comparison of development over twenty years 119–21
   full EMI programme 114–20
   growth of 111–13, 121–2
   language policy and planning 109–10
   partial EMI programme 114–20
   programmes in 1999 115–17
   programmes in 2019 117–19
   soft EMI programme 114–15
   university level 115–19
foreign language medium of instruction (MOI) 111–14, 121

higher education
   institutions 115, 117
   internationalization of 110
   regulations 111–13

UAE 14
   higher education in 71
United Kingdom 18
United States 18
University education, Sudan 169
University of Dammam 94
USAID 150, 164
Uzbekistan 130

Warburton, K. 92
Waters, J. 51

Yeditepe University 119

Zare-ee, A. 27, 28, 38

www.ingramcontent.com/pod-product-compliance
Lightning Source LLC
Chambersburg PA
CBHW061827300426
44115CB00013B/2284